*...the earth serves me to walk upon,
the sun to light me ...* Montaigne

Our Nation's
Great Heritage

*portrait illustrations of signers of
the Declaration of Independence
by Harry J. Schaare*

Our Nation's Great Heritage

The Story of the Declaration of Independence
and the Constitution

by Donald E. Cooke

HAMMOND INCORPORATED
MAPLEWOOD, NEW JERSEY

Library of Congress Cataloging in Publication Data

Cooke, Donald Ewin, 1916-
    Our nation's great heritage.

    Previously published in 1969 and 1970 as the author's
Fathers of America's freedom and America's great
document — the Constitution.
        Bibliography: p. 220
        1. United States.   Declaration of independence —
        Signers.   2. United States.   Constitution.
I. Title.
E221.C75   1972   973.3'092'2 (B)   72-5200
ISBN 0-8437-3715-8
ISBN 0-8437-3716-6 (classic ed.)

To all future generations
of the United States of America.
May they have the courage
to change what is bad in our society
and the wisdom to know
when tradition needs no improvement.

Contents

PART I

". . . these united colonies . . . ought to be free . . ."

THE STORY OF THE DECLARATION OF INDEPENDENCE

PART II

". . . to form a more perfect union . . ."

THE STORY OF OUR CONSTITUTION

Author's Introduction   131

PART I

"... these united colonies

. . . ought to be free . . .''

"Resolved that these united colonies are, and of right ought to be, free and independent States, that they are absolved from all allegiance to the British Crown and that all political connection between them and the State of Great Britain is and ought to be totally dissolved."

The Lee Resolution for Independence
June 7, 1776

Overleaf: Engraving by Paul Revere
for Revolutionary War currency.
THE GRANGER COLLECTION

The Story of the Declaration of Independence

To many people, the signing of the Declaration of Independence recalls the painting by John Trumbull — a formal gathering of elegantly dressed gentlemen who might have had nothing more momentous on their minds than the spice trade or growing tobacco. Romanticized pictures or brief historical accounts tell us little of the human drama in the lives of the fifty-six signers.

Not only were these men putting their signatures to an explosive document that would revolutionize political thinking for generations to come but, in the view of Britain's rulers, they were literally signing their own death warrants. The broad sweep of history establishes the signing of the Declaration as an event of national and worldwide importance, but it submerges the personal feelings and, in many cases, the disastrous consequences affecting the individuals involved.

While the Revolutionary War and the power struggles of Great Britain and France raged over two continents, what was happening to the men who "pushed the button," as it were, with the point of a quill pen?

This is the story of the Declaration of Independence and, above all, of the men who drafted it and signed it. Who were they? What sort of men could dare to pledge their lives, their fortunes and their sacred honor for a new and untried concept of "government by the consent of the governed"? In the following pages are biographical sketches that may shed some light on who and what they were up to the time of signing the Declaration. Then there is the aftermath — the consequences of their endorsement.

As each one took up the pen to sign his name, even the most courageous must have wondered what lay ahead. For most of them, trouble was inevitable. The only question was how serious the trouble would be. New York and New Jersey delegates faced almost immediate destruction of their properties by the invading British forces. Southerners may have felt temporarily more secure from the British, but were threatened by American loyalists in their own communities. New Englanders had already experienced their baptism of fire and had few illusions about the bleak future.

Nevertheless, the delegates signed the parchment bravely, and in most cases, cheerfully. Fortunately, the American army, under George Washington's remarkable leadership, managed to bring the war to a successful conclusion. Had it turned out otherwise, many of America's greatest men might have been remembered only as hot-headed rebels who wound up on the gallows, but it is doubtful that Thomas Jefferson's Declaration could have been buried with them. Within a few weeks after the adoption of the document, copies had been distributed throughout the colonies and it was being reprinted in France and circulated in the major capitals of Europe. Defeat of the Continental Army by Britain could probably have accomplished no more than to delay the inevitable revolution in political thought that had begun to grip the western world.

Again, this is the broad view of history. It tells us nothing of the anxiety, the pride, the anguish, the grief or the excitement experienced by each of the fifty-six signers after he had left his indelible mark on this great page of history. It is with such things, as well as with historical events, that this book is concerned.

D.E.C.
Wayne, Pa.

Colonial America in Maps

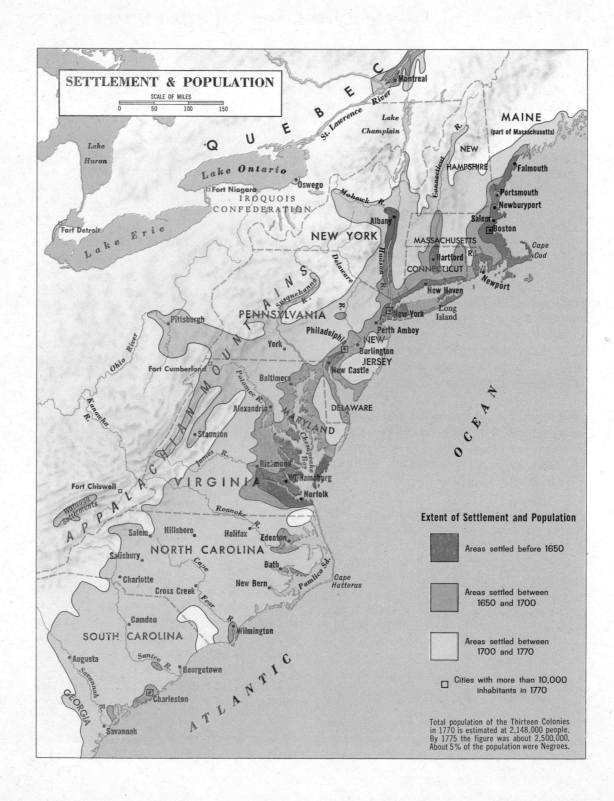

SETTLEMENT & POPULATION

SCALE OF MILES

0   50   100   150

QUEBEC

Lake Huron

Lake Ontario

Oswego

Fort Niagara

IROQUOIS CONFEDERATION

Fort Detroit

Lake Erie

St. Lawrence River

Montreal

Lake Champlain

Connecticut R.

MAINE
(part of Massachusetts)

NEW HAMPSHIRE

Falmouth

Portsmouth

Newburyport

Salem

Boston

Mohawk R.

Albany

MASSACHUSETTS

Hartford   R.I.

CONNECTICUT

Cape Cod

NEW YORK

Delaware R.

Hudson R.

New Haven

Long Island

Newport

Pittsburgh

PENNSYLVANIA

Susquehanna R.

York

Philadelphia

New York

Perth Amboy

NEW JERSEY

Burlington

New Castle

Fort Cumberland

Baltimore

DELAWARE

Ohio River

Kanawha R.

Alexandria

Staunton

Potomac R.

MARYLAND

Chesapeake Bay

OCEAN

Fort Chiswell

James R.

VIRGINIA

Richmond

Williamsburg

Norfolk

APPALACHIAN MOUNTAINS

Watauga Settlements

Roanoke R.

Salem

Hillsboro

Halifax

Edenton

NORTH CAROLINA

Salisbury

Cape Fear R.

Bath

Pamlico Sd.

Cape Hatteras

Charlotte

Cross Creek

New Bern

Camden

Wilmington

SOUTH CAROLINA

Augusta

Santee R.

Georgetown

Savannah R.

GEORGIA

Charleston

ATLANTIC

Savannah

Extent of Settlement and Population

Areas settled before 1650

Areas settled between 1650 and 1700

Areas settled between 1700 and 1770

Cities with more than 10,000 inhabitants in 1770

Total population of the Thirteen Colonies in 1770 is estimated at 2,148,000 people. By 1775 the figure was about 2,500,000. About 5% of the population were Negroes.

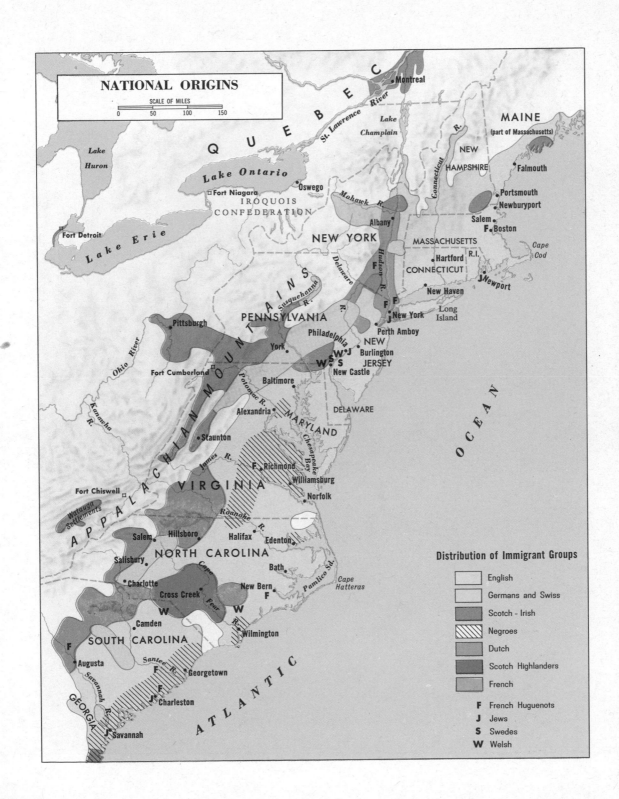

NATIONAL ORIGINS

SCALE OF MILES

0   50   100   150

Lake Huron

Lake Erie

Fort Detroit

Q U E B E C

St. Lawrence River

Montreal

Lake Champlain

Lake Ontario

Fort Niagara

Oswego

IROQUOIS
CONFEDERATION

Connecticut R.

MAINE
(part of Massachusetts)

NEW
HAMPSHIRE

Falmouth

Portsmouth
Newburyport

Salem
F. Boston

Mohawk R.

Albany

NEW YORK

MASSACHUSETTS

Hartford
CONNECTICUT

R.I.

Cape Cod

Hudson R.

Delaware R.

New Haven

Newport

M O U N T A I N S

Susquehanna R.

PENNSYLVANIA

Pittsburgh

F

F
J

New York

Long Island

Ohio River

York

Philadelphia

Perth Amboy

W. S. J
W. S. S

NEW
Burlington
JERSEY
New Castle

Fort Cumberland

Potomac R.

Baltimore

DELAWARE

A P P A L A C H I A N

Kanawha R.

Alexandria

M A R Y L A N D

Chesapeake Bay

O C E A N

Staunton

James R.

V I R G I N I A

F. Richmond

Williamsburg

Fort Chiswell

Watauga
Settlements

Norfolk

Roanoke R.

Salem

Hillsboro

Halifax

Edenton

Cape Hatteras

NORTH CAROLINA

Salisbury

Bath

Pamlico Sd.

Charlotte

Cross Creek

Cape Fear R.

New Bern

F

W

W

Camden

SOUTH CAROLINA

R.

Wilmington

F

Augusta

Santee R.

Savannah R.

F

Georgetown

F

F
J

Charleston

GEORGIA

Savannah

A T L A N T I C

Distribution of Immigrant Groups

☐	English
☐	Germans and Swiss
▨	Scotch - Irish
▧	Negroes
▨	Dutch
▨	Scotch Highlanders
▨	French

F   French Huguenots
J   Jews
S   Swedes
W   Welsh

13

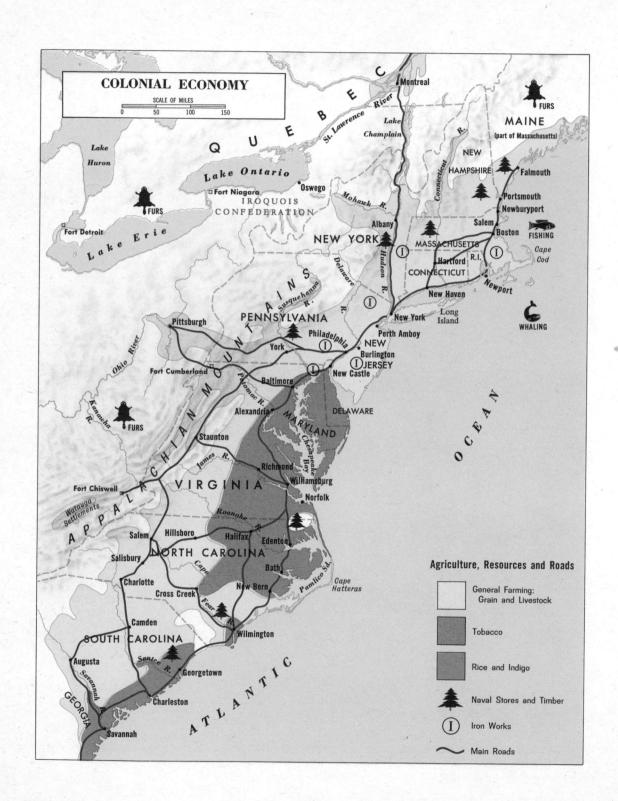

COLONIAL ECONOMY

SCALE OF MILES

0   50   100   150

QUEBEC

Lake Huron

Lake Ontario

Fort Niagara

Oswego

IROQUOIS CONFEDERATION

Fort Detroit

Lake Erie

FURS

St. Lawrence River

Montreal

Lake Champlain

Connecticut R.

Mohawk R.

Albany

NEW YORK

MASSACHUSETTS

Hartford

CONNECTICUT

R.I.

Newport

Delaware R.

Hudson R.

New Haven

New York

Long Island

MAINE
(part of Massachusetts)

Falmouth

Portsmouth
Newburyport

NEW HAMPSHIRE

Salem

Boston

FISHING

Cape Cod

WHALING

PENNSYLVANIA

Susquehanna R.

Pittsburgh

Ohio River

Fort Cumberland

York

Philadelphia

Burlington

New Castle

NEW JERSEY

Perth Amboy

Kanawha R.

FURS

Potomac R.

Baltimore

Alexandria

DELAWARE

MARYLAND

Chesapeake Bay

Staunton

James R.

Richmond

Williamsburg

VIRGINIA

Fort Chiswell

Watauga Settlements

Roanoke

Norfolk

APPALACHIAN MOUNTAINS

Salem

Hillsboro

Halifax

Edenton

Bath

NORTH CAROLINA

Salisbury

New Bern

Pamlico Sd.

Cape Hatteras

Charlotte

Cross Creek

Camden

Wilmington

Cape Fear R.

SOUTH CAROLINA

Augusta

Santee R.

Georgetown

Savannah

GEORGIA

Charleston

Savannah

ATLANTIC

OCEAN

Agriculture, Resources and Roads

General Farming:
Grain and Livestock

Tobacco

Rice and Indigo

Naval Stores and Timber

Iron Works

Main Roads

14

Chapter One

Eve of Decision

15

Philadelphia, July 1776

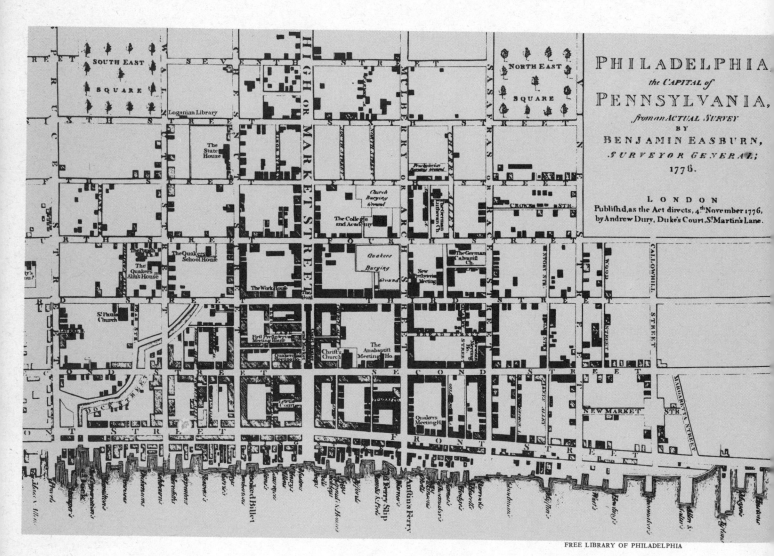

The month of July in 1776 began with typical Philadelphia summer humidity. The air was hot and oppressive, the sky was overcast, and thunder rumbled west of the town. It was as though the weather shared the mood of the populace, who were gathering political forces for a different kind of storm. The roll of thunder was scarcely distinguishable from a distant beating of the drums of war.

In colonial America, war with England was already a reality. The clash with redcoats along the country lanes between Lexington and Concord had occurred more than a year earlier, on April 18, 1775, and this had been followed by the bloody Battle of Bunker Hill, or more properly, Breed's Hill, in June. An alarmed Congress was torn between those who sought a reasonable accommodation with George III and those like the fiery Sam Adams or the soberly determined Ben Frank-

Opposite: Portion of a plan of Philadelphia by Benjamin Easburn drawn about 1776.

Below: The State House, later known as Independence Hall, where the delegates to the Second Continental Congress met.

lin who could see no other course but complete independence. George Washington was chosen to lead an army made up from all the colonies, and a new sovereign government of united American states began to take form.

Yet as late as January 6, 1776, the Continental Congress adopted a resolution stating that the colonies "had no design to set up as an independent nation." Many were strongly opposed to independence. Their reasons varied, but two considerations were paramount. First, the colonies were not ready for self-government, and, many believed, were incapable of defending themselves against the might of British military and naval power. Second, the colonies *were* British, and the thought of separation from the mother country was intolerable to sober men who had been brought up on traditional loyalty to the Crown.

The result was an almost unbearable politi-

17

cal tension. Tempers flared between members of the same family. Fights over political beliefs were common in the taverns, and impassioned speeches were being delivered from pulpits and in public squares from New Hampshire down to Georgia.

Only a day or two after the January 6 resolution had been passed by Congress, a sensational pamphlet was published in Philadelphia. It appeared under the innocuous title of *Common Sense,* but it did more to stir revolutionary fervor than anything said or written up to that time. The author was Thomas Paine, an Englishman who had come to America at the urging of Benjamin Franklin. Paine was no scholar, but he had a knack of penetrating hypocrisy and exposing the plain truth. His 25,000-word book was circulated all over America and in Europe, and it sold nearly 175,000 copies in the colonies alone.

Ripping into the concept of monarchy, Paine scorned men who pretended respect for the Crown while denouncing royal edicts. "The period of debate is closed," he wrote. "Arms, as a last resort, must decide the contest."

In another passage, Paine ridiculed remote rule by Britain: "There is something very absurd in supposing a continent to be perpetually governed by an island. In no instance hath nature made the satellite larger than its primary planet: and as England and America, with respect to each other, reverse the common order of nature, it is evident that they belong to different systems."

Common Sense rocked the political thought of the civilized world, and in America it whipped up the revolutionary storm to its breaking point as the stifling heat of summer settled over the eastern seaboard.

At the center of the political thunderhead was a handsome brick building known as the State House, now famous the world over as Independence Hall. In those days it was surrounded by dwellings and stables, while in its well-trodden, grassless quadrangle stood a crude wooden platform, erected several years before for making astronomical observations. This platform was an eyesore, but within a few days it was to serve as a stage for the reading of the immortal Declaration of Independence.

Sweltering in the July heat, delegates to the Second Continental Congress strolled across the cobbles of Chestnut Street. They wore the white stockings, knee breeches, ruffled cravats and three-cornered hats of the colonial period, and their costumes were by no means tailored to cool their tempers as they sat in the stifling interior of the State House.

Shortly after Congress had assembled in the State House on July 1, news was received that a large fleet of British warships had appeared off Sandy Hook. The report heightened the tension in a room already charged with anxiety and excitement. Hot as it was, the windows were kept closed for two reasons: the first, to insure secrecy of the proceedings; the second, to keep out horseflies that swarmed in a livery stable across the street. The resulting discomfort was nearly unbearable, particularly since a good number of the biting insects found their way into the hall anyway. Frequently the oratory was punctuated by the slapping of necks and ankles as the buzzing flies drew blood.

Presiding over the assembly was John Hancock from Boston, one of the wealthiest men in the 13 colonies. Since the convening of the Second Continental Congress, Hancock had become a familiar figure on Philadelphia streets. He enjoyed taking a stroll in his expensive clothes, attended by four or five servants. Amused residents laughingly referred to him as "King Hancock," or "Hancock, the Peacock."

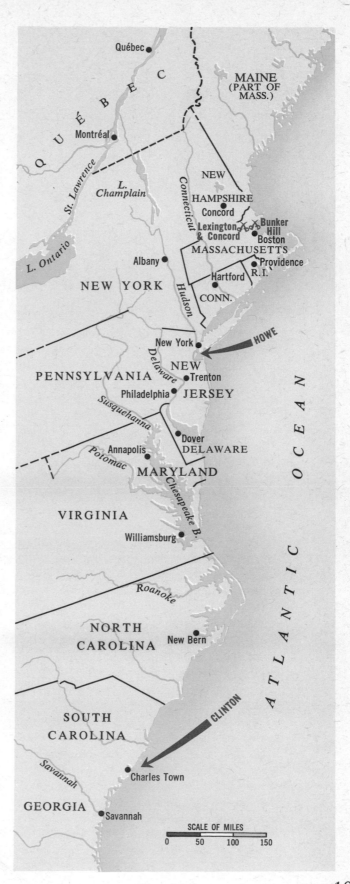

For all his finery and his royalist uncle, Hancock had no love for England's king, or for any royalty. He and Samuel Adams were the only two colonial leaders up to that time who were wanted for hanging. They were excluded from a general offer of pardon that had been extended by British General Gage in the hope of persuading the colonists to give up their "mad" quest for self rule.

The July 1 meeting opened with the reading of dispatches from General Washington, who asked for reinforcements to defend New York. As the heat of the day increased, the delegates grew restless. They listened impatiently to letters from various colonial legislatures, knowing that more important business was to be placed before them.

Assembled in the State House were between 50 and 60 men (the number fluctuated) who had been selected by various methods to represent the 13 colonies. Each colony had worked out its own plan and had made its own decision as to how many delegates it would send to the Congress. Yet each colony was permitted only one vote — always the majority opinion of that colony's delegation. If a delegation was equally split, the Clerk of Congress, Charles Thomson, recorded no vote for the colony. Delegates from Connecticut, New Jersey, New York and Maryland had been selected by their "Committees of Correspondence." These committees had been established originally to keep up secret contacts between towns and between colonies so that all sections of the country would be kept informed of developments during the growing crisis.

The colonial legislatures in Rhode Island, Massachusetts, Delaware and Pennsylvania chose their delegates to Congress, whereas in North and South Carolina, special conventions had been held for the express purpose of electing representatives. Josiah Bartlett of New Hampshire had been delegated by town

The Lee resolution of June 7, 1776,
called for independence from Great Britain.
Action on the resolution was postponed until July 1.

Resolved

That these United Colonies are, and of right ought to be, free and independent States; that they are absolved from all allegiance to the British Crown, and that all political connection between them and the State of Great Britain is, and ought to be, totally dissolved.

That it is expedient forthwith to take the most effectual measures for forming foreign alliances.

That a plan of confederation be prepared and transmitted to the respective Colonies for their consideration and approbation.

THE NATIONAL ARCHIVES

deputies. In Philadelphia, Bartlett was a busy man. As the sole representative of his colony he was expected to serve on all Congressional Committees, and this he did to the best of his ability.

After the routine reports, the Congress became alert when the chair announced that a roll call on independence would be recorded. This was to be an unofficial poll, but everyone present knew its significance. Although an effort was being made to carry a unanimous resolution, four of the colonies were still in doubt. New York representatives, who personally favored independence, were awaiting instructions. Despite the quiet persuasion of Philadelphia's senior diplomat, Benjamin Franklin, who spent most of his time trying to reassure wavering delegates, his own Pennsylvania was still opposed; so was South Carolina. The Delaware vote was evenly split — one for and one against, with a third member absent on urgent business.

While the off-the-record roll call was being taken, the sky darkened and thunder muttered close by. A motion was introduced to postpone a final vote on independence until the next day, and this was carried without opposition. Delegates scattered to their rooms or favorite ale houses as a shower spattered over the cobbled streets. The night would be tense and rainsoaked, with the great decision still to be made.

Yet in a very real sense, Congress remained in session. Much of the work — the committee meetings, the private gatherings in nearby taverns, the endless arguments — went on after the day's formal gathering adjourned.

While other delegations discussed the day's events, Thomas McKean's thoughts were concerned with his colleague, Caesar Rodney, who had returned to Delaware to help end strong loyalist activity near the town of Dover.

Realizing that the Delaware vote could be a crucial one in the effort to achieve a unanimous decision for independence, McKean had dispatched a rider with a message to Rodney, urging him to "get to Philadelphia at the earliest possible moment." As the weather was ominous, the roads poor, and the distance formidable (Dover was nearly 90 miles from Philadelphia), McKean feared that his friend would fail to arrive in time.

Caesar Rodney, the son of a prosperous planter, had been one of Congress' most active workers for independence. He was an odd-looking man — tall and lean with a face described by John Adams as "not bigger than a large apple." The left half of his countenance was concealed by a scarf which he wore to cover an advanced skin cancer. When he received McKean's message he prepared immediately for the long ride to Philadelphia. He set off in the early dusk, and rode north through torrential rain. With only a few essential stops to change horses and to take refreshment, he rode all night through downpours, wind and crashing thunder, but by dawn he was still many miles from the State House.

The other members of Congress were up early on Tuesday morning, July 2. It was customary for most of the delegates to rise at 5:00 A.M. They would breakfast, and by 6:00 were at work on committee reports or holding committee meetings prior to the general session at 9:00. On this particular morning little work was done by committees. There was only talk of the vote for independence, unofficial polling of delegates and the question of whether Delaware, South Carolina, Pennsylvania and New York could be persuaded to vote yes.

They gathered at the State House earlier than was customary. Stout old Benjamin Franklin was there, leaning on his walking stick, talking earnestly to a small group of delegates. Dr. Franklin's expression was serious, but his eyes twinkled with irrepressible humor. It was said that he refused to write the draft of the Declaration of Independence because he would be unable to resist poking fun at the British in a way that would detract from the solemnity of the situation.

Thomas Jefferson of Virginia was there. He sat near the rear of the chamber, slouched on one hip, in a careless attitude that did not in any sense reflect his inner nervous tension. It was Jefferson who had finally accepted the task of writing the Declaration.

Samuel Adams, a Massachusetts delegate was there — the unprepossessing little man with watery eyes who had done so much to start the break with England. Adams was one of the few men of modest means in that distinguished assembly. He wore good but plain clothes that had been given to him by friends when he was elected to the Congress. Throughout his life he remained poor, devoting virtually all his time and whatever property he acquired to the cause of democracy and freedom. No other man contributed more to the Revolution. His fiery speeches had roused people to the point where they attacked British troops in Boston on March 5, 1770, resulting in the Boston Massacre. It was Adams who organized and inspired the "Boston Tea Party" in 1773 to protest the arrival of a shipment of British tea. His activities with the Sons of Liberty and the Committee of Correspondence had made Boston the cockpit of rebellion.

Most of the men who would sign the Declaration of Independence — and some who did not sign — were at the State House that morning of July 2nd. The weather continued close and overcast. The streets remained wet from the night's showers. Missing still was Caesar Rodney as the hour of 9:00 approached and the rain began to fall again.

Notable for their absence were Pennsylvania delegates Robert Morris and John Dickinson. Since it was well known that they had been opposed to a declaration of independence, their failure to appear at this crucial moment was significant — an apparent gesture of unspoken approval. Delaware's Thomas McKean stood at the back of the hall, watching the door anxiously. Word was being passed among the delegates that Pennsylvania, New York and South Carolina had finally been won over. Now the Delaware vote was vitally important.

John Hancock, fashionably dressed as always, looked over the assemblage and prepared to open the meeting. At that instant, the clatter of hoofs sounded on the cobbles outside; a moment later a gaunt, bedraggled figure strode into the large room. It was Caesar Rodney. He still wore his mud-caked riding boots and spurs, and he was soaked to the skin. As he took his seat with McKean, the meeting was called to order. The clerk, Mr. Thomson read a resolution, the words of which were already familiar to the delegates. These courageous proposals had been penned and introduced to Congress on June 7 by Richard Henry Lee of Virginia:

"Resolved that these United Colonies are, and of right ought to be, free and independent States, that they are absolved from all allegiance to the British Crown and that all political connection between them and the State of Great Britain is, and ought to be, totally dissolved.

"That it is expedient forthwith to take the most effectual measures for forming foreign alliances.

"That a plan of confederation be prepared and transmitted to the colonies for their consideration and approbation."

Chairman of the Committee of the Whole to consider the resolution on independence was Benjamin Harrison, a large, jovial man who had skillfully chaired and moderated every meeting and debate on the measure.

Now the vote was being recorded. As was customary they began with the northernmost colonies and proceeded from New Hampshire southward to Georgia. The New England vote was solidly for independence. The New York delegates abstained once again, though all were sure by this time that their instructions, when they should arrive, would be to vote "aye." New Jersey voted affirmatively and, in the absence of Morris and Dickinson, Pennsylvania followed suit. Next Thomson asked for Delaware's vote. In behalf of that colony, Caesar Rodney rose to his feet and spoke in a weary but clear voice, "As I believe the voice of my constituents and of all sensible and honest men is in favor of independence and my own judgment concurs with them, I vote for Independence."

So it went, straight through the roll. The vote was, indeed, unanimous — 12 colonies in favor of separation from England, and one abstention. Charles Thomson made the appropriate entry in his journal, and the thing was done.

But the consequences could only be guessed. Every man in the room knew that the decreed British penalty for their action was death by hanging. Most of them must have been thinking of their homes and families and what might now occur in the various colonies during their absence. For the moment, however, little time was permitted to ponder the gloomy prospects. Thomas Jefferson's paper was now to be considered, and there was divergence of opinion as to the document's wording. As the day wore on and it became clear that the delegates were not prepared to approve the Declaration as it stood, it was decided to adjourn and to devote the next day to debating Jefferson's draft.

The great decision had been made. Now would come the work, the bloodshed and the heartache of implementing it.

The man who had been chosen to put America's quest for independence into words was Thomas Jefferson, the Virginia delegate who had been elected to the drafting committee. This committee, established three days after the introduction of Richard Henry Lee's resolutions, consisted of John Adams of Massachusetts, Benjamin Franklin of Pennsylvania, Roger Sherman of Connecticut, Robert R. Livingston of New York and the Virginian, Thomas Jefferson.

No committee of the Second Continental Congress bore a greater responsibility. On the statement they were expected to write rested the future of mankind, and the five committee members were well aware of it. At the outset, the committee debated among themselves as to who was best suited to do the actual writing. Thomas Jefferson originally urged John Adams to accept the task. When Adams refused, he pointed out that Jefferson himself was the logical author. "Reason first," he said, "you are a Virginian, and Virginia ought to appear at the head of this business.

Reason second, I am obnoxious, suspected and unpopular; You are very much otherwise. Reason third, you can write ten times better than I can."

"Well," replied Jefferson, "if you are decided, I will do as well as I can."*

The insistence of John Adams that a Virginian do the writing was soundly based. Delegates from all the colonies were familiar with Virginia's historic roll in the rebellion. In March 1775, a convention had been held at St. John's Church, Richmond, Virginia, and there George Washington, Thomas Jefferson, Richard Henry Lee and many other prominent Virginians heard Patrick Henry speak in a voice that would reverberate through the endless corridors of human history, "I know not how others may feel, but as for me, give me liberty or give me death!"

While others might argue that the greatest activists of the revolution were the two Massachusetts cousins, John and Samuel Adams,

---

* Adams to Timothy Pickering — The Works of John Adams

Left: Portable writing desk used by Thomas Jefferson in writing the Declaration.

Right: A portion of Jefferson's "rough draft."

the fact remained that much of the eloquence flowed from Virginia's scholars.

From his days as a young lawyer, Jefferson's views on freedom and human rights had been unorthodox for that time and place. As early as 1770 he had spoken out against slavery. In a court case involving the enslavement of a grandchild of a white woman and a Negro man, he argued, "Under the law of nature, all men are born free, everyone comes into the world with a right to his own person, which includes the liberty of moving and using it at his own will."

The court ruled his argument invalid.

However, other Virginians agreed with his ideas and supported him in the Virginia House of Burgesses. Despite his views on slavery he was considered to be less of an extremist than many of the Virginians of his generation.

During Jefferson's term with the Second Continental Congress he rented two second floor rooms in the house of Frederic Graff, a bricklayer by trade. The red brick house was on the southwest corner of Seventh and Market Streets in Philadelphia, a location considered to be "on the edge of town," and it was there that the Declaration of Independence was written. Jefferson worked on a portable writing desk which he held on his knees. He had invented and designed the desk himself and had ordered it made by a former landlord named Benjamin Randolph.

For several days he scratched away with his quill, crossing out phrases, inserting others, rewriting and refining. As he had also authored the recently adopted Virginia Bill of Rights, it was natural that he should paraphrase its opening words, ". . .all men are born equally free and independent and have certain inherent rights — among which are enjoyment of life, liberty and pursuing and obtaining happiness and safety."

Essentially, this was the thought expressed in the final Declaration, but the sentence was improved both in its literary style and in its directness, as Jefferson realized that while pursuing happiness was a basic right, obtaining it was not:

"We hold these truths to be self-evident: That all men are created equal; that they are endowed by their creator with certain inalienable rights; that among these are life, liberty and the pursuit of happiness."

Jefferson's first rough draft was generally approved by John Adams, who nevertheless felt that some passages showed the harshness — and consequent weakness — of anger. Adams questioned the anti-slavery passages which occupied a prominent place in the draft. He argued that direct reference to the evils of slavery might so antagonize the southern delegations that the entire cause might founder.

The early version included the phrase, "The King of Great Britain kept open a market where men were bought and sold, and prostituted his negative by suppressing Virginia's legislative attempts to restrain this execrable commerce." Jefferson insisted on keeping this sentence in the draft, but as Adams predicted, Congress struck it out.

Benjamin Franklin was less critical of the draft, though he did do some minor editing of the wording.

The other committee members, Roger Sherman and Robert Livingston, apparently made their contributions through discussion of specific points in the document. Roger Sherman, considered to be one of the most level-headed

When in the course of human events it becomes necessary for one people to dissolve the political bands which have connected them with another, and to assume among the powers of the earth the separate and equal station to which the laws of nature & of nature's god entitle them, a decent respect to the opinions of mankind requires that they should declare the causes which impel them to the separation.

We hold these truths to be self-evident; that all men are created equal, that they are endowed by their creator with...

members of the Congress, helped to temper Jefferson's fiery prose. He was a quiet, sober Puritan who had begun his career as a cobbler and had taught himself law by propping books before him on his cobbler's bench. John Adams said of him, "... he was one of the most sensible men in the world. The clearest head and the steadiest heart."

Although Robert Livingston served on the drafting committee, he never signed the document he had helped to create, as he was no longer in the Congress at the time of the actual signing, and in point of fact he was never enthusiastic about a full break with Great Britain. A prosperous New York lawyer and a landowner, his views were more conservative than those of most of his colleagues. He was elected to the committee at the urging of Sam Adams who felt it would help win votes of other conservative delegates to have a restraining hand involved in the drafting.

Regardless of any help or advice provided by the other committee members, Thomas Jefferson was the real author of the Declaration. After discussing the form of the composition with the committee, he agreed that not only must he make clear to Britain the reasons for separation, but he must justify the rebellious action with all the nations of the world. Further, the Declaration must serve as a catalyst to hold the separate colonies together and to help weld a solid union. It was an awesome assignment.

He titled his first draft, *A Declaration by the Representatives of the United States of America, in General Congress Assembled.* His beginning in the original read as follows:

"When in the course of Human events it becomes necessary for a people to advance from that subordination in which they have hitherto remained, & to assume among the powers of the earth the equal & independent station to which the laws of nature & nature's god entitled them, a decent respect to the opinions of mankind requires that they should declare the causes which impel them to the change."

Jefferson's quill pen rushed on, and the words began to flow with greater eloquence as he outlined the "truths" which he held to be "sacred & undeniable." It was here that he drew upon his earlier composition of the Virginia Bill of Rights, stating the fundamental concept of Man's natural freedom that would stand as the cornerstone for the entire human rights structure. Much of his philosophy could be traced to the writings of another Virginian, George Mason, and to John Locke's well-known *Treatises of Civil Government.* But to those earlier writings, Jefferson added a clarity and brilliant logic that was purely his own. Up to that time, nearly all discussions of human rights had considered ownership of property to be the justification for most other rights. While Jefferson agreed that every man had a right to own property, and that it was a function of government to protect that property, he recognized that the *lack* of possessions in no way diminished a man's right to take part in government or his right to life, liberty and the pursuit of happiness.

One of the momentous phrases in Jefferson's declaration was that "governments are instituted among men, deriving their just powers *from the consent of the governed."* Here was the foundation of the entire revolutionary movement — a concept that would shake the world and bring about the downfall of most

25

of Europe's monarchies. Yet he introduced the idea so casually and followed it with such reasonable statements about traditional, "long established governments," that the conservative delegates in Congress could find no fault.

"Prudence," he said, "will dictate that governments long established should *not* be changed for light & transient causes; and accordingly all experience hath shewn that mankind are more disposed to suffer while evils are sufferable, than to right themselves by abolishing the forms to which they are accustomed."

Still, he argued, the list of grievances against the British Crown was so long and so heavy with injustice that America must provide new guards for its future security.

The struggle to present the colonial case simply, and powerfully, and to include all the desired ingredients must have brought Jefferson near to a state of mental exhaustion by the time his draft was completed. When the day arrived for Congress to discuss his work— to criticize it and debate the value of each sentence — he must have suffered agony. Already he and the committee members had made more than thirty changes in the first draft. Probably the committee discussions had been heated at times. The paper, riddled with insertions and deletions was finally recopied by Jefferson, and it was this second draft that was now in the ungentle hands of Congress. It had been awaiting final approval since it was handed over on June 28.

When the delegates assembled on Wednesday, July 3, the rains of the past two days had ended. It was a fine, clear day — the kind that stirs the blood. While Jefferson nervously took a seat at the back of the hall, his portable writing desk on his lap, the representatives plunged into their task with enthusiasm. The first two paragraphs of the Declaration were read and passed almost as Jefferson had written them. The few minor alterations in the

introduction included changing "inherent & inalienable rights" to "certain unalienable rights." (Most experts believe that the *un* was a printer's error and not an editorial change requested by Congress.)

A heated discussion developed, as expected, over Jefferson's references to slavery and the African slave trade. Finally northern and liberal southern delegates acceded to the demands of southern slaveholders by deleting the slave trade charge. Jefferson himself made notes of the proposed changes, seethed inwardly, but said nothing. His chief defender was the dauntless John Adams whom Jefferson later described as "our colossus on the floor . . . not graceful nor eloquent, nor remarkably fluent, but he came out . . . with a power of thought and expression, that moved us from our seats."

John Dickinson of New Jersey still attempted to dissuade Congress from making any formal declaration of independence. In the earlier debate over independence, on July 1 he had asked, "What advantages are to be obtained from such a declaration?" Foreign powers would want to see deeds, not words, he argued; further, "this Declaration may weaken the Union, when the people find themselves engaged in a cause rendered more cruel by such a Declaration without prospect of an end to their Calamities, by a continuation of the war."

The conclusion of Dickinson's eloquent speech had been greeted by a chilling silence. Clearly the delegates who had begun the discussion with patriotic zeal were now moved to doubts and second thoughts. It was at this point that Edward Rutledge had come over to where John Adams was seated and begged him to speak in defense of the declaration. Adams did so, reluctantly, for he had used the arguments so many times he feared they had gone stale. Yet his spontaneous speech which was only partially recorded, was probably one

Silver inkstand
used in signing the Declaration.

INDEPENDENCE NATIONAL HISTORICAL PARK COLLECTION, PHILADELPHIA

of the best — certainly one of the most important — of his political career.

"This is the first time of my life," he told the delegates, "that I have ever wished for the talents and eloquence of the ancient orators of Greece and Rome, for I am sure that none of them ever had before him a question of more importance to his country and to the world."

Adams then proceeded to reaffirm the faith of the great majority of delegates in the fateful step they were about to take. Yet he made no attempt to gloss over the dangers confronting them: "If you imagine that I expect this declaration will ward off calamities from this country, you are much mistaken. A bloody conflict we are destined to endure."

The debate on July 3 lasted several hours, and the session adjourned without final approval of the document. On July 4, the merciless editing of Jefferson's writing continued, and it was in the latter portion of the document, the list of grievances against King George and the British government, that most of the changes were made. Out of the original 1817 words, 480 were cut while Jefferson suffered in silence.

The revision was completed some time in the evening of July 4, 1776, and the adoption of the Declaration of Independence "by the representatives of the United States of America in General Congress Assembled" was duly recorded as of that date. In spite of Jefferson's natural resentment of the extensive cuts in his work, the manuscript was, on the whole, improved by the work of those fifty-odd critics. The final result left only the essential points and a direct, uncluttered statement of principles. Possibly by the time the final vote of approval was taken, the delegates were too weary to argue further, or they might have overdone a good job.

The only person to sign the document that day was the president of Congress, John Han-cock, whose signature was attested by Secretary Charles Thomson. In the final action of the day Congress ordered that copies of the Declaration were to be printed that night, and that independence should be declared throughout the United *States*. The word "colony" no longer appeared in the records.

As Congress adjourned that evening, the great bell in the State House tower was rung. An expectant crowd that had been gathering in the square all afternoon cheered wildly. Suddenly the quiet town was aroused. Cannon boomed; church bells clashed and clanged from Front Street on the Delaware, to the Schuylkill River, two miles to the west, and riders were dispatched to carry the momentous story to other towns and colonies.

That night, printer John Dunlap ran off a number of large 15- by 18-inch copies of the Declaration. These were posted in prominent places and were read in village squares, markets, from the pulpits of churches and in army camps. General Washington directed that the Declaration was to be read to each brigade of the army on the evening of July 9.

For several days, spontaneous parades and celebrations were held in communities all over the country. Occasionally violence erupted. In Bowling Green, New York, a huge equestrian statue of George III was roped and pulled to the ground. Gleefully, the crowd hacked it to pieces and the chunks of royal metal were carted to the home of General Oliver Wolcott in Connecticut, where his wife and other ladies of the town melted them and cast the metal into more than 42,000 bullets.

The day for a formal signing of the Declaration was set by Congress, and in preparation for this, the document was ordered engrossed on parchment by a skilled calligrapher named Timothy Matlack.

In the meantime, there was a public reading of the Declaration at the State House yard in Philadelphia. Colonel John Nixon, standing

27

on the wooden observation platform and flanked by several important members of Congress, read the document to a large crowd of citizens on July 8. Not until July 9 did the New York State Convention vote to permit their delegates to vote approval of the Declaration. They formally cast their "aye" vote on July 15, and on that day the title of the document was changed to "The Unanimous Declaration of the Thirteen United States of America."

After the handsomely engrossed parchment copy was completed, on August 2, Congress gathered in the State House for the signing. Whether or not it had been intended from the beginning that all delegates should sign the Declaration is not clear, but at some point it was agreed that the general signing should be made for the protection of all. There was, perhaps, some safety in numbers, although none doubted that each signer was "putting his head in the noose" by his action.

Delegate William Ellery of Rhode Island took up a position where he could see each member as he wrote his name. "I was determined," he wrote afterward, "to see how they all looked as they signed what might be their death warrants. I placed myself beside the secretary, Charles Thomson, and eyed each closely as he affixed his name to the document. Undaunted resolution was displayed on every countenance."

John Hancock, who signed first, penned his large, flourishing signature which he had developed in penmanship class at a Boston Latin School. "John Bull can read my name without spectacles," he said, "and may now double his reward of £500 for my head."

The other delegates signed in the usual geographical order of states from north to south, so that George Walton of Georgia was the last to enter his name that day. Between July 4 when the final version of the Declaration was approved and the formal signing on

August 2, there had been a number of changes in Congress. Some delegates had left and been replaced. Others who had been absent for the vote were present at the signing. One of these was Robert Morris. New members on August 2 included Benjamin Rush, George Clymer, James Smith, George Taylor and George Ross of Pennsylvania. Virginia's Richard Henry Lee, who had initiated the original resolution for independence, was absent on the day of the vote as well as on August 2, but he returned to sign at an unknown later date. Samuel Chase of Maryland also signed later. One of the delegates who voted against independence, but who signed the document nevertheless, was George Read of Delaware. Probably the last signature to be added in 1776 was that of Matthew Thornton, Irish-born New Hampshire representative who was not elected to the Congress until the twelfth of September and was not seated until November. He signed the Declaration a few days after his arrival in Philadelphia.

When Congress moved from Philadelphia to Baltimore in December, 1776, all official papers were removed from the State House, including the Declaration. In Baltimore, a new printing was made, less hastily and with fewer errors. All names of the signers were included on this printing, with the single exception of Thomas McKean of Delaware. Evidently he signed last of all, some time in 1777.

The 56 courageous men who had put their names to the historic document had taken perilous steps in a direction from which there was no turning. Yet they wrote their names without the slightest hesitation. Only one signer's hand shook so that the signature was scarcely more than an irregular scratch. This was Stephen Hopkins of Rhode Island, the second oldest delegate who suffered from severe palsy. As he handed over the quill to Ellery, he remarked, "My hand trembles, but my heart does not!"

AMERICAN PHILOSOPHICAL SOCIETY

In CONGRESS, July 4, 1776.

A DECLARATION

By the REPRESENTATIVES of the

UNITED STATES OF AMERICA,

In GENERAL CONGRESS ASSEMBLED.

WHEN in the Course of human Events, it becomes neceſſary for one People to diſſolve the Political Bands which have connected them with another, and to aſſume among the Powers of the Earth, the ſeparate and equal Station to which the Laws of Nature and of Nature's God entitle them, a decent Reſpect to the Opinions of Mankind requires that they ſhould declare the cauſes which impel them to the Separation.

We hold theſe Truths to be ſelf-evident, that all Men are created equal, that they are endowed by their Creator with certain unalienable Rights, that among theſe are Life, Liberty, and the Purſuit of Happineſs—That to ſecure theſe Rights, Governments are inſtituted among Men, deriving their juſt Powers from the Conſent of the Governed, that whenever any Form of Government becomes deſtructive of theſe Ends, it is the Right of the People to alter or to aboliſh it, and to inſtitute new Government, laying its Foundation on ſuch Principles, and organizing its Powers in ſuch Form, as to them ſhall ſeem moſt likely to effect their Safety and Happineſs. Prudence, indeed, will dictate that Governments long eſtabliſhed ſhould not be changed for light and tranſient Cauſes; and accordingly all Experience hath ſhewn, that Mankind are more diſpoſed to ſuffer, while Evils are ſufferable, than to right themſelves by aboliſhing the Forms to which they are accuſtomed. But when a long Train of Abuſes and Uſurpations, purſuing invariably the ſame Object, evinces a Deſign to reduce them under abſolute Deſpotiſm, it is their Right, it is their Duty, to throw off ſuch Government, and to provide new Guards for their future Security. Such has been the patient Sufferance of theſe Colonies; and ſuch is now the Neceſſity which conſtrains them to alter their former Syſtems of Government. The Hiſtory of the preſent King of Great-Britain is a Hiſtory of repeated Injuries and Uſurpations, all having in direct Object the Eſtabliſhment of an abſolute Tyranny over theſe States. To prove this, let Facts be ſubmitted to a candid World.

He has refuſed his Aſſent to Laws, the moſt wholeſome and neceſſary for the public Good.

He has forbidden his Governors to paſs Laws of immediate and preſſing Importance, unleſs ſuſpended in their Operation till his Aſſent ſhould be obtained; and when ſo ſuſpended, he has utterly neglected to attend to them.

He has refuſed to paſs other Laws for the Accommodation of large Diſtricts of People, unleſs thoſe People would relinquiſh the Right of Repreſentation in the Legiſlature, a Right ineſtimable to them, and formidable to Tyrants only.

He has called together Legiſlative Bodies at Places unuſual, uncomfortable, and diſtant from the Depoſitory of their public Records, for the ſole Purpoſe of fatiguing them into Compliance with his Meaſures.

He has diſſolved Repreſentative Houſes repeatedly, for oppoſing with manly Firmneſs his Invaſions on the Rights of the People.

He has refuſed for a long Time, after ſuch Diſſolutions, to cauſe others to be elected; whereby the Legiſlative Powers, incapable of Annihilation, have returned to the People at large for their exerciſe; the State remaining in the mean time expoſed to all the Dangers of Invaſion from without, and Convulſions within.

He has endeavoured to prevent the Population of theſe States; for that Purpoſe obſtructing the Laws for Naturalization of Foreigners; refuſing to paſs others to encourage their Migrations hither, and raiſing the Conditions of new Appropriations of Lands.

He has obſtructed the Adminiſtration of Juſtice, by refuſing his Aſſent to Laws for eſtabliſhing Judiciary Powers.

He has made Judges dependent on his Will alone, for the Tenure of their Offices, and the Amount and Payment of their Salaries.

He has erected a Multitude of new Offices, and ſent hither Swarms of Officers to harraſs our People, and eat out their Subſtance.

He has kept among us, in Times of Peace, Standing Armies, without the conſent of our Legiſlatures.

He has affected to render the Military independent of and ſuperior to the Civil Power.

He has combined with others to ſubject us to a Juriſdiction foreign to our Conſtitution, and unacknowledged by our Laws; giving his Aſſent to their Acts of pretended Legiſlation:

For quartering large Bodies of Armed Troops among us:

For protecting them, by a mock Trial, from Puniſhment for any Murders which they ſhould commit on the Inhabitants of theſe States:

For cutting off our Trade with all Parts of the World:

For impoſing Taxes on us without our Conſent:

For depriving us, in many Caſes, of the Benefits of Trial by Jury:

For tranſporting us beyond Seas to be tried for pretended Offences:

For aboliſhing the free Syſtem of Engliſh Laws in a neighbouring Province, eſtabliſhing therein an arbitrary Government, and enlarging its Boundaries, ſo as to render it at once an Example and fit Inſtrument for introducing the ſame abſolute Rule into theſe Colonies:

For taking away our Charters, aboliſhing our moſt valuable Laws, and altering fundamentally the Forms of our Governments:

For ſuſpending our own Legiſlatures, and declaring themſelves inveſted with Power to legiſlate for us in all Caſes whatſoever.

He has abdicated Government here, by declaring us out of his Protection and waging War againſt us.

He has plundered our Seas, ravaged our Coaſts, burnt our Towns, and deſtroyed the Lives of our People.

He is, at this Time, tranſporting large Armies of foreign Mercenaries to compleat the Works of Death, Deſolation and Tyranny, already begun with circumſtances of Cruelty and Perfidy, ſcarcely paralleled in the moſt barbarous Ages, and totally unworthy the Head of a civilized Nation.

He has conſtrained our fellow Citizens taken Captive on the high Seas to bear Arms againſt their Country, to become the Executioners of their Friends and Brethren, or to fall themſelves by their Hands.

He has excited domeſtic Inſurrections amongſt us, and has endeavoured to bring on the Inhabitants of our Frontiers, the mercileſs Indian Savages, whoſe known Rule of Warfare, is an undiſtinguiſhed Deſtruction, of all Ages, Sexes and Conditions.

In every ſtage of theſe Oppreſſions we have Petitioned for Redreſs in the moſt humble Terms: Our repeated Petitions have been anſwered only by repeated Injury. A Prince, whoſe Character is thus marked by every act which may define a Tyrant, is unfit to be the Ruler of a free People.

Nor have we been wanting in Attentions to our Britiſh Brethren. We have warned them from Time to Time of Attempts by their Legiſlature to extend an unwarrantable Juriſdiction over us. We have reminded them of the Circumſtances of our Emigration and Settlement here. We have appealed to their native Juſtice and Magnanimity, and we have conjured them by the Ties of our common Kindred to diſavow theſe Uſurpations, which, would inevitably interrupt our Connections and Correſpondence. They too have been deaf to the Voice of Juſtice and of Conſanguinity. We muſt, therefore, acquieſce in the Neceſſity, which denounces our Separation, and hold them, as we hold the reſt of Mankind, Enemies in War, in Peace, Friends.

We, therefore, the Repreſentatives of the UNITED STATES OF AMERICA, in GENERAL CONGRESS, Aſſembled, appealing to the Supreme Judge of the World for the Rectitude of our Intentions, do, in the Name, and by Authority of the good People of theſe Colonies, ſolemnly Publiſh and Declare, That theſe United Colonies are, and of Right ought to be, FREE AND INDEPENDENT STATES; that they are abſolved from all Allegiance to the Britiſh Crown, and that all political Connection between them and the State of Great-Britain, is and ought to be totally diſſolved; and that as FREE AND INDEPENDENT STATES, they have full Power to levy War, conclude Peace, contract Alliances, eſtabliſh Commerce, and to do all other Acts and Things which INDEPENDENT STATES may of right do. And for the ſupport of this Declaration, with a firm Reliance on the Protection of divine Providence, we mutually pledge to each other our Lives, our Fortunes, and our ſacred Honor.

Signed by ORDER and in BEHALF of the CONGRESS,

JOHN HANCOCK, PRESIDENT.

ATTEST.
CHARLES THOMSON, SECRETARY.

PHILADELPHIA: PRINTED BY JOHN DUNLAP.

Key To Declaration of Independence Painting
by John Trumbull

1. GEORGE WYTHE, Virginia
2. WILLIAM WHIPPLE, New Hampshire
3. JOSIAH BARTLETT, New Hampshire
4. BENJAMIN HARRISON, Virginia
5. THOMAS LYNCH, South Carolina
6. RICHARD HENRY LEE, Virginia
7. SAMUEL ADAMS, Massachusetts
8. GEORGE CLINTON, New York
9. WILLIAM PACA, Maryland
10. SAMUEL CHASE, Maryland
11. LEWIS MORRIS, New York
12. WILLIAM FLOYD, New York
13. ARTHUR MIDDLETON, South Carolina
14. THOMAS HAYWARD, South Carolina
15. CHARLES CARROLL, of Carrollton
16. GEORGE WALTON, Louisiana

17. ROBERT MORRIS, Pennsylvania
18. THOMAS WILLING, Pennsylvania
19. BENJAMIN RUSH, Pennsylvania
20. ELBRIDGE GERRY, Massachusetts
21. ROBERT TREAT PAINE, Massachusetts
22. ABRAHAM CLARK, New Jersey
23. STEPHEN HOPKINS, Rhode Island
24. WILLIAM ELLERY, Rhode Island
25. GEORGE CLYMER, Pennsylvania
26. WILLIAM HOOPER, North Carolina
27. JOSEPH HEWES, North Carolina
28. JAMES WILSON, Pennsylvania
29. FRANCIS HOPKINSON, New Jersey
30. JOHN ADAMS, Massachusetts
31. ROGER SHERMAN, Connecticut
32. ROBERT L. LIVINGSTON, New York

33. THOMAS JEFFERSON, Virginia
34. BENJAMIN FRANKLIN, Pennsylvania
35. RICHARD STOCKTON, New Jersey
36. FRANCIS LEWIS, New York
37. JOHN WITHERSPOON, New Jersey
38. SAMUEL HUNTINGTON, Connecticut
39. WILLIAM WILLIAMS, Connecticut
40. OLIVER WOLCOTT, Connecticut
41. JOHN HANCOCK, Massachusetts
42. CHARLES THOMPSON, Pennsylvania
43. GEORGE REED, Delaware
44. JOHN DICKINSON, Delaware
45. EDWARD RUTLEDGE, South Carolina
46. THOMAS M'KEAN, Pennsylvania
47. PHILIP LIVINGSTON, New York

The Signers

From his vantage point close to the table where the parchment rested, William Ellery of Rhode Island observed the faces of fifty men as they affixed their signatures to the document. These were, for the most part, sober members of a well-to-do society—landowners, lawyers, merchants, doctors and educators. They came to the table in groups, by delegations. Each man dipped a large quill pen into a pot of ink, wrote his name, and moved toward the back of the hall to converse in low tones with his compatriots. The act of signing was a simple one, but its implications and long-range effects were vast.

Although the weather had moderated, the interior of the hall still retained the heat of the past few days, yet none of the delegates seemed to notice. Their mission absorbed their attention. Ellery knew them all, some intimately, others by reputation, and he could scarcely be blamed for taking pride in being a member of such a group. Their ages ranged

34

Members of the Second Continental Congress
pledged their lives and sacred honor
in declaring that the colonies were,
of right, free and independent.

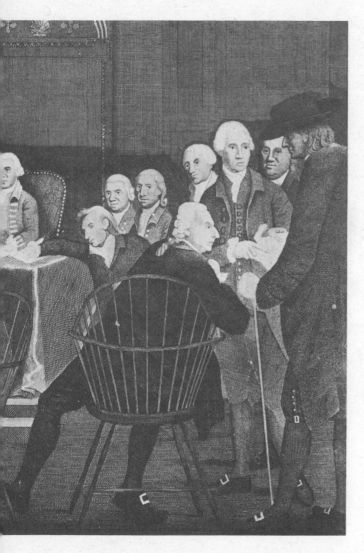

was already in progress—a war that so far was not going well for Washington's ill equipped army. Undoubtedly many of the signers glanced at the final sentence of the Declaration, just above their signatures, as they picked up the quill: "And for the support of this declaration, with a firm reliance on the protection of Divine Providence, we mutually pledge to each other our lives, our fortunes, and our sacred honor."

This was no mere rhetoric—no high-sounding phrase for effect. The pledge meant exactly what it said, and many of the men in that room were destined to sacrifice their lives and their fortunes to the cause they had endorsed.

What did William Ellery see in the faces of the delegates? What sort of men were they who dared to risk everything they had for a new and revolutionary idea? Here were no hot-blooded radicals from the universities, dreamers whose heads were filled with theoretical nonsense, no poverty-stricken outcasts with nothing to lose. From a standpoint of material well-being, most of them could gain nothing; many could—and would—lose great wealth. Why, then, did they sign the Declaration so eagerly?

The answer was in the character of the men and of the times. Believing absolutely in the rightness of the step they took, it was a matter of sacred honor to uphold it, come what may. They understood, as few men do, that wealth of the mind and of the spirit is more to be cherished than all the material possessions of a Midas. What brought them to the State House, what led each man to the table and to the signing of the Declaration varied with individual training and circumstances. They had debated the issue long and thoroughly; there had been disagreements. But having finally agreed on independence they were now determined as one to fight to the death for it.

from 26 (Edward Rutledge of South Carolina) to 70 (Benjamin Franklin of Pennsylvania). Though they were men of divergent background and temperament their common purpose in this gathering welded them into a mighty atom of political force. As Benjamin Franklin was reported to have said to them, "We must all hang together, or most assuredly we shall all hang separately."

The atmosphere in the State House that day was apparently calm enough, but a war

John Hancock

A New and Accurate
PLAN of the TOWN
of
BOSTON,
in
NEW ENGLAND.

William Ellery watched the first signer with particular interest, for here was not only the President of the Second Continental Congress and as such, a "ringleader" in British eyes, but he was one of the wealthiest and most influential men in America. His birthplace was Braintree (renamed Quincy), Massachusetts. His father, a Puritan clergyman, died when John Hancock was seven. He was afterwards supported by Thomas Hancock, an uncle, who was considered to be the most prosperous merchant in Boston. From the uncle, John inherited his luxurious home on Beacon Hill along with the uncle's shipping firm and a fortune in money and properties.

At the age of seventeen Hancock had graduated from Harvard College. Within ten years he was one of New England's foremost merchants, a leader in his community, and even wealthier than his uncle had been before him. British regulations restricting colonial trade were of direct concern to John Hancock's interests. He therefore vigorously opposed the 1765 Stamp Act, and one of his sloops, the Liberty, was seized by British authorities for his refusal to pay duties. His courageous stand made him a popular figure throughout New England. This remarkable man of fortune did not allow his love of luxuried living to stifle his anger over England's unjust behavior. He made it clear that nothing would deter him in the fight to rid Boston of British troops when he remarked, "Burn Boston and make John Hancock a beggar, if the public good requires it."

He was involved in politics as early as 1769, when he was elected to the Massachusetts legislature, known at that time as the "General Court." In 1770 he was in the forefront of a movement demanding withdrawal of British troops from Boston. After British General Gage issued an order forbidding the establishment of a provincial government, Hancock was elected president of the Massachusetts congress which first met in Concord.

It was on April 18, 1775, about six months after he had become president of the provincial congress, when Hancock and Samuel Adams were aroused in the night by Paul Revere, who had made a wild ride from Boston to warn them that the British were on their way to seize them. Hancock had been enjoying a pleasant dinner with his fiancee, Dorothy Quincy, at the parsonage of Rev. Jonas Clarke when the warning was brought by Revere. As Adams and Hancock made their departure, Revere rode on, urging citizens to arm themselves and to prepare to fight the British. The two patriot leaders had barely escaped when the first shots of the Revolution echoed along the country lanes near Lexington.

As an elected Massachusetts delegate to the Second Continental Congress, John Hancock took his seat in Philadelphia early in May 1775. Within a few days, the Congressional president, Peyton Randolph, resigned and Hancock was unanimously chosen to replace him. As efforts were made to organize a Continental Army, Hancock confidently expected to be made the commander-in-chief, but he was disappointed to learn that other delegates had selected George Washington of Virginia. The choice was partly political, since many northern delegates hoped, by this means, to assure the South's support in the coming struggle. Later, the egotistical Hancock showed his resentment by discussing military plans with subordinate generals without consulting Washington.

With the signing of the Declaration of Independence, John Hancock's name became immortal. Legend has it that John Hancock said that he had written his signature large enough for John Bull to read it without his glasses. His name stands out boldly so that even today it is synonymous with the word "signature."

Josiah Bartlett

Wm Whipple

Matthew Thornton

The New Hampshire delegation, composed of two members, followed John Hancock to the table. Second to sign the Declaration was Josiah Bartlett, a physician who had gained a wide reputation through effective use of a Peruvian bark called cinchona. His discovery of the medicinal qualities of this bark occurred years before the more concentrated quinine was extracted from it.

Bartlett was born November 21, 1729, in Amesbury, Massachusetts, and from his earliest years he had been determined to become a doctor. After he had learned medicine under the tutelage of another physician he began practice in Kingston, New Hampshire, at the age of twenty-one. Always a leader in his community, he was elected to the New Hampshire Assembly in 1765, and was appointed a colonel of militia by the royal governor of the colony. Although he was highly favored by the British authorities, Bartlett immediately joined with the colonists as the struggle for independence developed. His support of the patriot cause led to his dismissal as a justice of the peace and, presumably, to the burning of his house by a British agent in 1774. He worked on the New Hampshire Committee of Correspondence until his election to the Second Continental Congress. As Josiah Bartlett took up the quill to put his name to the document, William Ellery saw a rugged-looking man in his forties. Bartlett was tall, his curly hair had a reddish tint, and he moved with determination and vigor. When the vote for independence had been tallied, he had "made the rafters echo

with his approval," according to fellow delegates. Now he had the privilege of being the first of the regular delegates to sign the Declaration.

William Whipple was the second New Hampshire delegate to take up the quill. A well-to-do merchant, Whipple had at one time been the captain of a ship plying the West Indies trade. At twenty-nine, he took his savings, retired from the sea and entered into a successful mercantile partnership with his brother, Joseph. In 1775, he began to take part in meetings of New Hampshire patriots and was elected to the local Committee of Safety. This led to his selection by the legislature to serve as a representative of New Hampshire in the Second Continental Congress. By this time he had relinquished his

JOSIAH BARTLETT

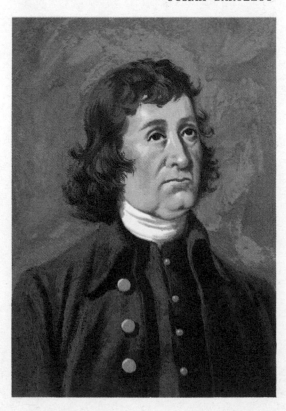

New England saltbox house
from colonial times.

38

part in the business in order to devote his full time to the struggle for independence.

New Hampshire had yet another signer, Matthew Thornton, also a physician. He was not present at the formal signing, as he was elected to the Continental Congress in September, and did not take his seat until November 1776. Thus although he had no opportunity to vote for independence, he asked permission to sign the Declaration and added his name to the document on November 19. He was sixty-two at the time. Thornton had served as a military surgeon in the British colonial army thirty years earlier, and had accompanied some five hundred New Hampshire militia on an expedition that attacked the French in Nova Scotia. A native of Ireland, he had come to America with his parents at the age of four. He was a spirited story teller who loved to regale listeners with humorous anecdotes and fables. He had a knack for capturing and holding the attention of those around him. After his early schooling in Massachusetts, Thornton had studied medicine under an established physician by the name of Grout, and had begun his own practice when he was twenty-six. A few years before the Revolution he became a member of the New Hampshire legislature. As trouble with England developed, he threw all his energy behind the patriot cause, was elected president of New Hampshire's provincial legislature, and as chairman of the regional Committee of Safety, was active in collecting arms and recruiting militia for the colony. After serving briefly as speaker of the newly organized New Hampshire house of representatives in 1776, he gave up this post to represent his state in Philadelphia.

WILLIAM WHIPPLE   MATTHEW THORNTON

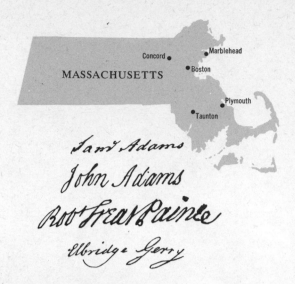

As William Ellery studied the next delegate to approach the table, he was reminded of some of the events that had culminated in this historic moment. Samuel Adams, known to many as the "firebrand of the Revolution," was a plain, unprepossessing man of medium build who dressed shabbily and appeared undistinguished in the company of so many wealthy delegates. But on close scrutiny, his penetrating steel-gray eyes revealed a man of unusual power. In business he had been a failure—he had no head for figures. But given an audience of concerned citizens he could charge the atmosphere in such a way as to arouse the most casual listener. From a distance men thought he was austere, yet in private gatherings he could be genial and entertaining. Sam Adams was born in Boston September 27, 1722, entered Harvard College, graduated from Harvard Law School, had tried his hand at becoming a merchant, and had finally turned to politics as the clamor for colonial rights began to stir the populace.

Here was the man, Ellery realized, who had led protests against the Stamp Tax, who had harangued crowds on the Boston water front, and who had organized the raiders who carried out the daring "Boston Tea Party," dumping chests of valuable tea into the waters of Boston harbor.

When he became clerk of the Massachusetts Assembly, he carried on a voluminous correspondence with patriot leaders in other colonies and in the course of this work he conceived the idea of setting up the "Committees of Correspondence." The plan was first put into operation in 1772 so that various groups in Massachusetts could keep each other advised of revolutionary activity. The idea spread rapidly through the colonies until it became a key factor in the unification of America.

Samuel Adams was one of the first leaders to suggest the formation of a Continental Congress. Long before most of the delegates to this congress were ready to accept the idea, Adams was speaking out for independence. He was a forceful, persuasive speaker but by no means a polished orator. His effectiveness was due to the depth of his conviction rather than to personality or eloquence.

Now, at fifty-four, he signed the document for which he had worked so hard. His hands shook, his eyes were watery, and his clothes were plain and ill-fitting. Yet here was one of the great architects of the American republic.

The other Adams was next in line. John, a second cousin of Sam Adams, was also a Harvard graduate. He was a native of the same town as John Hancock's birthplace—Braintree, Massachusetts—and was a leader in the patriot movement from its very beginnings when protests against the Stamp Act were being voiced in 1765. He was a powerful spokesman for independence, yet his keen legal mind was never clouded by prejudice or uncontrolled emotion. Even in the face of popular outrage, he defended British soldiers who had taken part in the "Boston Massacre," arguing at their murder trial that the true criminals were the supreme authorities in England, and that the troops were merely carrying out orders of their superiors. He won acquittal for all but two of the soldiers. The two were convicted of manslaughter and released without severe punishment.

This was a test of moral courage on the part of John Adams. He knew that he was risking his political career by defending the

SAMUEL ADAMS

soldiers, but as it turned out, the people of Massachusetts showed respect for his honesty and courage by electing him to the General Court, or legislature. From there, he went to the First Continental Congress, where he was prevailed upon by friends to restrain himself in expressing his views on independence. Though he was personally convinced that a break with England was inevitable, he went along with the more conservative delegates who believed that a formal protest to the British Government would suffice to bring the desired improvements. John and Samuel Adams, as well as a number of other delegates, including Patrick Henry and George Washington, bided their time, certain that they would be forced to fight.

At the Second Continental Congress, which convened May 10, 1775, it was John Adams who proposed that George Washington be

ROBERT TREAT PAINE   ELBRIDGE GERRY

appointed commander-in-chief of the Continental Army. The army was organized, the forces for independence grew stronger, and the inevitable break with Britain came as John had predicted it would.

The next Massachusetts signer was a distinguished-looking gentleman with a strong, determined face. Robert Treat Paine had won a wide reputation for his eloquent speeches condemning Britain's highhanded policies in America. He was, at the signing, forty-five years old and was generally considered the foremost attorney of Massachusetts. His Puritan background had given him an unbending code of behavior. What he lacked in humor he made up for in determination, honor and courage. At the urging of his parents he had studied theology, served as a chaplain in a New England regiment, and for a time delivered sermons in Boston churches. For some unexplained reason, he shifted to a study of law, paying for his own

JOHN ADAMS

schooling by teaching on the side. Paine began his law practice about 1759 in Taunton, Massachusetts, where he married a Miss Sally Cobb. Then, as people began to protest against edicts of the British governor of Massachusetts, Robert Paine joined the patriots and attended meetings and conventions. By a curious coincidence, at the historic signing of the Declaration, he followed the man he had opposed at the trial of British soldiers in Boston, for it was Paine who had been appointed special prosecutor in that celebrated case. As a delegate to the Congress he won the sobriquet of the "Objector," due to his constant opposition to motions and proposals. Generally, he supported united colonial action in the hope that Britain would accede to their demands. He did not favor independence until the outbreak of actual fighting in 1775. Then he chaired a committee for the purchase of guns and bayonets.

Paine finally voted for the Declaration, and he signed it without hesitation despite his earlier moderate position.

William Ellery looked in vain for the last of the Massachusetts delegates, Elbridge Gerry, a slender young man of thirty-two, a native of Marblehead, who had worked for independence from the earliest days of patriot activity. Another Harvard graduate, Gerry was a close friend of Thomas Jefferson and John Adams. He was serious, intense, and given to switching his support from one group in Congress to another. Nevertheless, he had voted for the Declaration, and despite his apparent indecision on many issues, he consistently supported legislation to strengthen the armed forces and served on a number of committees involved in arming and equipping troops.

On August 2, the day of the formal signing, Gerry was absent from Congress. He did not put his signature to the document until November 19, 1776.

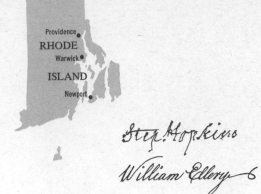

One of the elder delegates now stepped forward to sign the Declaration. He walked unsteadily, shuffling slowly to the table where he took up the quill in a hand that shook with palsy. This was Stephen Hopkins, sixty-nine, the signer who said, "My hand trembles, but my heart does not."

Hopkins had been involved in Rhode Island politics for nearly 50 years, having served in the Rhode Island legislature for many terms and having been elected governor of the colony nine times. Strongly in favor of the abolition of slavery, he had freed the slaves on his own estate. As early as 1759 Stephen Hopkins had advocated a union of the American colonies. As chief justice of the Rhode Island superior court he refused to have a group of colonists arrested after they burned a British revenue schooner, the *Gaspée*, in protest against restrictive Navigation Acts. From the beginning, Hopkins spoke vehemently in support of independence. He was one of the few delegates at the First Continental Congress who opposed any form of conciliation with Britain.

STEPHEN HOPKINS

The *Gaspée* burning in Rhode Island waters.

43

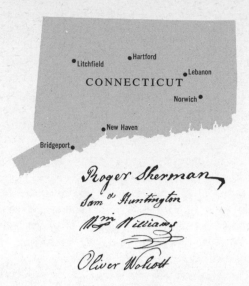

The self-appointed observer, William Ellery, the other delegate from Rhode Island, had come to know Stephen Hopkins well. He admired the elder statesman for his unshakeable courage and conviction, and was proud to follow him to the table and to add his name to the parchment. Ellery was a much younger man, forty-eight on this occasion. He was a native of Newport, a Harvard graduate, and had entered into a number of business ventures without much success. Finally he became a lawyer, in which profession his keen wit was a valuable asset. He soon built up a large practice in Rhode Island and became so well known that he was overwhelmingly elected to the Continental Congress. Since Rhode Island had already declared its independence from Britain at the time Ellery took his seat in May 1776, he was naturally one of the foremost advocates of independence for all the colonies and he had pledged his large fortune to Congress. He was an odd-looking fellow, rather short and stockily built with a head that appeared too large. He loathed physical exercise, but devoted his energy to mental and intellectual pursuits. His caustic remarks often brought laughter to the serious debates in the State House. Now under Stephen Hopkins' shaky signature Ellery wrote his name with a neat, confident flourish, then returned to his place to observe the rest of the proceedings.

The next signer was Roger Sherman of Connecticut, a self-taught lawyer who had started his career as a shoemaker's apprentice. His father was a Massachusetts farmer who had little money for the boy's education. As a result Roger read dozens of books on politics, theology and law. Meanwhile he continued to repair shoes and did some surveying until he had acquired enough money to set up his own law office. His courage and determination were demonstrated when as a young man he moved from Newton, Massachusetts, to New Milford, Connecticut, walking over a hundred miles with a heavy case of shoemaker's tools strapped to his back. Not only did he learn law from his reading, but he became an accomplished mathematician. He used this knowledge in his work as a surveyor and he even delved into astronomy. Ultimately he moved to New Haven, Connecticut, where he became a popular leader in political affairs. He was elected to the Connecticut legislature, became a judge of the superior court, and defended colonial rights against the unpopular edicts of the British Parliament. Shortly before the Revolution he headed the New Haven Committee of Correspondence. He was a sober, plainly dressed Puritan who, according to Thomas Jefferson, "never said a foolish thing in his life." When he was only forty-five, Sherman held four positions at one time, serving on the governor's council, the Connecticut upper house, as judge of the Connecticut high court and as treasurer of Yale College. Having helped to draft the Declaration, he signed it

with a stiff, clear hand as plain and un-
complicated as his Yankee upbringing.

Sherman was followed by two other Connecticut delegates: Samuel Huntington and
William Williams. Huntington was a quiet
man, dignified and reserved in his manner,
and although he could scarcely be numbered
among the fiery patriots, he was firm in his

To the Hon.ble Jonathan Law Esq.r Gov.r of CONNECTICUT in New Eng.d this Prospect of YALE COLLEGE is humbly dedicated by his Honour's most humble Serv.t James Buck

SAMUEL HUNTINGTON

WILLIAM WILLIAMS

OLIVER WOLCOTT

belief that the colonies should be independent. Although he had held the post of King's attorney right up to the outbreak of revolution, he never faltered in his work for the patriot cause once the colonies had set their course toward independence. Like Roger Sherman, he was the son of a Puritan farmer and he had largely educated himself. He had first been apprenticed to a cooper where he learned to make barrels, but he studied law in his spare time and was admitted to the bar when he was twenty-seven. From a successful law practice he entered politics and served in the Connecticut legislature, then in the Second Continental Congress. He was forty-five when he signed the Declaration of Independence.

William Williams, also age forty-five, next took up the quill pen. Here was another stern faced New Englander, son of a Congregationalist minister. Williams was a Harvard graduate who had at one time thought of following his father and grandfather into the ministry. However, during the French and Indian Wars, he served with his uncle, Colonel Ephraim Williams, the founder of Williams College, and he returned with a determination to become a merchant. In this he enjoyed some success, but his election to the Connecticut legislature in 1757 drew him into a lifelong political career. Sent as a delegate to the Second Continental Congress, he voted to break all ties with England. He pledged everything he had to the colonial cause, even signing promissory notes in 1775 to raise money for the army.

Another Connecticut delegate, Oliver Wolcott, did not sign the Declaration until September 4, as he had been forced to leave Philadelphia in June due to poor health. Nevertheless, he was an ardent patriot. It was Wolcott who had brought the New York statue of George III to his home in Windsor, Connecticut, where his wife and other ladies of the town melted it down to make bullets for the Continental Army. Wolcott was born in Windsor on November 20, 1726. He was as much a soldier as he was a politican; after graduating from Yale College with highest honors, he had accepted a captain's commission and fought on the northern frontier in the French and Indian War. He became a major general of the Connecticut militia and in 1776 he led fourteen regiments in the defense of New York City. This action prolonged his absence from Congress, but shortly after his units had joined with the main body of the Continental Army in New York, he returned to Philadelphia and added his signature to the Declaration.

The geographical order of delegates brought the New York representatives to the table next. The first of this group was William Floyd, a well-to-do young man of forty-one who had been active in community affairs on Long Island and was a major general in his local militia. His estate was particularly vulnerable to British seizure, for the redcoats had already occupied Staten Island in July and the number of British warships in New York harbor had been increasing daily until the masts of more than a hundred vessels were clustered like a leafless forest; their decks were crowded with the blue uniforms of German mercenaries and the scarlet of crack British units. Yet another enemy flo-

tilla appeared in the harbor, sailing in from the south almost at the time that William Floyd was signing the Declaration.

William Floyd was, therefore, well aware of the risk he took in supporting the patriot cause, yet he had thrown himself whole-heartedly into the struggle for independence. The son of a prosperous landowner, Floyd spent much of his boyhood and early youth in sport and social activities. What little education he received was largely from tutoring at home, but he was a logical thinker, and his consistent support of the patriot movement made him popular with the people in his community.

After Floyd had joined the Suffolk County militia, he rose to command of the unit. In 1774 he was chosen to represent New York at the First Continental Congress. He returned to his estate at a time when a British invasion of Long Island was threatened. Floyd immediately called his militia and prepared to fight any landings the British might attempt.

View of New York from the northwest shortly before 1773.

However, the invasion did not take place. At the Second Continental Congress, he served on a number of committees. Although he favored independence, along with the other New York delegates, he abstained from voting on the Declaration, pending instructions from the New York legislature. New York's approval was voted in time for them to sign the document on August 2.

Floyd was followed by a much older gentleman, a stout, stern-looking man of sixty-two, who had been born at Livingston Manor, his family's huge estate in Albany and who had conducted a highly profitable business as an importer in New York City. Philip Livingston was as stern in his beliefs and principles as in appearance. His temper flared over any injustice and he had been angered by the arrogance of British rule. At the same time, he was opposed to violence on the part of overzealous patriots. Repeatedly he tried to inject reason into protests to the royal governor of New York, and when he was selected to serve in the colonial assembly in 1768 he led that body in drawing up a set of resolutions demanding that the British Parliament recognize certain rights of the colonies.

This action was premature. The governor dissolved the assembly, and in a new election, pro-British Tories won a popular majority. But the relations of the colonies with England continued to deteriorate, and Philip Livingston was sent to the First Continental Congress in 1774. He and his brothers, William and Robert, were also delegates to the Second Continental Congress, but William left Philadelphia to command the New Jersey militia prior to adoption of the Declaration, and Robert, opposing independence as too radical a step, withdrew from the Congress after serving briefly on the committee to draft the Declaration. Thus, of the three brothers, only Philip was on hand for the signing. Having

tried to restrain the colonists from taking this drastic step, he nevertheless joined with the majority when the final decision was made.

It was to be an ironical fact of history that Livingston and other New York signers who had at first been lukewarm to independence, were among the men who were to suffer most at the hands of British troops. One of these was sixty-three-year-old Francis Lewis, the next delegate to affix his signature to the Declaration. Lewis was one of eight signers who were born abroad. He was a native of Llandaff in Wales, was educated in London, and had come to America at the age of twenty-four. He had settled in New York City where he developed a successful merchandising firm and accumulated a comfortable fortune. After an adventurous career which included being shipwrecked on the coast of Ireland and being captured by Indians during the French and Indian Wars in 1756, he retired from business at the age of fifty-two, to devote his talents to public

PHILIP LIVINGSTON

service. Lewis quickly became a leader in protests against the British Stamp Tax and other restrictive laws. He was outspoken in his denunciation of pro-British colonists, yet he was slow to accept the idea of complete independence, believing as did many New Yorkers that Parliament could be persuaded to take a more moderate course. As it became obvious that no amount of reason could change royal policy, he took a firm stand on independence and signed the Declaration without the slightest hesitation. For this he and his family were destined to pay a heavy price.

Last to sign for the New York delegation was Lewis Morris, age fifty. William Ellery saw him as an aristocratic gentleman with the proud bearing of a man who had been born to affluence. A grandson of the first royal governor of New Jersey, he had inherited "Morrisania," an estate of over two thousand acres covering a large area of what is now the Bronx in New York City. While most of his wealthy neighbors were Tories who supported British policy, Morris spoke out forcefully against England, and after making some fiery speeches in the New York Assembly, he was soon deeply involved in patriot activity. He worked with George Washington on plans for supplying a continental army, and was sent on a mission to western Pennsylvania in order to gain support of Indians in fighting the British.

In 1776, he was elected to serve in the Second Continental Congress, but as he was also a brigadier general of New York militia, his military duties kept him away from Philadelphia during the debates over the Declaration. However he was on hand for the signing on August 2. Tall, distinguished, and immaculately dressed, the fifty-year-old Morris stepped forward, took the quill and put his huge fortune on the line with a few strokes of the pen and a bold calligraphic flourish.

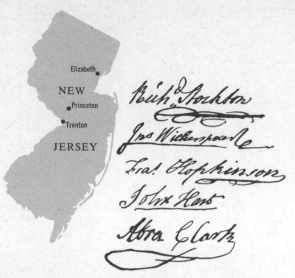

As the first of New Jersey's delegates moved to the table, William Ellery watched him with intense interest. Here was another man of considerable means, but one who had been known as a moderate, and who had at first resisted drastic measures in dealing with Britain. Richard Stockton, forty-five, a graduate of the College of New Jersey, wealthy landowner and successful lawyer, had been won over to the side of independence. He showed not the slightest hesitation in signing his name to the Declaration. If he had any premonition of the personally disastrous consequences of his act, he gave no sign of it as Ellery observed him.

Stockton's background could easily have led him to a Tory viewpoint. While serving as a trustee of the College of New Jersey he had gone to Scotland in 1766 for the purpose of finding a new president for the college. It was on this mission that he met John Witherspoon, and prevailed upon him to accept the college presidency. After his return to America, Stockton was asked to serve on the executive council of William Franklin, the royal governor of New Jersey. In this position he was surrounded by conservatives and loyalists to whom colonial independence was unthinkable. Stockton was naturally influenced by these men, and for a time he had believed that reconciliation between Britain and the colonies was possible. However, when it became clear that a break with England was inevitable he resigned from the governor's council. He was appointed to the supreme court of New Jersey in 1774, and

to the Continental Congress in June 1776, just in time for him to hear John Adams' plea for the Declaration of Independence. By this time he was wholeheartedly dedicated to the patriot cause.

The somberly dressed clergyman who followed Richard Stockton to the table was the Rev. John Witherspoon, the Scottish Presbyterian pastor, whom Stockton had brought to America in 1768 as the newly appointed president of the College of New Jersey — later Princeton University. Witherspoon was born in 1723 near Edinburgh and was a descendant of the great founder of Protestantism in Scotland, John Knox. Witherspoon entered Edinburgh University at the age of fourteen, graduated at eighteen, but continued to study theology for another three years. After accepting the pastorate of a parish in Beith, he became involved with the people in their attempts to restore "Bonnie Prince Charlie" to the throne. He was captured by English troops at the Battle of Falkirk in 1746, but was released after a brief term in prison. He rapidly gained a wide reputation for his writings on individual rights and human dignity. When Richard Stockton sought to bring him to America, Elizabeth Witherspoon, his wife, objected because she feared that life in the colonial "wilderness" would be too rugged for her and their five children. But a mutual friend, Benjamin Rush, an American who was studying medicine at Edinburgh at the time, joined Stockton in persuading the couple to go.

Witherspoon's direction of the College of New Jersey was highly successful. He quickly became a leading figure in colonial affairs, siding with the revolutionary groups from the beginning. During a debate over the course the colonies should take he once heard a remark that America was not yet ripe for a declaration of independence. He was reported to have replied, "In my judgment, we are

Nassau Hall and the president's house,
Princeton University.

JOHN WITHERSPOON

not only ripe for independence, but in danger of rotting for want of it." He needed no persuasion to vote for and then sign the Declaration.

In direct contrast to the dignified Reverend Witherspoon was Francis Hopkinson, an energetic little man with a lively manner and a habit of speaking in short, rapid sentences. Although he was a native of Philadelphia, where he was born in 1737, Hopkinson had settled in Bordentown, New Jersey, after his marriage to Ann Borden, a wealthy heiress.

His growing reputation as a lawyer brought him an appointment to the New Jersey governor's council. Nevertheless he supported the patriots and wrote such scathing articles about British rule that he soon had a large and enthusiastic following in the colonies.

Hopkinson's father, Thomas, had been a well-to-do lawyer and jurist, and was the American Philosophical Society's first president when the organization was founded in 1744. Young Francis had been educated at the College of Philadelphia (later to become

51

Left to right
FRANCIS HOPKINSON
JOHN HART
ABRAHAM CLARK

the University of Pennsylvania) and was a member of its first graduating class. He then studied law at the office of Benjamin Chew, attorney general of Pennsylvania.

Hopkinson visited England when he was twenty-eight, lived at his uncle's home for several months and met some of the most important British leaders, including the prime minister. Much as he enjoyed his stay, he returned to America with no great affection for Britain's rulers, and by the time the Second Continental Congress convened, Hopkinson was eager to serve in it.

"Honest John Hart," a plainly dressed Jersey farmer, was the next delegate to sign. Hart, now sixty-five, had been a tall, dark-haired youth whose good looks and good manners had endeared him to his neighbors. Although he had received a meager education, his honesty, hard work and common sense had marked him as a leader in his community. He had been born in Stonington, Connecticut, in 1711, but had been brought to New Jersey by his parents when he was a small boy. His life had been quiet and productive. His 380-acre farm prospered, and his wife, Deborah, presented him with 13 children. As a justice of the peace for Hunterdon County, he won a reputation for fair dealing, and in 1761 was elected to the New Jersey legislature. While serving on that body he voted opposition to the British Stamp Act and backed the refusal to pay British troops stationed in the colony. In 1774 he served as a member of the first congress called by New Jersey to elect delegates to the newly formed Continental Congress.

Because the original New Jersey delegation in Philadelphia opposed independence, the provincial legislature had voted to replace it with a new group, which included John Hart. As a result he was on hand August 2 to sign the Declaration and, like Richard Stockton, was destined to suffer tragic consequences.

Abraham Clark was the last of the New Jersey delegates to come forward. William Ellery saw a man of fifty, rather stout, dignified, with an expression of solemn determination. Born in Elizabethtown, New Jersey, in 1726, he had been a frail child whose parents considered him too sickly to be sent to school. He taught himself mathematics and the fundamentals of law. Although he had never been admitted to the bar, he offered free legal advice to the poor and as a result he earned the nickname of "The Poor Man's Counselor." An early champion of independence, he joined the New Jersey Committee of Safety in 1774, and when in June 1776, the state legislature arrested and imprisoned the royal governor, William Franklin, Clark was selected as one of the new patriot delegates to the Second Continental Congress. Along with the other New Jersey representatives he had voted for independence and adoption of the Declaration. Now, only a month after his arrival in Philadelphia, he was affixing his signature to the all-important document.

View of Philadelphia from the Jersey shore in 1768.

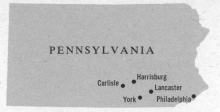

PENNSYLVANIA

Carlisle • • Harrisburg
• Lancaster
York • • Philadelphia

Rob Morris
Benjamin Rush
Benj. Franklin

John Morton
Geo Clymer
Ja. Smith
Geo. Taylor
James Wilson
Geo. Ross

The man who became the "Financier of the Revolution," and who was first of the Pennsylvania delegates to sign the Declaration, was Robert Morris, forty-two, a Philadelphia merchant who had cautiously abstained from voting for independence from Great Britain. Despite his early opposition to the Stamp Tax and his membership in the Philadelphia Committee of Safety, he had steadfastly opposed violence or any drastic action against British authority. He was born in Liverpool, England, in 1734, the son of a prosperous tobacco merchant who came to Maryland when Robert was still a young boy. He was sent to school in Philadelphia, and it was in that city that he learned the import business with the well-established trading firm of Charles Willing. After his father was accidentally killed by a cannon that was firing a salute to the arrival of one of

ROBERT MORRIS

the College at the age of fourteen. Young as he was, he took up the study of medicine under a Philadelphia doctor by the name of Redman. For six grueling years he worked with Redman, gaining much practical experience during one of the terrible yellow fever epidemics of that period. Then, in 1766, he sailed to England and continued his medical studies at the University of Edinburgh, Scotland. While there, he learned of his uncle's death, and was asked by Richard Stockton and other trustees of the College of New Jersey to speak to John Witherspoon about the vacant position at the College. It was partly due to Rush's persuasive arguments that Witherspoon finally accepted the post. Ultimately, they became fellow signers of the Declaration. Benjamin Rush, Richard Stockton and John Witherspoon all became fast friends, and Rush married Stockton's daughter, Julia, in 1776.

In London, Dr. Rush met Benjamin Franklin, who took such a liking to him that he made a 200-pound loan to the young physician for a trip to Paris. Rush spent much of his time in the French capital visiting hospitals and studying their facilities. After returning to Philadelphia, he won considerable fame not only as a leading physician but as a brilliant essayist on independence from Britain. In 1769 he became a professor of chemistry at the College of Philadelphia.

Elected to the Second Continental Congress in July 1776, he was seated too late to vote for the Declaration, but on August 2 he signed with genuine enthusiasm.

Now Ellery leaned slightly forward to watch the oldest member of the Congress who stepped to the table and took up the quill. Following the thirty-year-old Benjamin Rush, Dr. Franklin at seventy looked old indeed, and his silvered hair and his spectacles gave him an air of venerable dignity. Everyone loved and respected Benjamin

his ships, Robert Morris worked diligently in the Philadelphia company, becoming a full-fledged partner at the age of twenty. The firm, which became known as Willing, Morris & Company, was one of the leading shipping concerns in the colonies. Elected to the Pennsylvania legislature late in 1775, Morris was picked as one of that body's representatives in the Continental Congress, where he became a member of a vital committee to obtain arms from foreign countries. He also took part in laying plans for building an American navy. However, he did not appear for the vote on independence on July 2, or for the adoption of the Declaration two days later. He continued to argue that the colonies were not ready to break away from England; still, he signed the Declaration with a firm hand.

Morris was followed by the young physician, Benjamin Rush, who had played an important role in persuading John Witherspoon to accept the presidency of the College of New Jersey. From his station near the table, William Ellery saw a handsome fellow of thirty, and he marvelled at this youthful delegate's accomplishments. A native of Philadelphia, Rush had received his early education at his uncle's West Nottingham Academy in Maryland. The uncle, Samuel Finley, was later appointed president of the College of New Jersey, and Rush followed him there as a student. He graduated from

Franklin. When he took up the pen to inscribe his famous name on the parchment, all conversation in the hall ceased for a moment. He had already become such a giant of his time, that his connection with the Declaration seemed overshadowed by so many previous accomplishments.

Franklin had been born in Boston, January 17, 1706, the youngest son of a candlemaker by the name of Josiah Franklin. Ben had learned the printing trade largely because his parents were unable to afford the education necessary for him to become what they hoped would be his calling — that of a minister. After a five-year apprenticeship in his brother James' print shop, at the age of seventeen, Benjamin took passage on a ship to New York. He was now an established journalist, for unknown to James, he had been writing essays for his brother's newspaper, signing them, "Mrs. Silence Dogood." When Ben failed to find work in New York, he went on to Philadelphia where he obtained a job as a printer's assistant. While thus employed, he rented a room in the house of Deborah Read, whom he later married. A year or so afterward, the governor of Pennsylvania, Sir William Keith, took an interest in young Franklin, offered to set him up in business with a printing shop, and urged him to go to London to buy presses and type. Keith assured Franklin that he would send letters of credit to finance the enterprise. But after he arrived in England in 1725, Franklin found that Governor Keith had not lived up to his promise. Forced to find work with a London printer, Franklin spent eighteen months enjoying life in the British metropolis. Then a wealthy Philadelphia merchant, who was in London on business, met Franklin and persuaded him to return to America and to work for him in his shipping firm. Back in Philadelphia, he spent only a brief period in Thomas Denham's business, then returned to printing when the merchant died. Franklin began to save his money for the purpose of acquiring his own shop. He founded the Junto, a philosophical club, from which grew the American Philosophical Society. At the same time, he built up the Junto's library and in 1731 he used this as the basis for the first circulating library — the Library Company of Philadelphia. Mean-

while, in 1729, he began publishing *The Pennsylvania Gazette* with the help of a printer partner, Hugh Meredith. Three years later, in 1732, he established *Poor Richard's Almanack*. This quickly became the leading American periodical with its witty commentary and maxims. When he was thirty, Franklin became a clerk in the legislature of Pennsylvania. This began for him a political career that included such offices as postmaster of Philadelphia (later of the colonies), representative in the Pennsylvania legislature and delegate to the Continental Congress. Meanwhile his scientific experiments led to the invention of the famous Franklin stove, bifocal glasses, an electric storage battery, and to the discovery that lightning was an electrical charge.

As early as 1754, when the French and Indian Wars threatened American security, Franklin outlined a plan for uniting the colonies under a representative government, but the plan was never adopted.

Franklin spent five years in London representing Pennsylvania in a tax dispute between the colonists and the "proprietors" of Pennsylvania who were descended from William Penn. The British proprietors claimed tax exemption for their lands, but Franklin won his case for the colony. The tax exemption was withdrawn for all but land that had never been surveyed. On a later visit to London in 1765, he worked successfully for repeal of the Stamp Act, but this unpopular tax measure had permanently damaged relations between Britain and the American colonies. Franklin continued to serve in England as a diplomatic representative of Pennsylvania, Georgia, New Jersey and Massachusetts. Despite his wise council, British authorities took an increasingly dim view of Franklin's efforts to present the colonial viewpoint, and with war imminent, he returned to America, arriving May 5, 1775.

He was promptly elected to the Continental Congress, served on the Pennsylvania Committee of Safety, and was appointed Postmaster General of the colonies.

Having helped Jefferson to draft the Declaration of Independence, he now signed it with an elaborate flourish.

After the great Dr. Franklin came John Morton, a fifty-two-year-old delegate from Ridley Township, near the town of Chester, Pennsylvania. Joining with Franklin and James Wilson, he had cast the deciding Pennsylvania vote for independence on July 2, the day when John Dickinson and Robert Morris were absent and when Charles Humphreys and Thomas Willing voted against the Declaration. His key support of independence turned many of his friends and neighbors against him, since there were many loyalist Quakers in his community.

Morton was born in 1724, the son of John and Mary Richards Morton. The father died before the birth of his son, and as a result John Junior was brought up by a stepfather, John Sketchley, who taught the boy surveying and mathematics. At thirty-two Morton was elected to the Pennsylvania legislature, on which he served for over 20 years. He strongly opposed British tax policies, a stand that made him a popular figure throughout the colony. For three years he served as sheriff of Delaware County, was elected speaker of the house of representatives, then became an associate judge of the Pennsylvania supreme court. When he was sent to the First Continental Congress in 1774, he worked for healing the rift with Britain, but in the Second Congress he began to support the independence movement.

John Morton was followed by a much younger man, George Clymer, thirty-seven, a Philadelphia merchant who had been working diligently for the break from England. Clymer, a partner in the shipping

firm of Meredith and Clymer, was a close friend of George Washington. He was reserved, quiet, but thoroughly informed on the trends and events of his time. After graduation from the College of Philadelphia he had learned the importing business in the counting house of his uncle, William Coleman. At twenty-six he married Elizabeth Meredith, daughter of another prosperous Philadelphian who took him into the firm as a partner. Early in the period of tension with Great Britain, Clymer took an active part in the colonial cause, attending protest meetings and speaking in defense of colonial rights. He joined the local militia, became a captain, and was elected to the Pennsylvania Committee of Safety. When the Continental Congress began to seek funds for the army, George Clymer was appointed treasurer with the task of raising money to support Washington. He exchanged all of his personal assets for Continental paper money and prevailed upon most of his wealthy friends and business acquaintances to follow suit. When the Pennsylvania delegation to Congress expressed opposition to independence, several delegates were recalled and replaced by popular demand, and among the new appointees was George Clymer. He took his seat July 20, 1776, too late to vote for the Declaration, but just in time to sign the historic document.

Next of the Pennsylvania delegates was James Smith, Irish born son of a York County farmer who had settled in Pennsylvania in 1729. Like George Clymer, he had attended the College of Philadelphia, and had been elected to the Congress as a replacement for anti-independence delegates on the same date as Clymer. Smith's career had previously been devoted largely to law and surveying. Not until 1774 did he become involved in politics. His conviction that war with England was inevitable led him to organize the first Pennsylvania Company of patriot troops, and

he was elected its captain. Shortly afterward he became colonel of a full regiment. In 1775 and 1776 Smith served as a delegate to patriot conventions, and was finally sent to the Second Continental Congress on July 20, 1776, in time to join in the signing, August 2.

Smith was followed closely by George Taylor, another Irish immigrant. Taylor was a comparative unknown to Ellery and other veterans of the Continental Congress. He had come to America when he was about twenty-one, an indentured servant who had been forced to earn his freedom by hard work in an iron foundry near Durham, Pennsylvania. When it became clear that he was not strong enough to endure the strenuous furnace stoking, he became the firm's bookkeeper. Eventually, he married his employer's widow, Anne Taylor Savage, became the owner of the foundry and built up a large and prosperous business. With the spread of revolutionary fever in the colonies, Taylor accepted the commission of colonel in the local militia and was elected to the Pennsylvania legislature in 1775, an outspoken patriot who urged a full break with England. Now, at the age of sixty, as one of the five replacement delegates who had joined Congress on July 20, he proudly signed his name to the Declaration.

The next Pennsylvania signer was better known to William Ellery, who knew him as one of the most scholarly men in America. James Wilson was born in Scotland, had received his education at the universities of Glasgow, St. Andrews, and Edinburgh. When he was only twenty-three he decided to find a career in America, and he arrived in New York some time in 1765 when the first rumblings of discontent were being heard in the colonies. Wilson found employment as a Latin teacher at the College of Philadelphia. Shortly afterward he began a study of law in the firm of John Dickinson. Wilson lived for a time in Carlisle, Pennsylvania, where he

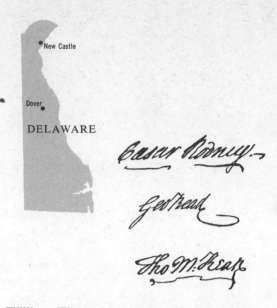

practiced law and married Rachel Bird. During this period, between 1767 and 1775, he became recognized as an outstanding patriot writer. His pamphlet, *Considerations of the Nature and Extent of the Legislative Authority of the British Parliament,* had wide circulation and was probably a factor in winning him election to the Second Continental Congress in 1775. Although his legal tutor, John Dickinson, opposed the Declaration, Wilson voted for it, and he proudly inscribed his name to the parchment on August 2. He was one of the younger signers, only thirty-three at the time.

Finally, George Ross signed for the Pennsylvania delegation. Ross was a real veteran of the Congress, having been a delegate to the First Continental Congress as well as the Second. In the earlier period he had been a loyalist, voting opposition to drastic action against England. Ross was of Scottish descent, but had been born in New Castle, Delaware, the son of an Episcopal minister. When the senior George Ross became assistant rector of Christ Church in Philadelphia, the family moved to Pennsylvania, and it was in Philadelphia that young Ross grew up and received most of his education. He studied law, and was admitted to the bar in 1750, at the age of twenty. He practiced law in Lancaster, Pennsylvania, and in 1768 was elected to the Pennsylvania legislature. His conservative views gradually changed as Britain continued to show its disdain for colonial petitions. Though not at first a delegate to the Second Continental Congress, he worked tirelessly for the Pennsylvania Committee of Safety, helped to draft the Pennsylvania State Constitution, and was chosen as one of the five replacements for the anti-independence delegates to the Congress. His tall, distinctive script at the bottom of the large list of Pennsylvania signatures stands out boldly as testimony that his earlier caution had been tossed aside.

William Ellery, his chin on his hand, was studying the countenance of the next signer. Caesar Rodney, the first of the Delaware delegation to come to the table, had won the eternal admiration of his Congressional associates with his wild ride from Dover, Delaware, on the night of July 1. Ellery found this man's appearance fascinating. Rodney was tall and thin. His small, wrinkled face seemed even smaller because of the green scarf he used to cover the left cheek that was afflicted by an advanced case of skin cancer. Despite his ill health, his eyes blazed with an indomitable spirit and a keen sense of humor. Born near Dover October 7, 1728, Caesar Rodney had been raised on his father's prosperous plantation. The father had died when Caesar was still a small boy, but his mother, acting as his tutor, had trained him to manage their large estate. At thirty he was elected sheriff of his county, became justice of the peace at the end of his term, and in 1761 was elected to the colonial legislature. In 1765 he was sent to the Stamp Act Congress in New York City.

Throughout his service in the Delaware legislature, Rodney supported the most liberal acts. He voted to prohibit the importation of slaves into Delaware, but the act was defeated. As speaker of the lower house of the legislature, he worked tirelessly for the patriot cause and was ultimately given chairmanship of the patriot convention. The convention elected him to the First and Second Continental Congresses.

The long night ride from Dover
to Philadelphia to vote for Independence.

Smallest of the colonies after Rhode Island, Delaware represented an important link between the north and the south. Unfortunately loyalists were everywhere, especially in the vicinity of Dover, and as the independence movement had gained momentum, so had violent opposition to it among Delaware's Tories.

In an effort to combat this opposition, Caesar Rodney was recalled from Congress in 1775 and given the task of building up a powerful and well-drilled force of volunteers. This was, to say the least, a difficult assignment. Patriots with sufficient enthusi-asm to leave their farms or their trades and professions to prepare for war with local Tories — many of whom were friends and neighbors — were hard to find. Yet Rodney set to work with his usual energy. He not only enlisted the required number of troops but within six months had made them one of the best disciplined units in all the colonies. Their presence alone helped to keep Tory activity to a minimum during 1775 and early 1776.

Nevertheless, the situation continued to be so tense that Rodney had been prevented from joining the debate over independence in

59

Philadelphia. Reports continued to circulate that an armed uprising in Delaware was imminent. Meanwhile Rodney had been commissioned a brigadier general to take command of the Delaware militia. It was because his military duties had kept him in Dover that his associate Thomas McKean had to summon him to the crucial vote in Congress on July 2. By voting for independence and signing the Declaration, Rodney knew that he had sealed his own death warrant, though not for the reason that he was guilty of treason in the eyes of Britain's rulers. His was a more personal problem, hopeless of solution. He had planned to go to London where a famous surgeon might have been able to save him. Now such a trip would be impossible, and there was no one in the colonies who knew how to treat his ailment.

The next signature to the Declaration is that of George Read. When he picked up the quill on August 2, 1776, he was forty-two years old, a cool, dignified jurist whose austere manner sometimes awed his compatriots. William Ellery, like most of the other delegates, had found him difficult to approach. He seemed to frown on familiarity and, as a result, had few close friends. Though he was a native of Maryland, he had studied law in Philadelphia and had set up his practice in New Castle, Delaware. A member of the colonial assembly of the Three Lower Counties, (originally administered by the governor of Pennsylvania) he took a strong stand against the Stamp Act, but was more cautious in his views on independence. His opposition to the Declaration prompted Thomas McKean to summon Rodney in order to provide the tie-breaking vote. Nevertheless, he signed the document with a firm, neat hand, and as far as Ellery could see he evinced neither doubt nor regret in taking this action.

Thomas McKean, the third and last representative of the newly formed state of Delaware was a forty-two-year-old lawyer from New Castle County. One of the most ardent patriots in the State House, tall, handsome Thomas McKean had been a fighter for freedom for the past 15 years, yet unfortunately he was not on hand to sign the Declaration on August 2. He was elected to the Delaware legislature in 1762, and he had served on this lawmaking body ever since. Delaware had sent him to the Stamp Act Congress in New York in 1765. On the basis of McKean's recommendation that each colony represented at the Stamp Act Congress have one vote, the equal voice rule was not only applied there, but in the Continental Congresses, and would be applied later in the Senate of the United States. During that same year of 1765, McKean became a justice of the peace in the court of common pleas in New Castle County. Under his jurisdiction, this court was the first in America to ignore the Stamp Act and to use unstamped documents in the conduct of its business. McKean was becoming increasingly popular in his community. In 1772 he was elected speaker of the Delaware house of representatives. He was then sent to the First Continental Congress, while he continued to serve as a delegate to the Delaware legislature and as a militia colonel for the state. In the Second Continental Congress, Thomas McKean favored independence from the very beginning of discussions on this explosive issue. William Ellery, watching for this ardent patriot, was disappointed not to see him in the gathering. When he inquired of a fellow delegate, he learned that McKean was absent on a tour of military duty with Washington's forces in New Jersey. McKean was not in a position to sign the Declaration until much later — probably some time in 1781. Although the exact date of his signing is not known, it is generally believed that he was the last of the delegates to affix his name to the document.

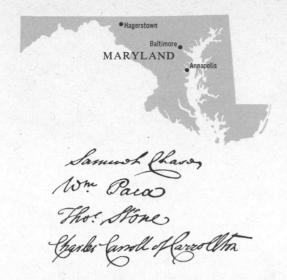

MARYLAND

SAMUEL CHASE

A heavyset gentleman led the four-man Maryland delegation to the table. He was Samuel Chase, who had been described by a leading citizen of Annapolis as "a busy, restless incendiary, a ringleader of mobs, a foulmouthed and inflaming son of discord and faction. . . a promoter of the lawless excesses of the multitude."* Chase was indeed a fiery patriot and a hot-tempered, argumentative politician. His florid face became easily reddened in the heat of debate. He was given to table- or desk-pounding as he spoke, and his Maryland compatriots nicknamed him "Bacon Face." Chase was only thirty-five when he signed the Declaration. He looked older. Ellery was amused by the angry expression on the Maryland delegate's face as he picked up the quill. Unlike the calm deliberation of the majority of signers, Chase wrote his name as though he wished the ink were pure venom that could somehow bring death to King George.

Samuel Chase was born on April 17, 1741 in Somerset County, Maryland. His father, Thomas Chase, was an Episcopal minister who became rector of St. Paul's Church in Baltimore. Under his father's tutelage, Samuel received a classical education, but as his mother had died at his birth, he apparently lacked training in gentlemanly manners. In 1759 he undertook the study of law in Annapolis, and he was admitted to the bar in 1761. Shortly afterward, when he was only

* Whitney, David C., Founders of Freedom in America, Chicago, Ill., J. G. Ferguson Publishing Company, 1964, p. 63.

twenty-three, he was elected to the Maryland legislature. From the start of his political career he showed his opposition to the royal governor and to external British rule. When the Stamp Act was passed in 1765, Chase led violent mob actions in protest, and burned in effigy the local stamp distributor, a royal agent. At the same time, he openly criticized other Maryland citizens and legislators for not being more outspoken in denouncing the tax.

After Chase took part in organizing the Maryland Committee of Correspondence, he was sent to the First Continental Congress where he was one of the few delegates to speak out passionately for rebellion against the Crown. In the Second Continental Congress he was pleased by the swing toward independence, and he was sent on a mission to Canada, along with Benjamin Franklin, John Carroll and Charles Carroll, in an effort to persuade the Canadians to break away from England. Since the mission failed, as did an abortive military expedition into Canada, Chase returned to Philadelphia in time to join in the debate over independence. To his dismay, he found that his own Maryland delegation had been instructed to vote *against* independence. He and Charles Carroll therefore took horses and rode to Maryland to address the legislature at Annapolis. They also travelled throughout the colony, making impromptu speeches in villages and on planta-

tions, urging the people to support the independence movement. So successful was this campaign that patriotic fervor swept Maryland. As a result, the legislature reversed its position and on June 28, Chase wrote a letter to John Adams saying, "I am just this moment from the house to procure an express to follow the post, with an unanimous vote of our convention for independence."*

Chase then mounted his horse and in a wild day-and-night ride, managed to arrive in Philadelphia in time to vote for independence with the other Maryland delegates on July 2.

William Paca followed Samuel Chase to the table. In contrast, here was a man of quiet dignity whose calm, legalistic appraisal of situations won the respect and confidence of his associates. Paca was born in Abingdon, Maryland, October 31, 1740, the son of John Paca, a wealthy plantation owner. After completing academic studies at the College of Philadelphia, he studied law in Annapolis and then in London. On his return to Annapolis, he set up a thriving law practice, married an heiress by the name of Mary Chew, and soon became a leader in his community. In 1768 he won election to the Maryland legislature where he became a close political ally of Samuel Chase. Although they were of entirely different temperaments, both men strongly opposed British efforts to rule by proclamation, and both took an early stand for independence. On one occasion, Paca and Chase led a crowd to the public square where they conducted a mock "hanging" of a governor's proclamation of taxes to be imposed on the colony. The proclamation was then buried under the gallows in solemn ceremony. Paca was appointed a delegate to the First Continental Congress in 1774, and to the Second Continental Congress a year later. He again worked closely with Samuel Chase dur-

* Whitney, David C., Founders of Freedom in America, p. 65.

ing the campaign to pressure the Maryland legislature into releasing their delegates for an affirmative vote on independence. As a result, Paca was permitted to vote for the Declaration which he now proudly signed.

The next signer from Maryland, Thomas Stone, was one of the younger delegates. At thirty-three, he was tall and lean, and his face had the pallor of a serious scholar. He was born on his father's plantation in Charles County, Maryland, some time in 1743. The exact date is not recorded. He learned horsemanship at an early age, since he had to ride 20 miles to school every day. As a younger brother, he inherited nothing of his father's large estate, but he acquired a loan so that he could study law under Thomas Johnson in Annapolis. By the time he was twenty-one he had passed his bar examination and was practicing law in Frederick. Ironically, he was appointed by the Maryland government to prosecute patriots who were defying the tax laws, although his sympathies were with his fellow colonists. When he was sent to the Second Continental Congress in 1775, he tried to pursue a moderate course in respect to England, but as it became evident that independence was the only honorable solution to the colonial problem, he voted with the majority and was on hand for the historic signing on August 2. Quiet and undemonstrative, he was not well known to the delegates from other states.

Better known to William Ellery and to others in the hall was Charles Carroll, thirty-eight, who now accepted the quill pen from Thomas Stone. Carroll was the sole Roman Catholic in the Congress, a fact that intrigued Ellery, who knew that according to old Maryland law, Catholics were not permitted to enter politics. Consequently, Carroll's desire for independence and freedom from the old regime had been stirred not only by the usual motives but by a personal determination to

bring genuine religious freedom to Maryland. Not that the Carroll family had suffered privation. Their estate at Carrollton Manor and their other tracts were among the great land holdings in America; their wealth and position could be traced through their ancestry to ancient Irish royalty. Charles Carroll, the younger, was born in Annapolis on September 19, 1737. At the age of eight, his father took him to France where he received his early education from Jesuit fathers at a school in St. Omer. Because of the religious and educational restrictions against Roman Catholics in Maryland, the senior Charles Carroll attempted to acquire a tract of land in French Louisiana where he proposed to resettle American Catholics, but he was unsuccessful in this mission. Meanwhile, young Charles continued advanced studies in Paris and Rheims, then he took up the study of law at the Inner Temple in London. He returned to Maryland in 1764, fluent in the French language and with the manners of a European aristocrat. When his father presented him with the huge Carrollton Manor plantation, he became known as Charles Carroll of Carrollton, as distinguished from the elder Charles Carroll of Annapolis. He married his cousin, Mary Darnall, at a time when he was becoming an active participant in the patriot movement. Unable to seek a seat in the Maryland legislature, he wrote newspaper articles and pamphlets which he signed "Second Citizen." His theme was the illegality of law by proclamation, and his writings became so popular that citizens of Annapolis gratefully awarded him the title of Maryland's "First Citizen." More than any other leader in Maryland, and for good reason, Carroll spoke forthrightly for revolution and a clean break with England. It is said that he once debated this point even with the fiery patriot Samuel Chase. When Chase stated that the colonists had already won their points against the British with sound written arguments, Carroll is reported to have replied, "And do you think that writing will settle the question between us?" "Certainly," replied Chase. "What else can we resort to?" "The bayonet!" exclaimed Carroll without hesitation.

Carroll soon became active on Maryland's Committee of Safety and Committee of Correspondence. Early in 1775 he became a member of a "Committee of Observation," an unofficial but powerful ruling body that ignored royal decrees and took Maryland law into its own hands. Though he still could not legally be elected to the Continental Congress, he was nevertheless chosen by the Philadelphia body to accompany Benjamin Franklin, Samuel Chase, and Carroll's own cousin, John Carroll, on the mission to Canada in hope of enlisting Canadians in the fight for independence from England. On his return from this unsuccessful expedition he worked tirelessly to get the Maryland legislature's approval of the Declaration of Independence. Finally, on July 4, 1776, the day of the Declaration's adoption, the Maryland state convention appointed him to the Continental Congress. He arrived at the State House on July 18 and was thus on hand for the signing. As Carroll came forward, William Ellery heard someone remark, "There goes another fortune!" Carroll smiled and inscribed with a flourish, *"Charles Carroll of Carrollton."*

other liberal arts subjects. At age fourteen, upon his father's death, he fell heir to a huge estate comprising over two thousand acres and about three dozen slaves. At seventeen he entered William and Mary College in Williamsburg, Virginia, graduating two years later, in 1762. He then undertook a study of law with George Wythe who was destined to become a fellow signer of the Declaration. Jefferson was an enthusiastic student of contemporary politics. He spent considerable time at the Virginia House of Burgesses, listening to the speeches and forming his own ideas of how a government should operate. When he heard Patrick Henry lash out against the Stamp Act, he was deeply affected by Henry's eloquence. For a few years Jefferson practiced law in Williamsburg, earning a comfortable income. During this time he also earned the reputation of being a radical thinker, for his views on individual freedom often clashed with the slave-owning members of his society. He won a seat in the Virginia House of Burgesses in 1769 and continued to serve on this body until the Revolution.

In 1772, Jefferson married Martha Wayles Skelton, a wealthy widow whose land holdings equalled his own. During this period he had begun the building of his famous home, Monticello, and he and his bride moved into the partially completed mansion.

As the colonies began to talk of open rebellion against England, Jefferson became a close friend of Richard Henry Lee, Patrick Henry, and Francis Lightfoot Lee. These three, together with Jefferson and his brother-in-law, Dabney Carr, held meetings at the Raleigh Tavern in Williamsburg. There they formed a Virginia Committee of Correspondence, and because the others recognized Jefferson's writing ability, they asked him to draw up appropriate resolutions which Carr presented to the House of Burgesses. On the prompt passage of the resolutions, Jefferson

No other group of delegates had been more influential in bringing about the break with England than the gentlemen from Virginia. In fact, of all the 13 colonies, Virginia stood out boldly as the leader in revolutionary thought and action. Here were the men who conceived of American independence as a legal right which sprang from the illegality of foreign tyranny, and who saw individual freedom as a God-given, inalienable right common to all peoples. Curiously, most Virginians had not applied such advanced thinking to the subject of Negro slavery, but the principles they expounded were nonetheless sound, and their concepts transcended their own narrow application of them. First of the Virginia signers to come under William Ellery's observation was Thomas Jefferson, author of the Declaration of Independence. The sandy-haired, thirty-three-year-old delegate signed his own composition in a large, stiff hand as he leaned down over the table from his six-feet-two-inch height.

Jefferson's cool courage, his candor and his inflexible determination to build a nation of free and independent states had won universal admiration and respect among his associates. Though he possessed a quiet dignity, he was warm and cordial to his friends and was known to have remarked, "My habit is to speak only of men's good qualities."

Born April 13, 1743, Jefferson had grown up on his father's plantation in Albemarle County, Virginia, and had attended a local school where he studied Latin, Greek and

The College of William and Mary.

THOMAS JEFFERSON

was appointed a member of the Committee of Correspondence.

Due to illness, Jefferson was not originally a delegate to the First Continental Congress, but in 1775, after his recovery, he was sent to replace his cousin, Peyton Randolph. Soon he was deeply involved in committee work. His paper on "the causes and necessity of taking up arms," attracted the attention of the delegates and established his reputation as a polished and persuasive writer. As a result, he was the overwhelming choice of the Congress to head a committee for drafting a declaration of independence. This committee of five, formed on June 11, 1776, consisted of Thomas Jefferson, chairman, John Adams, Benjamin Franklin, Robert Livingston, and Roger Sherman.

In the meantime, Jefferson had also been writing a proposed constitution for the state of Virginia, but by the time he submitted his draft, the Virginia convention had already adopted one written by George Mason. Nevertheless, the convention voted to use Jefferson's preamble.

The distinguished young Virginian now relinquished the pen to fifty-year-old Benjamin Harrison, the stout, jovial chairman of "the committee of the whole" who had presided over Congress during the vital debates on independence, July 1 and 2. Harrison was a gourmet and looked the part. A prosperous

65

Virginia planter, he owned several large plantations and lived lavishly. Nothing pleased him so much as a good wine, rich food and congenial company. He was an entertaining story teller who laughed infectiously at his own jokes and who was affectionately known as the Falstaff of Congress. For more than 25 years he had held a seat in the Virginia House of Burgesses, having several times been speaker of the house. For all his love of luxury, he had never hesitated to endorse the patriot cause and thereby to risk his life and fortune. Watching him sign the Declaration, William Ellery chuckled as he recalled a remark Harrison had made recently. Turning to slightly built Elbridge Gerry, fat Ben Harrison had said that when it came to hanging the signers, "I shall have all the advantage over you. It will be all over in a minute, but you will be kicking in the air half an hour after I am gone!"

Looked upon as an elder statesman of Virginia, Harrison wielded much influence. He was an intimate friend of George Washington and of Peyton Randolph, who had been president of the Congress until his death in 1775. Of Harrison's many children, seven survived childhood, and one of these, William Henry Harrison, was destined to become the ninth President of the United States. The twenty-third President, Benjamin Harrison, was a great grandson of the signer.

Now Harrison inscribed his name on the great document, his red face serious, but his eyes twinkling with humor. No doubt, thought Ellery, he would offer some wry comment concerning the occasion when he rejoined the other delegates.

Another Virginia delegate noted for his obesity and good humor followed Harrison. He was Thomas Nelson, age thirty-seven, son of a well-to-do merchant of Yorktown, Virginia. He was born December 26, 1738, spent his boyhood in Yorktown, but was sent to

Hackney preparatory school in England at the age of fourteen. For eight years he continued his studies abroad, attending Trinity College of Cambridge University, and not returning to Virginia until 1761. As he was then of age, his wealthy father presented him with a plantation and a large house in Yorktown. There Nelson and his wife, the former Lucy Grymes, enjoyed a life of luxury and ease, disturbed only by the natural turmoil created by 11 children. At twenty-six, Nelson had been elected to the Virginia House of Burgesses, where he served until 1774. In that year, the royal Governor Dunmore was presented with a number of resolutions calling upon the British Parliament to redress wrongs done to the colonies. Dunmore promptly dissolved the House of Burgesses, which merely moved in a body to a nearby tavern. There, they formed a provincial legislature and called upon the other colonies to join Virginia in a Continental Congress. Thomas Nelson was elected to the revolutionary legislature and was sent to the Continental Congress in August 1775. Meanwhile he had been commissioned a colonel of a Virginia regiment.

Nelson returned from Philadelphia to attend a session of the Virginia legislature early in 1776, and while there he offered a resolution asking that the Continental Congress declare American independence from Great Britain. When his resolution was passed, he carried it on horseback to Philadelphia, thus setting the stage for Richard Henry Lee's independence resolutions, which in turn led to the formal Declaration of Independence.

Despite his tendency to overweight, Nelson was a vigorous man. His joviality and apparently boundless energy won him a host of friends in the Congress as well as at home in Virginia.

As the next signer came forward, Ellery experienced a sense of disappointment, seeing

that it was Francis Lightfoot Lee, and not the older brother, Richard Henry, author of the original independence resolutions. Richard was still absent from Congress, having rushed to Virginia in June when he learned of his wife's serious illness. Francis, a less colorful political figure than his brother, was nevertheless a staunch patriot. He was born October 14, 1734, at the Lee mansion in Westmoreland County. Brought up with all the easy living of a Virginia country gentleman, he was more prone to seek social pleasures than his serious older brother. The father, Thomas Lee, served for a time as governor of Virginia, and he saw that his sons received a good education from private tutors.

When the elder Lee died in 1750, Francis acquired one of the Lee estates in Loudoun County, Virginia. Eight years later he became a member of the Virginia House of Burgesses, but he was not elected to the Continental Congress until one of the older Virginia delegates resigned in August 1775. A quiet, reticent man, Francis Lee took little part in debates on the floor of Congress, but was a persuasive talker at social gatherings or in small, private groups. As a result, he was an excellent committeeman. He strongly supported his brother's resolutions, voted for independence, and now signed the vital document.

Last of the Virginia delegates to sign on August 2 was Carter Braxton. William Ellery observed that this was the first of the signers who showed no enthusiasm for the task. Braxton's expression was dull, resigned, without emotion, as he lifted the quill pen. Searching his memory, Ellery thought he understood something of the man's feelings, for after the early death of his Virginia-born wife, Judith Robinson, Carter Braxton had gone to England where he made many friends among the leaders of British society. In 1761, he

married again, this time to Elizabeth Corbin, daughter of a British colonel who held the post of Receiver of Customs in Virginia for the King. Braxton's magnificent home became a center of social activity where officials from England as well as leading citizens of Virginia were lavishly entertained.

Braxton was born on his father's tobacco plantation in Newington, Virginia, on September 10, 1736. He received a liberal arts education at William and Mary College, and was still in his teens when he inherited the family estate upon the death of his father. In 1761 he was elected to the Virginia House of Burgesses, where he became intimate with George Washington, Thomas Jefferson, Patrick Henry, and Richard Henry Lee. However, because of upbringing and his family connections he did not share these patriots' zeal for independence from Britain. He did protest mildly against some of the early import taxes, and was prevailed upon to sign a non-importation agreement which had a serious effect on his own business interests. Elected in 1774 to the convention of Virginia patriots, then to the Committee of Safety and the Second Continental Congress, he pursued a conservative course, arguing and voting for conciliation between the colonies and England. He helped to restrain Patrick Henry and some of Henry's angry followers when they threatened to march on Williamsburg to seize a store of gunpowder that Governor Dunmore had impounded. In order to keep the peace, Braxton persuaded his father-in-law, Colonel Corbin, to pay the colonists for the powder and the proposed attack on Williamsburg was abandoned.

Braxton finally went along with the majority, and he now entered his name beneath those of the other Virginia delegates.

Not present for Virginia on August 2 were George Wythe and Richard Henry Lee, both of whom signed at a later date. Wythe was

the lawyer who gave Thomas Jefferson his law instruction. He was born some time in 1726 near Yorktown, Virginia, and like so many of the Virginia signers he grew up in the affluence of a prosperous plantation. He was tutored by his mother in Latin, Greek and mathematics, and this education proved valuable to him when his parents died and his older brother inherited the entire estate. He continued his education at William and Mary College, then studied law as a clerk in the law office of an uncle. About 1750 he began to practice, enjoying considerable success. By the time he was twenty-six, he was a member of the Virginia House of Burgesses. Meanwhile he achieved such a high reputation in his profession that he became generally rated as the foremost lawyer in Virginia.

When the hated Stamp Tax stirred patriot rebellion throughout the colonies, George Wythe wrote the "Resolutions of Remonstrance" which were among the strongest protests to be approved by the Virginia legislature. When the House of Burgesses was dissolved by the governor in 1775 Wythe was elected to the Virginia provincial congress. From there he was sent to the Second Continental Congress where he enthusiastically supported Richard Henry Lee's resolutions on independence. Since he was called back to Virginia to participate in the framing of a state constitution, he took Jefferson's draft with him, but he was absent from Philadelphia during the July debate on independence, and was not on hand for the formal signing on August 2. However, he returned to the Congress later in the month and signed his name to the Declaration August 27, 1776.

Richard Henry Lee, as has been stated earlier, was absent because of his wife's illness, but no man had contributed more to the cause of independence. From the opening session of the Second Continental Congress, Richard Lee was looked upon as a leader, and as Virginia's most illustrious delegate. As Lee was extremely wealthy, handsome, and influential, much of the early action of the Congress had revolved around him. Although he was a distinguished member of Virginia's landowning class, he favored the abolishment of slavery. He applauded the revolutionary ideas of New Englanders like John and Samuel Adams, and he often expressed a wish to move North, away from the Southern aristocracy.

Born on the Lee plantation in Westmoreland County, January 20, 1732, Richard Henry Lee had known only wealth and graceful living, and had received an excellent education at Wakefield Academy in England. The father, Thomas Lee, was acting governor of Virginia when he died, leaving his property to Richard Henry, who found himself owner and manager of huge plantations at the age of nineteen.

One of Lee's first encounters with British arrogance was in 1755 when, as a captain of the Westmoreland County militia, he offered his troops to General Braddock for a campaign against the French in the French and Indian War. Braddock rejected the Colonials whom he looked upon as untrained and undisciplined provincials. As a result, Lee began to develop an intense dislike for British authority.

In 1757, Richard Henry Lee was elected County Justice of the Peace, and he was sent to the Virginia House of Burgesses a year later. In his first speech to that distinguished body he startled the delegates by advocating abolition of slavery. His association with George Washington and Patrick Henry led him to an early conviction that the colonies had no honorable course but to fight for self government. He helped to establish the Virginia Committee of Correspondence, which he had conceived as early as 1768. There is still some question as to whether he or Samuel

Adams first thought of the idea as a means of unifying the colonies in their quest for independence.

When the House of Burgesses was dissolved, only to carry on their sessions in a nearby tavern, Richard Henry Lee prepared a request to the other colonies, urging that a Continental Congress be established in order "to deliberate on those general measures which the united interests of America . . . require."

Lee organized citizens of his own county to boycott British goods. Called the Westmoreland Association, it was the first group of its kind in America. As a result of his vigorous efforts in behalf of colonial justice, he was sent to the First Continental Congress in 1774. There he served on most of the

RICHARD HENRY LEE

major committees, and as leader of the Virginia delegation and as a polished writer, he was the author of most of the important resolutions adopted by the Congress. One of his more radical resolutions was not passed, however. In it he declared, ". . . as North America is able, willing, and, under Providence, determined to defend, protect and secure itself, the Congress do most earnestly recommend to the several colonies, that a militia be forthwith appointed and well disciplined, and that it be well provided with proper arms."

Later, when he became a delegate to the Second Continental Congress, Lee argued for drastic action with much greater success. Finally, his resolution of June 7, 1776, was adopted:

"Resolved: That these United Colonies are, and of right ought to be, free and independent States, that they are absolved from all allegiance to the British Crown . . ." and so forth.

This document adopted by the Congress was the first official blow to be struck by the United Colonies for independence. In introducing the resolution, Lee spoke with all the eloquence of a deep and abiding conviction.

"Why, then. . .do we longer delay? Why still deliberate? Let this happy day give birth to an American republic. Let her arise, not to devastate and to conquer, but to reestablish the reign of peace and of law."

One can only guess how keen must have been the disappointment of Richard Henry Lee when he could not be present on August 2 for the formal signing of the Declaration. Of greater historical importance was the fact that he would have been the logical choice of Congress to write the Declaration itself, but his enforced absence resulted in the selection of Thomas Jefferson for this important task.

Lee finally returned to Philadelphia and signed the Declaration on September 4, 1776.

North Carolina

Salem • • Hillsboro • Edenton

• Charlotte • New Bern

• Wilmington

Wm Hooper

Joseph Hewes,

John Penn

As William Hooper of North Carolina came forward, William Ellery was reminded that this Southern patriot was a Bostonian by birth and had studied law under a veritable firebrand of the Revolution, James Otis. Hooper had moved south to a colony where there had been strong loyalist sentiment, especially since an abortive uprising against a royal governor had failed in 1771. At that time, dissension between "uplanders" and "lowlanders" had led to the arrest of upland leader Harmon Husbands who was imprisoned in Governor Tryon's palace at New Bern. An uplander attack on the palace had been smashed when many North Carolinians rallied to the support of Tryon. Hooper's own father, a Scotch Congregationalist minister, supported the king and was deeply distressed by his son's political activities. Nevertheless, William Hooper steadfastly worked for the colonial cause.

Hooper was born June 7, 1742. Contrary to his father's wishes, who wanted him to enter the ministry, he decided to study law. After graduating from Harvard, he worked in the law office of James Otis who was already engaged in legal battles with the British over the enforcement of various tax measures. Young Hooper absorbed much of Otis' viewpoint in these matters, and he rapidly became an accomplished orator in his own right. After he had passed his bar examination he decided to go south where he was told there were wider opportunities for lawyers. In Wilmington, North Carolina, he met and married Anne Clark, became a success-

ful lawyer, and in 1770 was appointed deputy attorney general for the colony. While he served in this post, the rebellion against the royal governor broke out on North Carolina's western frontier. Hooper urged the use of militia to put down the insurrection, and he fought on the side of the government troops who crushed the frontier forces at the Battle of Alamance, 1771. Two years later, Hooper was elected to the colonial legislature, then to the First Continental Congress in 1774. As a member of the Second Continental Congress he had consistently voted for resolutions condemning British rule, and finally cast his vote for independence on July 4. Although he had initially opposed any form of violent dissent, he saw that compromise with Britain was becoming impossible. In 1775 he wrote, "That our petitions have been treated with disdain, is now become the smallest part of our complaint: ministerial insolence is lost in ministerial barbarity."

Hooper entered his name just to the left of John Hancock's signature, but in a much smaller, neatly executed script.

Next came Joseph Hewes, the second North Carolina delegate who had also been born in a northern colony. Hewes, a prosperous merchant at forty-six, was born in Kingston, New Jersey, January 23, 1730. As a boy he had been interested in ships and trade, had been apprenticed to a merchant in Philadelphia, serving as a countinghouse clerk, and had learned the trade so well that immediately after completing his apprenticeship he set up his own trading firm.

When he was twenty-nine he moved his business to Edenton, North Carolina, an active port on the Albemarle Sound. Soon he acquired a fleet of ships and was admired and respected in his county. In 1766 the community chose him as their representative to the North Carolina legislature. Re-elected time after time, he showed increasing distaste

for British rule. He reflected the sentiment of most of his constituents when he spoke vehemently against the Stamp Act, supported various patriot resolutions and became a member of the local Committee of Correspondence. Hewes was a logical choice to serve with North Carolina's delegation to the First Continental Congress. Although he

WILLIAM HOOPER

Royal Governor's residence at New Bern.

had been brought up as a Quaker, he did not go along with many Quakers who urged loyalty to King George. Instead, he voted for discontinuance of trade with England if colonial demands were not recognized, despite the serious effect such action would have on his own shipping business. In the Second Continental Congress Hewes served as chairman of the naval committee. When the American navy's first warship was commissioned, Hewes put John Paul Jones in command of the vessel. Having voted for independence on July 4, he now signed the Declaration with a firm hand.

Completing the trio of North Carolina delegates was John Penn, who had only recently moved to Granville County, North Carolina, from Virginia in 1774. Thus none of the three men of this delegation was a native of the state he represented. Penn was born in Caroline County, Virginia, on May 6, 1740, the son of a moderately successful planter. He had received almost no formal education until after his father's death in 1759, when he was

encouraged by an Edmund Pendleton to study law. Pendleton, a justice of the peace, possessed an excellent library, the use of which he offered to young Penn. By the most intensive study, Penn was able to pass his bar examination at the age of twenty-one, but his early years of law practice in Virginia were unrewarding. Finally, in the hope of finding better opportunities, he took his wife, the former Susannah Lynne, and their three children to Williamsboro, North Carolina. There the course of his life suddenly altered for the better. As he interested himself in the patriot movement, he quickly became a leader in his community, was elected to the provincial legislature in 1775 and then to the Second Continental Congress. William Ellery saw Penn as a fresh-faced and pleasant-looking man who appeared to be younger than his thirty-six years. He was quiet, not given to speechmaking and as a result, not too well known to his fellow delegates. But he had voted consistently for independence and now signed the document with enthusiasm.

View of Charleston, South Carolina, 1739.

SOUTH CAROLINA

Camden

Georgetown

Charles Town

Thomas Lynch Junr

Arthur Middleton

Edward Rutledge /.

Thos Heyward Junr.

The next signer was the youngest of them all — Edward Rutledge, twenty-six, who had only recently returned to America after studying law at the Middle Temple in London. He was born in Charles Town (now Charleston), South Carolina, November 23, 1749, the youngest of seven children. After a period of being privately tutored, he worked in the law office of his older brother, John, who hoped Edward would follow him in the legal profession. When he was nineteen, Edward went to England to complete his study of law, and by the time he came home, in 1773, the colonies were stirring with rebellion. John filled him with genuine fervor for the colonial cause, though both men believed at first that England would be persuaded to see reason in granting the rights Americans demanded.

In 1774, the two brothers, along with Edward's wealthy father-in-law, Henry Middleton, were chosen by the South Carolina legislature to represent the colony in the First Continental Congress. Whatever impression twenty-four-year-old Edward Rutledge may have made on other delegates, he certainly did not impress John Adams favorably. Adams called the young man "a peacock" and "excessively vain, excessively weak... and puerile."

Nevertheless, Edward supported the more conservative resolutions and acquitted himself well enough to warrant his being elected to the Second Continental Congress, as was his brother. Not long afterward John was summoned home to prepare the new state constitution and he was elected president of South Carolina.

Without his brother's experienced guidance Edward showed his weakness as he vacillated over the issue of independence. At his request Congress delayed the final vote on the matter from June 7, 1776, the day Richard Henry Lee offered his resolutions, until July 1. When the time for a decision finally arrived, Rutledge and his delegation voted negatively, but on July 2, he reversed himself and voted for the Lee resolutions. Then on July 4, he voted for the Declaration, which he now signed unhesitatingly. Opposition to Britain had only recently been aroused to a high pitch in South Carolina when ten British warships arrived off Charleston on June 4, 1776, and landed troops with the intention of attacking the fort on Sullivan's Island. The offensive was actually launched on June 28, with British infantry under General Clinton attempting to cross the narrow strait from Long Island to Sullivan's, while the fleet pounded the fort with its guns. But the Colonials had returned shot for shot and after a sweltering day of carnage, the British withdrew. They did not return to South Carolina until 1780.

The South Carolinians were a surprisingly youthful group. The oldest member was only thirty-four, and Thomas Heyward, Jr., who now came forward, was thirty. Here was another heir to a prosperous tobacco plantation who had been sent to the Middle Temple in London to study law. Heyward was born July 28, 1746, in St. Helena's Parish, South Carolina, was tutored in Latin and Greek at an early age and apprenticed in a law office for a time before going to England. During his stay in the British Isles he was embittered by the arrogant and contemptuous attitude of Britons toward the "backwoods colonials." By the time he returned to South Carolina, in 1771, he was ready to join the patriots in their efforts to throw off British rule. He became a

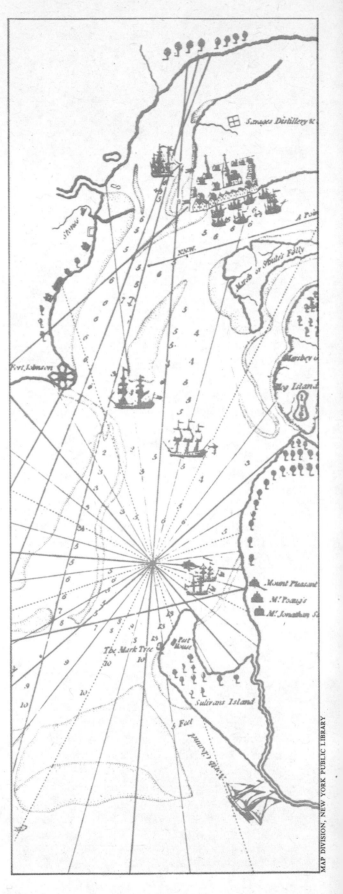

EDWARD RUTLEDGE

member of the South Carolina Committee of Safety and was appointed with ten other patriots to draw up a state constitution.

When he was twenty-seven, Heyward married Elizabeth Matthews. He had just been elected to the South Carolina assembly, and he served in the provincial Congress after Parliament's passage of the "Intolerable Acts" aroused all of the American colonies to a state of rebellion. Sent to the Second Continental Congress in 1776, young Heyward spoke in favor of the Richard Henry Lee resolutions, voted for them and for the Declaration of Independence.

After Heyward came Thomas Lynch, Jr.,

Left to right
THOMAS HEYWARD, JR.
THOMAS LYNCH, JR.
ARTHUR MIDDLETON

who was Edward Rutledge's senior by less than four months, and was, therefore, the second youngest member of the Congress. He was born on August 5, 1749 in Prince George's Parish, South Carolina, and he grew up on the Lynch plantation while receiving his early education at the Indigo Society School in Georgetown. When he was twelve years old he was sent to school at Eton College in England, and from there to Cambridge University and the Middle Temple in London. However, he took little interest in law, and when he returned home after ten years abroad, he told his father that he had no desire to become a practicing attorney. The senior Lynch generously acceded to his son's wishes and presented him with a large plantation on the Santee River. Young Thomas Lynch then married Elizabeth Shubrick and settled down to become a planter. This was in 1773. But with the exciting political events of the pre-revolutionary period, it was virtually impossible for a young man of Lynch's standing to remain aloof. He was soon commissioned a captain in the South Carolina militia and was appointed to the state constitutional committee.

In the summer of 1775, Thomas Lynch, Jr. was sent on a military recruiting mission that took him into some wild backwoods country. He contracted a fever (possibly malaria) from which he never fully recovered. Shortly after this he learned that his father, who was serving in the Continental Congress in Philadelphia, had suffered a stroke. Young Lynch tried without success to obtain a leave of absence from the militia, but friends used political influence to have him elected as an alternate delegate to the Congress. This automatically released him from military duty and he hastened to Philadelphia, arriving in that city in May 1776. As the father remained critically ill, Thomas Junior took his seat in Congress. He joined in the debate on indepen-

dence, voted for the Declaration, and proudly signed the document in place of his father on August 2. Observing the pallor of this young delegate, William Ellery wondered if he would be able to serve in Congress much longer. As it was to turn out, Thomas Lynch, Jr.'s signing of the Declaration of Independence was the high point of his short life, for from that day he was destined to know only tragedy.

Last and oldest of the South Carolina delegates was Arthur Middleton, thirty-four. He was reputed to be the wealthiest of the delegation, for he owned vast rice and indigo plantations which were worked by hundreds of slaves. He was born June 26, 1742, at the family mansion near Charles Town. His father, Henry Middleton, had been elected president of the First Continental Congress. Like the other three South Carolina delegates, he was educated in England. He attended the Hackney and Westminster preparatory schools, then obtained a bachelor of arts degree at Cambridge. Shortly after his return to South Carolina in 1763 he served as a delegate to the provincial assembly. Young Middleton was handsome, aristocratic and a polished gentleman, yet he plunged heart and soul into the patriot effort to gain colonial rights, raising funds, working on the Committee of Safety, and helping to organize the defenses of "Charles Town," or Charleston. Far more radical in his opposition to the British than was his rather conservative father, he took part in public gatherings and favored a declaration of independence at an early date. In 1776 he became a member of the committee assigned the task of drawing up a state constitution. Then, when his father resigned from Congress in the spring of 1776, Arthur was elected to fill his place. He arrived in Philadelphia in time to vote for independence and to take part in the historic August 2nd signing.

75

As the last of the thirteen delegations now approached the table to sign the Declaration, William Ellery experienced a sense of pride and achievement. This was the climax of bitter debate and prolonged tension. Only three men remained to endorse the document that was to rock the world. The first of the Georgia delegates was not well known to Ellery, but he remembered the man's name because of its oddity: Button Gwinnett. In a small, cramped script he penned what was destined to become the rarest of the 56 signatures near the left-hand margin of the parchment.

The exact date of Gwinnett's birth is unknown, but it is generally listed as 1735, in a village called Down Hatherley in Gloucestershire, England. The father was a Welsh clergyman. Evidently the family was not a wealthy one, and Gwinnett received a mediocre education. As a young man he established a small export firm in Bristol, and when he was about twenty-eight he and his wife sailed to America. He settled in Savannah, bought some land on St. Catherine's Island, and established a prosperous plantation. Although he served in the Georgia legislature beginning in 1769, he did little to distinguish himself. But in May 1776, he was elected to the Second Continental Congress. There he argued in favor of independence, voted for the Declaration, and now signed it with a kind of angry determination.

Despite a strong Tory element in Georgia, the members of the Georgia delegation were among the most outspoken supporters of the patriot cause. Such was certainly the case with Lyman Hall, the next signer, who had come originally from New England and who had been largely responsible for getting Georgia represented at the Continental Congress.

Hall was born in Wallingford, Connecticut, on April 12, 1724. With the encouragement of an uncle, he studied theology at Yale University where he graduated in 1747. Soon afterward he married Abigail Burr, and feeling himself unfit for the ministry he decided to take up medicine. By the time he was ready to practice, he decided to move to the south. He went to South Carolina in 1754, but after two years there he settled in Sunbury, Georgia. His medical practice prospered and he bought land to establish a successful rice plantation.

When the Georgia legislature at first refused to send any representatives to the Continental Congress, Lyman Hall summoned an independent citizens' meeting, many of whom were from his own St. John's Parish where patriot sentiment ran high. This convention elected Hall as a delegate to the Second Continental Congress in 1775, but because of the unofficial nature of his selection, he was not at first permitted to vote. However Georgia officially confirmed him as a delegate the following year and sent two other delegates to join him in Philadelphia. The oldest of the signers from Georgia, Hall spoke forcefully for independence and was an enthusiastic signer of the Declaration on August 2nd.

The last of the signers to inscribe the parchment on August 2nd was George Walton, a small, dapper man who appeared younger to William Ellery than he actually was. Walton was thirty-five when he signed the Declaration. He was born in 1741 in Farmville, Virginia, the son of a poor couple who could not afford to send him to school. He was the only Southern delegate who was not a plantation aristocrat. Apprenticed to a car-

Plan of the City SAVANNAH and Fortification.

Profile upon a N.15.E. Line, shewing the Street, Houses, &c Wharfs and Fortification.

penter, he worked for a man who expected him to keep at the job during daylight hours and did not want him to study at night. Since the master carpenter allowed him no candles, young Walton gathered scraps of wood and shavings from the shop and managed to burn them in the privacy of his room where he studied borrowed books. When he was finally released from his apprenticeship he continued to study law books. Then he moved to Savannah, Georgia, obtained a job in the law office of Henry Young, and was eventually admitted to the Georgia bar in 1774. As it turned out, Henry Young was a dedicated loyalist, but Walton became interested in a group of patriots who supported the actions of Boston citizens in their resistance to the British. The Georgia group set up a Committee of Correspondence, and at a meeting in Savannah in early 1775, Walton was appointed secretary of the provincial legislature. He also served as president of the Georgia Committee of Safety.

When Georgia's patriot congress learned of the action of St. John's Parish in sending Lyman Hall to the Second Continental Congress, they decided that they should elect a full delegation to represent them in Philadelphia. But one of these newly appointed delegates was exposed as a loyalist and was recalled. George Walton, elected to replace him, arrived in Philadelphia sometime in March 1776. He voted for independence and he now concluded the signing ceremony with a strong, clear hand, entering his name at the left of the document below the signatures of Button Gwinnett and Lyman Hall.

William Ellery rose from his seat and shook hands with his fellow signers. The job was done; it had not been difficult, nor had it required much time in its accomplishment. But for better or worse, America was now fully and officially committed to go it alone in the face of Britain's military and naval might. It was too sobering a thought for the signers to indulge in a celebration.

Chapter Three

The Aftermath

Time of Testing

Such were the men who signed the Declaration of Independence. With few exceptions they were men of property — sober, respected leaders in their communities. Yet the document they had produced and signed broke with centuries of tradition and committed their country to a desperate revolutionary war, the outcome of which appeared dubious even to the most optimistic among them.

Perhaps there were some members of the Congress who still hoped that in the face of such a drastic declaration Britain would recant and enter into negotiations with the newly established United States. Others in their enthusiasm may have believed that aroused Americans would quickly defeat the British troops. It is difficult to imagine exactly what was in the mind of each delegate as he signed his name, but for the most part the signers had no illusions.

For better or worse these courageous rebels had personally endorsed the break from England. Now they must accept the consequences. On that historic day, August 2, 1776, none could predict exactly what these conse-

Opposite: On July 9, on orders from George Washington, the Declaration was read to all troops in New York.

Below: That night, after the announcment of independence, a mob pulled down the statue of George III on Bowling Green.

NEW-YORK HISTORICAL SOCIETY

quences would be. To some the aftermath would bring new opportunities and greater success; to others . . .

Not long after the formal signing of the Declaration of Independence on August 2, 1776, General Howe and a British force of 25,000 men landed on the southwest shore of Long Island, and in a major battle on August 27th the redcoats inflicted nearly twenty percent casualties on the colonial army. General Washington called a staff meeting in Brooklyn Heights at the country estate of signer Philip Livingston, and there it was decided that the American forces should be withdrawn from Long Island. Leaving their campfires burning, the Colonials quietly moved in the night to Harlem Heights. In the morning the British found Washington's camp deserted.

The enraged redcoats proceeded to lay waste much of the countryside. In early September they burned to the ground the fine home of Francis Lewis at Whitestone. Evidently someone had advised the British that Lewis was a leading patriot, for they not only destroyed his property but seized his wife and

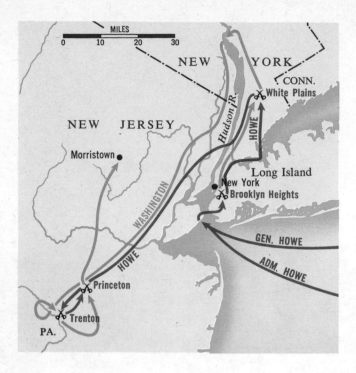

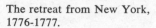

The retreat from New York, 1776-1777.

threw her into a military prison where conditions were intolerable. With no bed and no change of clothes for several months, she suffered cold and privation and her health was permanently impaired. Released two years later in a prisoner exchange, she died shortly after rejoining her family. Lewis was by this time heartbroken and virtually penniless. He nevertheless continued to serve in the Continental Congress until 1779, offering his valuable business experience to committees for the purchase of arms and supplies for the Continental Army. Lewis died on December 31, 1802, at the age of eighty-nine.

Philip Livingston likewise suffered serious losses at the hands of the British forces. His great estate, covering roughly 150,000 acres in Dutchess and Columbia counties, was seized by the occupying army, yet Livingston continued to furnish money to Congress for the conduct of the war. The strain and anxiety he suffered during the first two years of the Revolution had a serious effect on his health. In 1777, after the British had occupied Philadelphia, the Congress fled first to Lancaster, then to York, Pennsylvania. It was there, on June 12, 1778, that Livingston died, less than two years after he had signed the Declaration.

As the British advanced in the fall of 1776, they plundered one farm after another.

While still serving Congress in Philadelphia, William Floyd learned that his estate in Suffolk County, New York, had been seized. Local Tories aided in ruining what was left of Floyd's farm. They stole his machinery and livestock and removed everything from the house. Meanwhile Mrs. Floyd managed to escape with other members of the family by boat across Long Island Sound to Connecticut. For the entire seven years of the war, William Floyd was unable to return to his home. Nevertheless he served both the Continental Congress and the New York state senate. Later he became a New York representative of the first United States Congress. Floyd died on August 4, 1821, at the age of eighty-six, a highly respected leader of his community.

Another victim of the British campaign in New York was Lewis Morris, whose fine estate in Westchester County, "Morrisania," was sacked and burned while Morris was serving as a militia officer. Morris was one of those signers who clearly foresaw that destruction of his property was likely to follow his endorsement of the Declaration, for the British fleet had been hovering ominously close to New York during the tense debate in Philadelphia. As he had anticipated, British troops despoiled nearly a thousand acres of forest on his estate, ruined the fine house, butchered his cattle and drove his family into seeking shelter with neighbors. At the war's end, he returned to Morrisania and restored it, devoting the rest of his life to managing the estate and serving in the New York senate. He died on January 22, 1798, at seventy-one.

In the autumn, General Howe pushed methodically into Manhattan, and in the end, Washington again was forced to withdraw, this time into New Jersey. Newark fell to British and Hessian troops, and the Colonials retreated toward Trenton.

Members of the New Jersey state legislature followed these reports with great anxiety. Signer John Hart, who had recently left Philadelphia to take his seat in the legislature at Princeton, was personally concerned since his farm lay in the path of the advancing enemy. His fears proved to be well founded. A contingent of Hessian mercenaries who took up quarters in Trenton laid waste Hart's estate, killed his livestock, burned and looted his home and destroyed his valuable grist mills.

Meanwhile, with the British so close, the state legislature fled from Princeton and held meetings when and where the members could assemble in comparative safety. John Hart was sometimes forced to sleep in barns or out-of-doors, as he was never certain of support from local residents, some of whom were loyalists. All this time, he suffered intense anxiety over the situation of his ailing wife and 13 children, since the plundering of his farm had occurred at a time when his wife was gravely ill. By the time Hart was able to return home he found that his wife had died — probably due to lack of care and the hardships imposed by the destruction of their home — and his children were scattered, having taken refuge with various neighbors and friends. As a result of these personal disasters, John Hart's own health began to fail. In 1779, he was forced to retire from the state legislature, and for a brief time he attempted to repair the damage done to his property. But the effort proved too much for him. He died May 11, 1779, at the age of sixty-eight, less than three years after he signed the Declaration and before any end to the war was in sight.

* * *

The British Forces were spreading out and attempting to trap the illusive George Washington. But the wily old fox, as they began to call the American general, was waging the war on his own terms. Washington engaged and withdrew; attacked unexpectedly, only to disappear time and again when the British thought they were about to smash his pitiful army.

But if the British were frustrated, the Americans were close to desperation. Congress was forced to flee time and again, and the members were confronted with one crisis after another. One of the signers, Joseph Hewes of North Carolina, who had at first shown reluctance to approve the Declaration, plunged wholeheartedly into the overwhelming problems of creating a Continental Navy and in helping Washington to plan a campaign. He is said to have worked 12 to 14 hours at a stretch without even taking time to eat. This superhuman effort inevitably took its toll on his health. In the summer of 1779 he began to lose his strength. In the fall he suffered a collapse in Philadelphia and died on November 10, 1779, at the age of forty-nine.

Before the British troops occupied Princeton in 1776 John Witherspoon, president of the College of New Jersey, had closed the college. While the enemy used Nassau Hall as a barracks and destroyed the library with its hundreds of valuable volumes, Witherspoon devoted his time to the Congress. He served on the Board of War as well as on committees involved with foreign relations. Meanwhile his friend and fellow signer, Richard Stockton, had been experiencing serious troubles. Hearing that his family was facing danger in Princeton, he rushed home and managed to take them safely out of the town before the British troops arrived. But as he was attempting to return to Philadelphia, he was betrayed by a loyalist and was captured by enemy soldiers. They threw him into a foul prison because of his part in signing the Declaration of Independence. He was frequently beaten and nearly starved.

Stockton was finally released through the

efforts of Witherspoon and other members of the Congress who arranged an exchange. But by this time Stockton was in poor health. He found that the British had ruined his beautiful mansion, having burned his library and private papers and damaged or removed the furnishings. He remained an invalid until his death at his home, February 28, 1781.

Witherspoon continued as a leading delegate in Congress. He was a strong supporter of confederation of the states, and in 1778 signed the Articles of Confederacy for New Jersey. After the war ended, he spent most of his time working to restore the College of New Jersey. He died November 15, 1794 at the age of seventy-one.

Francis Hopkinson, the lively little man from New Jersey who composed songs and was an accomplished artist, stayed with Congress throughout the war and served as chairman of the Continental Navy Board. He drew up the first sketch of the stars and stripes that was finally adopted as the official United States flag. Hopkinson also designed various government seals, as well as the Great Seal of New Jersey. In late 1776 and again in early 1777, the British ransacked Hopkinson's home in Bordentown. Yet his zeal for the colonial cause never wavered. Besides serving as a popular member of Congress he wrote biting satires criticizing British policies. In 1789, President George Washington appointed him as a federal circuit judge in Pennsylvania. On May 9, 1791, Hopkinson had an attack of apoplexy. He died that day, at the age of fifty-three.

Along with Hopkinson, another New Jersey signer worked in the Congress throughout the war. This was Abraham Clark, as determined a patriot as any of the delegates. As the fighting progressed, his contempt for the British and for American loyalists increased, due in part to the fact that two of his sons fighting for the Continental Army were captured and cruelly treated by their British captors. In 1777, Clark spoke out angrily against General Washington's offer of amnesty to any former loyalists who would swear allegiance to the United States. Abraham Clark was convinced that the proclamation would permit many traitors to go unpunished. Meanwhile he was keeping a watchful eye on expenditures by the new government. He opposed special bonuses for army officers who, he felt, had sacrificed no more than had many civilians whose only reward was the winning of independence.

Clark served in the New Jersey state legislature between 1784 and 1787 and was sent as a delegate to the Annapolis convention in 1786, when he urged strengthening of the Articles of Confederation. He also represented New Jersey at the Constitutional Convention. With several other signers of the Declaration, he opposed ratification of the Constitution until it should include a Bill of Rights. From 1791 to 1794, he served in the United States House of Representatives, where he favored aiding France in its war with Britain. Abraham Clark died of sunstroke on September 15, 1794, three months after his retirement from Congress. He was sixty-eight.

In the summer of 1777, British General Howe had embarked a large force of 15,000 men on 260 ships and transported them from New York to the northern part of Chesapeake Bay. This massive operation which was a month in its execution was designed to enable the British to take Philadelphia from the south, while General Burgoyne approached the American capital from Albany to the north. Meanwhile, Washington had gathered his army to oppose Howe's advance. At the battle of Brandywine Creek on September 11, the Americans were defeated but, as usual, Washington withdrew with his army still intact, menacing the British occupation of Philadelphia. And although Washington's

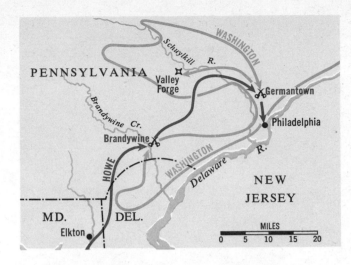

The campaigns in Pennsylvania, 1777-1778.

attack at Germantown in October miscarried, it so upset the British that they abandoned further offensive plans for the balance of the year and the ensuing winter while Washington and his men endured the rugged encampment at Valley Forge.

During their advance toward Philadelphia, British troops captured John McKinley, the president of Delaware. As a result, one of the signers of the Declaration, George Read, vice president of Delaware, was called upon to take McKinley's place. After receiving the news in Philadelphia, Read packed up his family and set off for Delaware. On the way he narrowly missed being captured by a British patrol.

After Read arrived home, he took over the administration of the state government, relieving signer Thomas McKean who had assumed the office temporarily. Read served until 1778 when Caesar Rodney was elected. In 1787, George Read was a delegate to the Constitutional Convention and, at his urging, Delaware became the first state to ratify the Constitution. As a member of the Federalist party he was elected U.S. Senator and served in Congress from 1789 to 1793. He then was appointed chief justice of the Delaware supreme court. At age sixty-five, on September 21, 1798, Read died at his home near New Castle, Delaware.

After serving in Congress for a brief period following the signing, Caesar Rodney returned to Delaware. The advancing skin cancer on his face was becoming painful, yet he worked ceaselessly for the war effort. Appointed a major general of the Delaware militia, he led his troops into battle during the bitter winter campaigns of 1776-77. His unit took part in the unsuccessful attempt to defend Philadelphia in 1777. In that year, a loyalist uprising in Sussex County, Delaware, forced Rodney to lead his militia against citizens of his own state, but his decisive action quickly quelled the rebellion which received little popular support. Rodney was elected state president by the Delaware legislature, and despite his serious affliction, he served for four difficult years, during which time the state was menaced by frequent British raids along the coast. By 1782, his health had deteriorated to the point where he was forced to decline reelection as president of Delaware. He was nevertheless appointed a delegate to Congress, although it was understood that he would be unable to serve. Caesar Rodney died on June 29, 1784 in his fifty-fifth year.

Caesar Rodney's friend and associate, Thomas McKean, became acting president of Delaware immediately after John McKinley's capture by the British on September 13, 1777. In a letter to John Adams, McKean described some of his experiences during that period. "I was hunted like a fox by the enemy," he wrote, "and compelled to remove my family five times in a few months." Finally he settled his family in a small log cabin on the Susquehanna River, over a hundred miles from his original residence. McKean signed the Articles of Confederation in 1779, and was chosen the first President of the Congress under the articles on July 10, 1781. McKean also served as chief justice of Pennsylvania, as he had at different times taken residence in both states. Although he did not take part in drafting the Constitution, he was sent to the Pennsylvania ratification convention in 1787. When he was sixty-five he was elected governor of Pennsylvania, serving in this high office from 1799 to 1808, at which time he retired from public service. On June 24, 1817, Thomas McKean died at the age of eighty-three.

Further Trials and a Taste of Victory

Pennsylvania delegates were next in line to suffer losses at the hands of rampaging enemy soldiers. After the British took control of Philadelphia in September 1777, George Clymer's home in Chester County was sacked and Clymer retired from Congress in an effort to take care of his family and to rebuild his fortune. But by December 1777 he was back in Congress. He made a perilous trip to Fort Pitt in severe winter weather to investigate reports of Indian massacres, which he proved were being instigated by the British. In response to Clymer's report, Congress sent a force of 500 men to attack Detroit, but the expedition bogged down for lack of communication and supplies.

Clymer worked closely with financier Robert Morris to set up the first national bank in the United States — The Bank of North America. Morris was having personal troubles of his own. In the course of the war he lost more than a hundred ships, yet he somehow avoided bankruptcy and managed to keep funds flowing into the treasury of the struggling new government. Morris and Clymer remained in Philadelphia when Congress withdrew to Baltimore. Even during the British occupation, they continued their activities in raising money for the war. Robert Morris led a dangerous life during this critical period, often riding alone in the dead of night to meet secretly with European agents at taverns outside of Philadelphia. Many of these agents were persuaded by Morris to furnish large sums of money, arms and other supplies to help the colonial cause.

On one occasion, in 1780, a member of the Congressional War Board by the name of Richard Peters received a letter from Washington stating that the army had nearly exhausted its supply of bullets. At a lavish reception given by the Spanish minister that night, Peters met Robert Morris who noticed that the Congressman looked unusually depressed. Learning of the crisis, Morris disappeared from among the guests, but after a time he reappeared with the news that a privateer had just arrived at his wharf with 90 tons of lead in her hold as ballast. They then arranged to round up 100 volunteers who unloaded the lead while others cast it into cartridges. By morning a great supply of ammunition was on its way to Washington's hard-pressed army.

In 1781, Morris issued over a million dollars of personal credit and raised a loan of $200,000 from France for the final campaign which led to the British capitulation at Yorktown. After the victory, Morris continued to struggle with huge public and personal debts. At one point he wrote a letter of resignation, but Congress persuaded him to stay on. Meanwhile his shipping firm of Willing, Morris and Company, prospered in its trade with China and France. He was elected Senator from Pennsylvania to the first United States Congress in 1788, and he entertained George Washington at the luxurious Morris home at the time of Washington's inauguration as President. Then in 1798 Morris' widely extended finances collapsed and he was sent to debtors' prison in Philadelphia. He was not released until 1801. Embittered and in failing health, Morris lived for a time on an annuity of $1500 a year, but he grew continually weaker and died in comparative obscurity May 8, 1806 at the age of seventy-two.

Morris' wartime associate George Clymer moved to Princeton at the end of the war so that his sons could attend the College of New Jersey. He attended the Constitutional Convention in 1787, was elected to the first United States House of Representatives, and accepted a number of special assignments for President Washington. In his latter years he devoted his time to personal interests, serving as president of the Philadelphia Academy of Fine Arts and the Philadelphia Agricultural Society. He

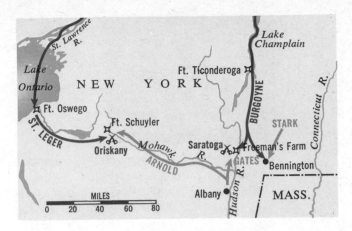

died on January 23, 1813, age seventy-three.

John Morton of Pennsylvania was the first of the signers to die. Morton had rendered an important service in the cause of independence when he cast the deciding vote for Pennsylvania in favor of the Declaration. The opposition to a complete break with England had been strong among the Pennsylvania delegates, and when John Dickinson and Robert Morris were absent, there remained two votes for independence — Franklin and Wilson; and two opposed — Willing and Humphreys. John Morton then broke the tie by voting for independence, although he had been undecided up to that point. As a result of his action many of his friends turned against him. Some of Pennsylvania's conservative Quakers considered him a traitor, and their denunciation of his stand greatly depressed him. In the spring of 1777, he fell ill with a raging fever. Shortly before the end, he told members of his family at his bedside that he was proud of signing the Declaration. "Tell them," he said, "that they shall acknowledge it to have been the most glorious service that I ever rendered to my country." Morton died shortly afterward in April 1777.

During the discouraging winter of 1777-78, the Congress moved to York, Pennsylvania, where its sessions were filled with the gloom of defeat and uncertainty. Then, following the news of the British abandonment of offensive action around Philadelphia, came word of stunning victories in the north. General Burgoyne suffered a major defeat at the hands of General Horatio Gates at Freeman's Farm on the Hudson River, and the British began an agonizing retreat toward Ticonderoga on October 8. But the Americans attacked their rear, then cut off their approach to Ticonderoga, and Burgoyne was forced to surrender on October 17, 1777. These successes bolstered the hopes of the hard-pressed members of Congress, but the dreary winter of 1778

produced little further news to relieve their anxieties.

* * *

One of the vital tasks of the Congress after declaring independence from Britain was the establishment of foreign relations and the enlistment of aid from other governments. At about the time of Washington's encampment at Valley Forge, Benjamin Franklin was in France seeking to persuade King Louis XVI and his war ministers to become an active ally of America. He had been on this mission for many months, having set sail from Philadelphia on October 27, 1776, not long after signing the Declaration. Before leaving, he had given his entire fortune of about 4,000 pounds to the Congress. In Paris, this indefatigable elder statesman proceeded quietly and with his famous good humor to persuade the French that their best interests would be served by sending military aid to the United States.

The surrender of General Burgoyne at Saratoga in October 1777 electrified France, and after months of frustration Franklin began to gain a sympathetic hearing among the French leaders in Paris. He held many talks with the French Minister of Foreign Affairs, Comte de Vergennes who had already been successful in granting arms and money to the beleaguered American Colonies. Finally, Franklin signed a treaty of alliance with France on February 6, 1778. This prompted an offer from the British to negotiate a peace treaty, but as there was no mention of American independence in the offer, Franklin refused to consider it further. Franklin remained in Paris where he helped to implement

the French aid and to represent the American government in European councils.

Franklin signed the final treaty of peace with England on September 3, 1783. By this time, he had become universally admired by the people of France and by the diplomats of other nations. There is no doubt that Benjamin Franklin was responsible more than any single individual for winning respect among world powers for the new United States. Not until 1785, when Thomas Jefferson relieved him as American minister to France, did Franklin return to Philadelphia. He arrived in his home city September 14, 1785, to a wild reception — bells rang, bonfires were lighted and artillery salutes were fired.

Yet Franklin's service to his country was not ended. He was elected president of the state of Pennsylvania in 1785 and in 1787, age eighty-one, as a delegate to the Constitutional Convention, he signed the United States Constitution. Three years later, on April 17, 1790, Franklin died in Philadelphia.

A man who played an important role at the Constitutional Convention by assisting the aging Benjamin Franklin was James Wilson of Pennsylvania. After he signed the Declaration, Wilson had withdrawn from Congress and moved to Annapolis during the British occupation of Philadelphia. Until 1782 he devoted most of his time to law practice and to land speculations. Because he had defended some wealthy Philadelphians charged with treason, he became unpopular with the public, and at one time a mob of tradesmen and militia gathered outside his house, opened fire on it with rifles and cannon, while Wilson and his friends fired back. Three people were killed before a troop of cavalry broke up the attack. Later, however, Wilson was elected to Congress and his legal activities were forgotten. As a delegate to the Constitutional Convention in 1787 he became Franklin's spokesman and actually delivered many of

the old gentleman's speeches. Wilson strongly advocated popular vote selection of the President and of members of Congress. He also took part in writing the draft of the Constitution and exerted a major influence on Pennsylvania's ratification of the document. In addressing the state convention, he said, "I am bold to assert that it is the best form of government which has ever been offered to the world." In 1790, James Wilson became an associate justice of the U.S. Supreme Court. He continued to serve in this capacity until his death on August 28, 1798, at the age of fifty-five.

Throughout the bitter winter of 1777, Benjamin Rush, the great Pennsylvania physician, served with Congress while reports of suffering in the field poured in from Washington's headquarters. In April 1777, Rush was appointed physician-general of military hospitals for the Continental Army, and he looked after hundreds of wounded men following the battles of Princeton and Brandywine. Partly because of his desire to improve discipline in the medical department of the army, and partly because of other disagreements with the high command, Rush began to work for the replacement of Washington as Commander-in-Chief. He resigned from his post as physician-general and held no government position until the end of Washington's Presidency. In 1783 he joined the staff of the Pennsylvania Hospital and was instrumental in setting up the first free medical clinic for poor people. When the terrible yellow fever epidemic swept through Philadelphia in 1793, Rush remained and treated hundreds of patients. He contracted the disease, but he recovered and was on hand to attend the sick when a second, equally virulent epidemic struck in 1798. Always politically active he attended the Pennsylvania convention to ratify the U.S. Constitution, and in 1797 he was given the position of Treasurer of the United States

Mint in Philadelphia. Rush was sixty-seven when he died, April 19, 1813.

* * *

As the war ground on, William Paca, signer from Maryland, continued to serve in Congress, and was a member of Maryland's state senate from 1777 to 1779. He was also appointed chief judge of Maryland's superior court in 1778. All this time he was pouring thousands of dollars of his personal fortune into outfitting and arming American regiments. He worked on the committee that drafted Maryland's state constitution, and at the war's end he became governor of Maryland, from 1782 to 1785. In 1789, President Washington appointed him as a United States district judge. Paca died in 1799 at the age of fifty-eight.

While Paca worked so vigorously to establish a new state government for Maryland, Charles Carroll, the only Roman Catholic signer, was also serving on the Maryland legislature and on the state constitutional drafting committee. Carroll made certain that full religious freedom became an integral part of the Maryland constitution. He was re-elected as a state senator for over 25 years, and he was also elected to the first United States Senate that convened in 1789, resigning from this position in 1792 to keep his Maryland senate seat. Carroll retired from public service in 1804, but he enjoyed an active life for many more years. In 1828 he took part in marking the foundation of the Baltimore and Ohio Railroad. He was the last surviving signer of the Declaration when he died at the age of ninety-five on November 14, 1832.

Samuel Chase of Maryland was one of the most active members of Congress during the first two years following the signing of the Declaration. He is credited with serving on at least 30 committees, among them one having the responsibility of restricting Tory ac-

tivity. But in 1778, Chase was accused of dishonest business practice when it was claimed that he had used information received in Congress to make a personal profit from selling flour to the army. As a result Chase was recalled from Congress. He went back to his law practice and gradually regained the confidence of the people in Maryland. In 1791 he was appointed chief justice of Maryland's general court, and five years later, George Washington chose him as an associate justice of the Supreme Court. Despite a fine legal mind, Chase became involved in political attacks on Jeffersonians being tried under the notorious Sedition Acts. His bias led to impeachment proceedings in 1804. He was acquitted and remained on the bench for the rest of his life. He was seventy when he died of gout on June 19, 1811.

A less colorful member of the Maryland delegation was Thomas Stone, whose quiet modesty kept him in the background of Congressional debate. He nevertheless worked diligently on committees, including the one assigned to drafting the Articles of Confederation. In 1777 he was elected to the Maryland state senate where he served for the rest of his life. He attended the Congress of Confederation at Annapolis in 1783 and was selected to represent Maryland at the Constitutional Convention of 1787. However, he declined this honor as his wife was seriously ill. When Mrs. Stone died that summer at the age of thirty-four, Stone retired from public life. He became deeply melancholy and died on October 5, 1787. He was only forty-four at the time of his death.

While many of the signers of the Declaration were suffering privation and hardships brought on by the war and by British vengeance, a number of them continued to serve in Congress, suffering more anxiety than actual hardship. Both Josiah Bartlett and William Whipple of New Hampshire remained in Philadelphia during the balance of 1776, and Whipple remained with Congress during the anxious months of 1777-1778. Bartlett helped to draft the Articles of Confederation for a proposed union of states, then in 1779 he served his home state as chief justice of the court of common pleas. Later he became chief justice of the New Hampshire superior court. When the states were voting to ratify the United States Constitution in 1788, Bartlett was a leader in persuading the people of New Hampshire to go along. When the first National Congress assembled, Josiah Bartlett was appointed by the state legislature to attend as a senator, but he refused the appointment because of his age and waning health. He did, however, accept the presidency of New Hampshire in 1790, serving one term. Within a year afterward, in 1795, he died at the age of sixty-five.

Bartlett's fellow signer, William Whipple, remained active in Congress until 1779. As he had been appointed a brigadier general of militia in New Hampshire, he spent some of this time in his home state recruiting and training troops, and he led a New Hampshire brigade in the Battle of Saratoga in October 1777. It is said that on this expedition he took a Negro slave with him, and prior to the engagement, Whipple told his man that he was expected to fight bravely for his country. The slave shook his head, saying that he had no reason to fight, but would be inclined to defend his liberty, if he had it, to the last drop of his blood. Whipple gave the slave his freedom on the spot.

Upon Burgoyne's surrender, Whipple was assigned by General Gates to the task of escorting the prisoners of war to a Boston campsite. He later took part in an unsuccessful campaign to drive the British from Rhode Island. In 1780 Whipple was elected to the New Hampshire legislature, and two years later he became associate justice of the state superior court. He died in 1785 of a heart ailment.

Meanwhile another New Hampshire delegate, Matthew Thornton, had also served the Congress for about a year after the signing, then returned to New Hampshire to become an associate justice of the superior court. He retained this office until 1782, when he retired at the age of sixty-eight. For the remaining years of his life he lived on his farm near Merrimack, New Hampshire, and he died June 24, 1803, age eighty-nine.

Proud and vain as he was, no member of the Independence Congress was more openhanded or more courageous than John Hancock. After he resigned as President of the Congress in 1777 he retained a seat as a delegate from Massachusetts, but for a time he took more interest in military matters. In 1778 he took command of the Massachusetts militia. Commissioned a major general, he led some 6,500 men in a campaign designed to drive the British from Rhode Island. The plan called for naval support from a powerful French fleet that had arrived in American waters to aid the Colonials on July 8, 1778. The French Navy was to bombard the British at Newport, Rhode Island, then land a body of French troops while Americans under General John Sullivan, along with John Hancock's New Englanders, attacked from the land side. Hancock led his men out of Providence in mid-July, and the battle began to unfold. But dissension between Sullivan and the French command slowed the campaign, and by August a full scale offensive had not been launched. Before the French troops could be put ashore, a violent storm scattered the fleet, and the French sailed north to Boston for repairs. The Americans engaged a strong British force, but were forced to withdraw.

John Hancock's brief military career ended in 1779 when he took part in the Massa-

Unfinished portrait
of American peace commissioners
in Paris.

chusetts constitutional convention and, upon adoption of the state constitution, was elected the first governor in 1780. For five years he served as the Massachusetts chief executive, living and dressing as lavishly as any previous royal governor. His magnificent coach was pulled by six horses, and his liveried servants accompanied him wherever he went. Elected again in 1787, he continued as governor for the rest of his life. Selected to head the Massachusetts convention to ratify the United States Constitution, Hancock played an important role, persuading his delegates to vote for ratification. By this action he won great popularity and hoped to be put forward as the first President of the United States, but as with his ambition to take supreme command of the army, this hope was dashed — again by George Washington. Hancock died, still in the office of governor of Massachusetts, on October 8, 1793.

It is a curious fact of the signers' story that one of the most colorful delegates, Samuel Adams, led a comparatively quiet life after the signing. For a few months, during late 1776 and the gloomy year of 1777, Adams continued to be one of the resolute Congressmen who helped to keep the shaky government from falling apart. He encouraged wavering delegates to have faith in their cause. "Better tidings will soon arrive," he insisted. "Our cause is just and righteous, and we shall never be abandoned by Heaven while we show ourselves worthy of its aid and protection." In 1779, Sam Adams helped John Adams compose a state constitution for Massachusetts, but he soon retired from Congress. He served the Massachusetts state senate for a time, and he opposed ratification of the United States Constitution until a bill of rights was added to it. As time went on, he seemed to lose his old revolutionary zeal, and although he was elected lieutenant governor of Massachusetts under Governor John Han-

cock, he accomplished little of importance during that period. In 1794, after Hancock's death, he was elected governor, an office he held for three more years. At the age of seventy-six, in 1798, Adams retired. He spent his remaining years weighed down by illness and poverty, and he died October 2, 1803.

By contrast, Samuel's cousin, John Adams, remained in the national limelight and was destined to become the second President of the United States. In the early years of the Revolution he served on numerous Congressional committees and is credited with being chairman of at least twenty-five of them. As chairman of the Board of War, he occupied one of the key positions in the new government. Then he followed Benjamin Franklin to Paris in February 1778, to assist in the vital negotiations for French aid.

On his return to America, John Adams was elected to the Massachusetts state constitutional convention, where he played a major role in drafting a document that became a model for many other states. When Franklin notified Congress in 1779 that Britain was making overtures toward peace, Adams was appointed minister plenipotentiary to negotiate a treaty of peace with Great Britain. He set sail in October 1779, but did not arrive in Paris until February 1780. By that time England was no longer desirous of making peace. Unable to accomplish his original mission, Adams was assigned a new task — to negotiate a loan from the Netherlands. For two years he struggled to win the confidence of the Dutch, finally succeeding in gaining from them recognition of the United States. The Netherlands signed treaties of trade in 1782 and authorized a loan of eight million guilders.

Governor Elbridge Gerry's role
in redistricting Essex County, Massachusetts,
into a dragon-like shape
gave rise to a new political word —
"gerrymander."

This move, coupled with the French assistance that Franklin had arranged, and the British military reverses in America, finally brought Britain to the conference table, and John Adams joined Henry Laurens, John Jay and Benjamin Franklin in Paris for the peace talks. A temporary treaty was signed November 30, 1782, but a final agreement was not reached until September 3, 1783.

Adams remained in Europe as a foreign minister to the Netherlands and England until 1788. Immediately after his return to America he became involved in the selection of a chief executive in the new federal government. Many of his friends were endeavoring to elect him President, but as Washington was clearly the popular choice, John Adams was proposed for Vice President. He won this position in 1789, but looked upon it with considerable disdain. "My country," he said, "has in its wisdom contrived for me the most insignificant office that ever the invention of man contrived."

After Washington's retirement, a genuine political campaign developed between the Federalists, supporting John Adams, and the Anti-Federalists who backed Thomas Jefferson. Under the regulations of that time, Adams was elected President with 71 electoral votes, while Jefferson, with 68 votes, automatically became Vice President.

Adams' presidency was not a particularly happy one. He became increasingly unpopular with the public for his determined stand to avoid involvement in a war between England and France. There was strong pressure for supporting France, and this became an issue in the election of 1800. Adams lost the election by only a handful of votes, and bitterly resented Jefferson's selection which, because of a tie vote between Jefferson and Aaron Burr, was decided in the House of Representatives.

John Adams retired to his home in Quincy, where he led a quiet life for 25 years. He lived to see his oldest son, John Quincy Adams, elected President in 1825. The following year, on July 4, 1826, Adams lay near death. "Thomas Jefferson still survives," he whispered. But Jefferson also died on the same day — the fiftieth anniversary of the adoption of the Declaration of Independence.

Signer Elbridge Gerry of Massachusetts was especially interested in military affairs, and he served on several Congressional committees involved in furnishing arms and supplies to the army. In 1785 he returned to Massachusetts where he was elected to the state legislature. Representing his state at the Constitutional Convention, he objected to many of the Constitution's provisions, and in the end refused to ratify it. As time went on he took a cynical view of democracy which, he felt, was "the worst of all political evils." Nevertheless he was elected to the U.S. House of Representatives in 1789, and spent much of his term arguing for amendments to the Constitution. He was sent by President John Adams as one of three commissioners to France in 1797. The other two men, Charles Pinckney and John Marshall soon left France in a disagreement over demands by French officials seeking bribes, but Gerry remained and for doing so, was severely criticized in America.

After his return home, Gerry was elected governor of Massachusetts in 1810 and served until 1812. He was then nominated to run for Vice President of the United States with James Madison, and was inaugurated March 4, 1813. He never completed his term, for on his way to the Capitol on November 23, 1814, the seventy-year-old Vice President became ill and died in his carriage.

Soon after signing the Declaration, Oliver Wolcott of Connecticut took an active part in the army. As a brigadier general, then major general of militia, he was in the thick of fighting in New York and Connecticut. He

Roger Sherman's home
in New Haven.

commanded several thousand volunteers and marched to Saratoga where he joined the forces of General Gates. In October 1777, he participated in the capture of British General Burgoyne and his army. For a brief period in 1778, Wolcott served again in Congress while it was meeting in York, Pennsylvania, but the following summer he was once more in command of a Connecticut division, charged with defense of the state's seacoast. During this difficult period the British invasion of Connecticut laid waste the towns of Fairfield and Norwalk. Families fled to the woods for safety while enemy soldiers looted and burned their homes. Wolcott's army fought the invaders constantly through 1779, and was ultimately successful in driving the British out. Following the war, in 1786, Wolcott became lieutenant governor, then governor of Connecticut ten years later. After a little over a year in office, he died on December 1, 1797, age seventy-one.

* * *

Meanwhile a number of other signers devoted their energies to serving in Congress or in other branches of government. Robert Treat Paine served Congress until late 1777 when he became attorney general of Massachusetts. He was appointed a justice in the Massachusetts supreme court and retired in 1804 at the age of seventy-three. He died May 11, 1814. After the signing, Stephen Hopkins remained in Congress a brief time, did not attend any sessions in 1777, but returned as a delegate in 1778. He retired to his home in Providence in 1779, and died there in 1785 at the age of seventy-eight.

William Ellery, the man who had watched the faces of the signers so intently on August 2, 1776, had remained in Congress and served on a number of committees. While thus engaged, he was informed of the British invasion of his home state of Rhode Island and learned that his home in Newport had been burned. After the British withdrew from Newport, late in 1779, Ellery returned home to look after his family and property. He repaired his home and attended to his law practice and business interests in Rhode Island, then returned to Congress where he served from 1781 to 1785. Ellery's legal knowledge was invaluable to some of the committees on which he served. He was chosen to study the peace treaty with Britain, and he supported a resolution in 1785 to abolish slavery in the United States. After President Washington gave him the post of collector of customs for Newport, he served in that capacity for 30 years. On February 15, 1820, when Ellery was ninety-two years old, his physician stopped in to see him. Feeling no pulse, he insisted that the old gentleman take a glass of wine. "I have a charming pulse," said Ellery, "but why concern yourself. I am going off the stage of life and it is a blessing that I go free from sickness, pain or sorrow." Later that day he went quietly to his room where, propped up in bed, he read a copy of Cicero. In the evening his daughter found that he had died. He appeared to have fallen asleep over his book.

Roger Sherman of Connecticut devoted his time during the war to serving in Congress and on the superior court of his home state. He was on the committee to draft the Articles of Confederation, signed the Articles in 1778, and worked hard to see that they were ratified by all the states. At sixty-six, in 1787, he was selected as a representative of Connecticut to the Constitutional Convention, which met in Philadelphia. When serious arguments arose at the convention over the inequalities of representation between large and small states, Sherman made a number of proposals that satisfied the delegates and became known as the "Connecticut Compromise." By this compromise all states were given equal representation in the Senate. He signed the Constitution on September 17, 1787, and gave his wholehearted support to it in essays he wrote for Connecticut journals. When he was sent to the House of Representatives in 1789, Sherman helped to prepare the Bill of Rights and fought for its inclusion as an amendment to the Constitution. His final service to the country was as United States Senator. He died at age seventy-two, while still in office, on July 23, 1793.

In his efforts to keep the struggling Revolutionary Government from collapsing, William Williams sacrificed most of his personal wealth. He signed promissory notes to help finance the offensive against Ticonderoga, and in 1779 he converted large amounts of gold and silver to Continental paper money that became virtually worthless. During the campaigns of 1780 and 1781, he invited French officers to occupy his house in Lebanon, Connecticut. After helping to establish the Articles of Confederation, and later the Constitution, he served on the Connecticut governor's council for nearly 20 years. He died in 1811, at the age of eighty.

Samuel Huntington, of Connecticut, was a member of Congress for ten years following the Declaration of Independence. In 1778 he signed the Articles of Confederation, and when John Jay resigned as president of the Congress in 1779, Huntington was elected to fill his place. He was still the leader of Congress when the Articles of Confederation were ratified by Maryland, the last of the states to do so, in 1781. Shortly afterward, due to poor health, Huntington resigned and returned to Connecticut. There he served as an associate justice of the superior court. He then returned to Congress in 1783 while the legislature was meeting in Princeton, New Jersey. He was lieutenant governor of Connecticut in 1785 and governor one year later, winning reelection each year thereafter for ten consecutive years. Huntington was sixty-four when he died on January 5, 1796.

Like Huntington, James Smith of Pennsylvania served Congress for a time, then resigned to become a judge of the Pennsylvania court of appeals. Reelected to Congress in 1785, he refused the position because of his advancing years. He continued in law practice for a few more years but was no longer active in politics. He died July 11, 1806, at eighty-seven.

Less than a year after signing the Declaration, George Taylor of Pennsylvania returned to his home in Easton because of ill health. For a time he served on the Pennsylvania executive council, but he soon was forced to give this up, too. He died on February 23, 1781, at the age of sixty-five.

Although signer George Ross of Pennsylvania took little part in Congress after 1776, he devoted himself to work on relations with the Indians, and helped to consummate a treaty with the tribes in northwestern Pennsylvania. Ross was the uncle of Betsy Ross' husband, John Ross. Legend has it that he accompanied George Washington and Robert Morris to the widow Ross' upholstery shop on Arch Street in Philadelphia where the first stars and stripes banner was being made. George Ross suffered a severe case of gout, attributed to his love of rich foods. He was only forty-nine when he died in Philadelphia on July 14, 1779.

* * *

Some of the Virginians who had played important roles in the independence movement were less prominent in the affairs of the new United States. George Wythe, for example, became involved in Virginia affairs after signing the Declaration. He became a judge in 1778, then accepted a position as professor of law at William and Mary College. This was the first such chair of law in an American college. In 1790 he founded his

The duel between Button Gwinnett and General McIntosh.

own law school. There were suspicious circumstances surrounding his death at age eighty in 1806, as a Negro cook in the household testified that Wythe's grandnephew and heir to the estate had poisoned the old man. However, under Virginia law at that time, a Negro's testimony was not admissable and the case was dropped.

Richard Henry Lee, whose famous resolutions provided the first real step toward independence, lost popularity with Virginia voters when rumors were falsely spread that he was really a Tory, loyal to England. An official inquiry by the Virginia legislature cleared him of the charges, but for a time he seemed to lose prestige. During his term in Congress, he signed the Articles of Confederation. In 1778, while commanding a unit of Westmoreland County militia, he and his men engaged British forces that were plundering the Virginia countryside. After a brief period of army service, he was elected to the state legislature. In 1784 he became president of Virginia, but remained in that office for only a year. He was elected to the United States Senate in 1789, served for three years, then retired due to failing health. Lee was sixty-two when he died at his estate in Westmoreland County on June 19, 1794.

The stout, jovial man who had presided over the debates on independence as chairman of the committee of the whole, Benjamin Harrison, returned to Virginia in the fall of 1777. There he served in the Virginia legislature for a time, then became governor of Virginia in 1782. He was a firm administrator during the difficult period of the state's formation as an independent commonwealth, and was reelected for another term. He retired to private life at the end of his second term, though almost immediately afterward he was sent to the House of Burgesses. Again, in 1791, he was elected governor, but following a lavish party on the day

after his election, he fell seriously ill and died that night, April 24, 1791.

Francis Lightfoot Lee of Virginia retired from Congress in 1779. Although he spent several years in politics, serving on the Virginia legislature, his later life was comparatively uneventful. He lived quietly on his plantation in Richmond County, and died there at the age of sixty-two on January 11, 1797.

Only nine days after signing the Declaration, Carter Braxton returned to Virginia where he took his former seat in the state legislature, representing King William County. He continued to hold this position for many years and chaired a number of important committees, including the committee of the whole. As the war progressed, virtually every one of the merchant ships in which he had an interest was sunk or captured by the British. As a result he was forced to sell his land holdings and he fell more and more deeply into debt. Still, his neighbors continued to send him as their representative to the state legislature. On October 10, 1797 in his sixty-first year, he died of a stroke.

* * *

Farther south, in Georgia, a signer with military ambitions had ended his career in tragedy. Given the governorship and a military command in 1777, Button Gwinnett found himself at odds with General Lachlan McIntosh, who objected to Gwinnett's assuming supreme command of the Georgia troops. As governor, Gwinnett felt he had the right to direct the army and he ordered an ill-fated expedition against British positions in Florida. When McIntosh publicly denounced this poorly executed campaign, Gwinnett challenged the general to a duel. Early in the morning of May 16, 1777, the two men, with their seconds, met in a pasture, and with great formality took their stands several paces apart. They fired pistols almost simultaneously. Both men were hit, and although they were apparently not seriously hurt, Gwinnett died of his wounds on May 27. He was forty-two years old.

* * *

Late in 1778 and early in 1779, the war began to shift toward the south. British warships began to appear off the coasts of Georgia and South Carolina, while transports from New York, loaded with troops, landed a large fighting force at the mouth of the Savannah River. Another British unit was ordered north from Florida, threatening to squeeze Savannah in the jaws of a pincer movement.

To meet this threat the Americans had a force of about 1,000 men under North Carolina's General Robert Howe. This pitiful army was quickly overwhelmed as the British seized Sunbury, Savannah and Augusta. Soon the entire state of Georgia was in enemy hands.

This occurred while Lyman Hall was still serving Congress in Philadelphia. He learned some time later that his rice plantation had been leveled by the British in 1778, but fortunately his family managed to escape to the north. Eventually he was able to bring them to Philadelphia. In 1782 Hall returned to Georgia where he was elected governor. He held the office for only a year and retired to a newly established plantation in 1784. He died on October 19, 1790, age sixty-six.

In 1778 signer George Walton was appointed colonel of a Georgia regiment by the state legislature. American General Robert Howe was charged with defending Savannah when British forces under Colonel Campbell were landed for an attack on the city. With only 800 men in his command, Howe hoped to block the enemy's entrance into Savannah, and he might have succeeded had not an American defector shown Campbell a safe route across a swamp for an attack on the defenders from the rear. During the ensuing battle, George Walton was wounded in the thigh and captured. Shortly afterward he was released in a prisoner exchange. Walton was almost immediately appointed to the governorship of Georgia, and less than a year later, in January 1780, he was returned to Congress. He next served a full term as governor, then became chief justice for the state of Georgia. In 1798 he was elected to the United States Senate. He retired a year later and died on February 2, 1804, at the age of sixty-four.

In the spring of 1780, British General Sir Henry Clinton landed a strong contingent of troops on the coast near Charleston, South Carolina. While British warships lay offshore to blockade Charleston, Clinton led his army inland, crossed the Ashley River and surrounded the city. By May, cut off by land and sea, the American General Benjamin Lincoln was forced to surrender.

During the attack on Charleston, signer Edward Rutledge was captured by the British. Rutledge had left Congress early in 1777, to lead contingents of South Carolina militia and to shore up the defenses of his state. In command of a corps of artillery during the siege of 1780, he attempted to bring his troops to the aid of General Lincoln and was seized in the course of the resulting battle. He was held in Charleston as a prisoner of war, but after General Lincoln's unconditional surrender, British General Cornwallis grew nervous about the possibility of a secret uprising of the citizens. One night squads of soldiers were sent through the city to round up civil and military officers, many of whom were

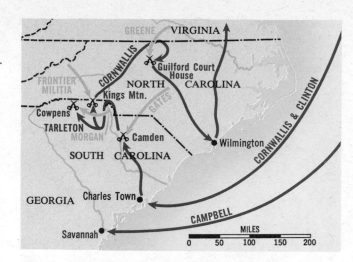

The campaigns in the South, 1778-1781.

roused from their beds and herded into the Exchange near the waterfront. Rutledge was among the assembled prisoners. His mother was taken from their country home and placed under house arrest in the city. Next day Rutledge, along with a large number of other prominent citizens, was put on a British guard ship that soon set sail for St. Augustine, Florida. He was held in a military prison for over a year before being released in a prisoner exchange. He then returned to a practice of law in Charleston. For several years, until 1798, he was a member of the state legislature. Then he was elected governor of South Carolina. He was only fifty when he died before the end of his term, on January 23, 1800.

Thomas Heyward, Jr. had left Congress in 1778 to become a circuit judge in his native South Carolina. At the time he took office his responsibilities exposed him to considerable danger, for the British were consolidating their positions near Charleston, and some Tories in the vicinity threatened to betray him. Nevertheless, Heyward showed no hesitation in trying a number of men accused of aiding the enemy. While the British advanced to within a few miles of Heyward's court, he calmly sentenced the convicted traitors to hanging and saw that the executions were carried out. As the British moved on Charleston in 1779 he donned his uniform as an artillery captain and led his unit into heavy fighting around Port Royal Island. He was with Edward Rutledge in a skirmish with the British at Beaufort in 1780, and in that action was seriously wounded. Then, shortly after the capture of Charleston, he was taken prisoner by enemy troops and sent with Rutledge to the St. Augustine prison. While he was confined there for several months British soldiers raided his plantation, burned the buildings and carried off his slaves. His wife became ill and died before he was released. In 1781

he returned to Charleston where, despite his losses, he vigorously resumed his work as a circuit judge and continued in this office until 1789. He died at age sixty-two on his plantation in 1809.

Another South Carolina signer to be captured and imprisoned by the British was Arthur Middleton, who returned from Congress early in 1778 to participate in the defense of his state. Although he had been elected the first governor of South Carolina under its newly adopted state constitution, he declined acceptance of the position as he doubted the legality of some of the assembly's actions. During the British invasion, Middleton's large estate was ravaged along with most of the plantations in the area, but he made no attempt to protect it, realizing that his first duty was to the state militia. He instructed his wife to take the family out of the area and joined with Rutledge in the defense of Charleston. When the city fell to the British, he was taken prisoner and sent to St. Augustine. Released in a prisoner exchange a year later, he returned to Congress in Philadelphia, where he served until 1782. Then at the war's end he devoted his energies to rebuilding his estate. While serving in the state legislature, he contracted a fever in 1787, and died on January 1, 1788, at the age of forty-four.

The only South Carolina delegate not involved in the defense of Charleston was Thomas Lynch, Jr. This unfortunate young man, who had signed the Declaration for his father when the latter became ill, had left Philadelphia in the fall of 1776. The father and son were both in poor health as they journeyed slowly to the south, and Thomas

97

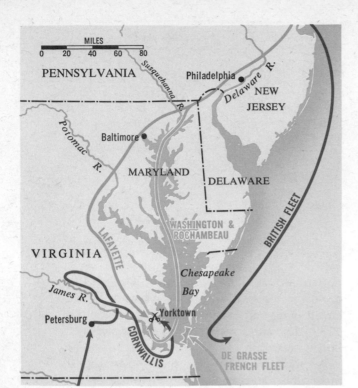

senior died before they reached home. For two years young Lynch fought unsuccessfully to regain his health, but finally on the advice of his doctor, he and his wife set sail for the south of France. But the ship disappeared at sea with all on board. It was never heard from again. This was in 1779, and at age thirty, Lynch was the youngest of the signers to die.

With nearly all of Georgia, and with Charleston, the jugular of South Carolina, under British control, General Clinton confidently wrote a dispatch to London in June 1780, indicating that war in the South was nearing a successful conclusion for the Crown. He then turned his command over to Lord Cornwallis and returned by ship to New York. To the Americans, the situation was perhaps the bleakest of the war.

As the war moved into North Carolina, signer William Hooper was engaged in law practice in Wilmington and was serving on the state legislature, having left Congress in 1777. The British advance in 1780 brought them to Wilmington, close to Hooper's plantation. Somehow the British were advised that a notorious patriot lived not far away, for they dispatched a band of raiders to capture Hooper. Warned of the approaching enemy party, Hooper sent his family into Wilmington where he felt they would be safer under the

British occupation than they would be as hunted fugitives. For himself, he chose the latter course and fled before the raiders arrived. With their usual vindictiveness, the British troops burned the estate and left Hooper's home in ruins. Hooper continued as a member of the North Carolina legislature till the end of the war, then resumed law practice. He died at the age of forty-eight on October 4, 1790.

About the time of Hooper's flight from the British, John Penn of North Carolina returned home from Congress. He was immediately given a powerful position on the North Carolina board of war, charged with the responsibility of supplying the militia. Partly due to his successful efforts, Francis Marion and his guerrillas were kept supplied, and the American troops succeeded in forcing the army of Lord Cornwallis into retreat before the end of 1780. John Penn remained in Stovall, Granville County, North Carolina, practicing law. Like Hooper, he died at an early age, forty-seven, in September 1788.

* * *

In 1780, the war in the South began to move to its conclusion, and although the American cause in many respects appeared hopeless, some signs appeared that foretold the ultimate British collapse. The daring lightning cavalry attacks of Francis Marion's guerrillas were beginning to take a serious toll of the Cornwallis forces as they moved north through North Carolina. General Nathanael Greene's army was steadily gathering strength while the British Army was being eroded. Early in 1781, Greene moved against the British encampment in Hillsboro, North Carolina, with a force of some 4,000 men. In March 1781 there was a violent battle at Guilford Court House, from which the Americans withdrew only after inflicting heavy casualties on Cornwallis' army.

Greene began a series of attacks on British supply lines in South Carolina, while Cornwallis' main army struggled northward toward Virginia. Action slowed as the raging heat of summer burned the swamps and plains of the Carolinas.

Meanwhile the great state of Virginia, virtually immune from military action until late in the war, was experiencing the terror and destruction of an invasion. British-Tory troops under Benedict Arnold had landed near Westover in January 1781, and were soon overrunning the eastern countryside. When Arnold encamped along the James River for the winter, Washington decided to send a well-trained force of about 1500 men to Virginia with support of elements from the French Navy. While the Americans marched south, Cornwallis moved up into Virginia to augment Arnold's smaller army. By the time the Americans under Lafayette had reached Richmond, they numbered about 3,000, while the augmented British Army had swelled to nearly 7,500. Then began a series of engagements in which the Continentals fought their usual harassing actions, always withdrawing before a full-scale battle could destroy them.

One of the Virginia signers became deeply involved in the climactic period of the war. This was Thomas Nelson, Jr. who had returned to Virginia from Congress due to an illness in 1777. Before the end of that year, Governor Patrick Henry commissioned Nelson a brigadier general in command of Virginia militia. The appointment came at a time when a British invasion of Virginia appeared imminent. But then the enemy warships turned north and the threat was ended.

When the British finally did invade Virginia in 1781, Thomas Jefferson was ending his term as governor. Jefferson recommended that Nelson, a military man, take his place. While Nelson struggled to defend the state with inadequate forces at his command, he was forced to call hundreds of young men from their farms. Realizing the hardships being imposed on their families, General Nelson assigned many of his own field hands to help smaller farms with their harvests. He also distributed huge sums of money to more than a hundred families. Then in August 1781, he was advised by General Washington that the French fleet, acting in unison with General Greene's army from the south and Lafayette's forces from the north, would attempt to trap Cornwallis at Yorktown.

Nelson himself led some 3,000 Virginia militia against the British, and on September 18, 1781 he met with Washington, Lafayette and their aides on board the French flagship of Comte de Grasse to plan the siege of Yorktown. During the siege that followed, the house of Nelson's uncle was commandeered by the British to serve as Cornwallis' headquarters. While some 16,000 American troops closed in, the guns of the French fleet bombarded the town, and the elder Nelson's fine home was leveled. Meanwhile, Thomas Nelson, Jr. was observing the action of his own artillery. Noticing that the gunners were shelling all parts of the town except the vicinity of his mansion, he asked the crews why they avoided that particular section.

"Out of respect to you, sir," was the reply.

Nelson stepped up to one of the cannon, aimed it directly at his house and lit the fuse.

An old account of this incident is a masterpiece of understatement: "Governor Nelson

... at once directed fire upon his house. At that moment a number of British officers occupied it, and were at dinner enjoying a feast, and making merry with wine. The shots of the Americans entered the house, and killing two of the officers, effectively ended the conviviality of the party."

After three weeks of siege, Cornwallis asked for a parley. His historic surrender came on October 19, 1781.

Thomas Nelson, Jr. remained in the office of governor for only a month after the siege of Yorktown was lifted. His health had been steadily deteriorating and he retired permanently from public life. Although he was elected a delegate to the Constitutional Convention, he declined. He died on January 4, 1789, at his quiet country home in Hanover County.

* * *

The author of the Declaration of Independence, Thomas Jefferson, did not remain long in Congress after he had signed the document. Instead he decided to serve his own state and accepted a seat in the Virginia Assembly to which he had been elected. In the fall of 1776, when Franklin was appointed to negotiate a treaty with France, Jefferson declined an offer to accompany the elder statesman and continued to work with the state legislature. He assisted George Wythe and Edmund Pendleton in revising Virginia laws. In the course of this assignment he proposed the first laws in the South forbidding the importation of slaves, establishing public schools, and guaranteeing broad rights in religious freedom.

As Governor Patrick Henry's term ended in June 1779, Jefferson was elected to take his place. Then, within a few months, Virginia was invaded by Benedict Arnold's troops, and the army of Cornwallis moved up from the south. A large section of Richmond was de-

stroyed; fires raged all along the James River, and when the marauding army approached Jefferson's home, he narrowly escaped capture. He was greatly relieved, in 1781, to turn the governorship over to General Thomas Nelson, Jr., fellow signer of the Declaration.

Jefferson then retired to his estate, but again he was threatened with capture, this time by the notorious Colonel Tarleton. Jefferson had been warned that a British raiding party was in the vicinity and had sent his family away in a carriage. He had then returned to his room to gather up some papers when he saw a troop of enemy cavalry coming up a hill toward the house. He seized a sheaf of papers from his desk, rushed to a side door and leaped into the saddle of his horse just as the cavalry came clattering up the carriageway at the front of the house. Jefferson spurred his horse across a meadow and into the woods without a second to spare.

The war had barely ended when Jefferson was overcome with grief at the death of his wife in 1782. To keep his mind occupied, he sought a return to public service and was appointed minister plenipotentiary to assist in negotiating a final treaty with Great Britain. But before he could leave for England, an acceptable treaty draft was submitted to Congress and his trip was canceled. He then served in Congress for two years, during which time he conceived of the decimal money system and the dollar unit for the United States. In May 1784, he sailed to France, accompanied by his eldest daughter, Martha, to join Franklin and John Adams in a mission for establishing trade relations with various European countries. Jefferson then took Franklin's place as minister at the French court, and served in this capacity until 1789. He next became Secretary of State in George Washington's first cabinet. As time went on, Jefferson found himself differing more and more with Washington's

The White House,
executive mansion for two presidents
who were signers of the Declaration,
John Adams and Thomas Jefferson.

policies and more particularly with those of Secretary of the Treasury, Alexander Hamilton. Finally he resigned in 1793.

In the Presidential election of 1796, Jefferson opposed John Adams. He received the second largest number of popular votes and became Vice President in accordance with the law at that time. Again, in 1800, Jefferson sought the Presidency. This time he succeeded after a tie electoral vote was settled in the House of Representatives. In his inaugural address, Jefferson commended the nation to "a wise and frugal government, which shall restrain men from injuring one another, which shall leave them otherwise free to regulate their own pursuits of industry and improvement, and shall not take from the mouth of labor the bread it has earned."

He was reelected in 1804 by an overwhelming vote. During his eight-year administration he negotiated the Louisiana purchase and authorized the Lewis and Clark expedition to explore the continent west of the Mississippi. His management of foreign relations was exceptionally skillful at a time when the fledgling nation was attempting to gain respect.

Although Jefferson and John Adams had become political enemies, after Jefferson's retirement to Monticello the two signers reestablished their former friendship and engaged in voluminous correspondence. In 1818 Jefferson founded the University of Virginia. He acted as its rector for the remainder of his life.

The end came in 1826, when Jefferson was eighty-three years old. He became very ill in June of that year, and on the third of July he asked those at his bedside what day of the month it was. On being told, he expressed a wish that he might live until the Fourth, which would mark the fiftieth anniversary of the country's independence. The next morning he handed his daughter a leather case in which he had placed his epitaph:

Here was buried
THOMAS JEFFERSON
Author of the Declaration of Independence,
Of the Statute of Virginia for
Religious Freedom,
And Father of the University of Virginia

By noon of the Fourth of July 1826, Thomas Jefferson had died. He was not aware that by an uncanny coincidence his friend John Adams died on the same day.

The story of America's quest for independence had come full circle, but the great Declaration that had flowed from Jefferson's pen 50 years earlier belonged to every generation. It will continue to inspire new generations as long as mankind struggles to free itself of tyrannical government.

"I have sworn upon the altar of God, eternal hostility against every form of tyranny over the mind of man."
— THOMAS JEFFERSON

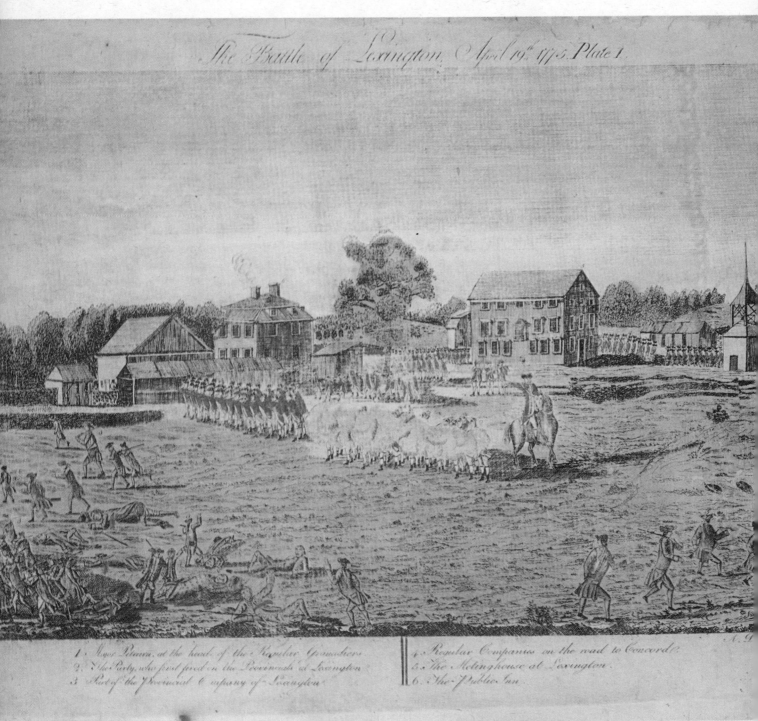

The Battle of Lexington, April 19th 1775. Plate 1.

1. Major Pitcairn at the head of the Regular Granadiers.
2. The Party who first fired on the Provincials at Lexington.
3. Part of the Provincial Company of Lexington.
4. Regular Companies on the road to Concord.
5. The Metinghouse at Lexington.
6. The Public Inn.

Opposite: A one-sided engagement
between British troops and American minute men
on the Lexington green
began the struggle for independence.
Print by Amos Doolittle was engraved
shortly after the event.

Below: At North Bridge in Concord,
real resistance to the British began.
In this Doolittle print, British regulars
are shown retreating under
heavy American fire.

Plate III The Engagement at the North Bridge in Concord.

1 The Detachment of the Regulars who fired first on the Provincials at the Bridge

2 The Provincials headed by Colonel Robinson & Major Buttrick 3 The Bridge

A. Doolittle Sculp

Opposite: The American invasion of Canada in late 1775 failed to achieve its goal. The American commander, Richard Montgomery, was killed in the assault on Quebec. Engraving is based on painting by Trumbull.

Below: A British invasion force under Burgoyne a year and a half later also failed in its objective. Here John Stark directs American forces at the Bennington rout, a prelude to British disaster at Saratoga.

Washington at the Battle of Princeton,
January, 1777, rallied his troops to defeat
British regulars and boost colonial morale
at a critical point in the war.
Painting is by William Mercer, son of an
American general killed in the action.

Left: Molly Pitcher took the place of her fallen husband in the Battle of Monmouth. The battle, fought on a hot June day in 1778, was a draw and was the last major clash in the Northeast.

Below: The year 1780 was one of gloom for the patriot cause, with mutiny in the North and the British victorious in the South. Shown here is the defeat of American forces at Camden, South Carolina. Baron de Kalb falls in a last brave stand of regulars.

Cornwallis at Yorktown found himself besieged on land and hemmed in by sea. On October 19, 1781, the British force of 8,000 men laid down their arms. The Trumbull painting here shows British General Charles O'Hara surrendering to General Benjamin Lincoln. Cornwallis stayed in his quarters. The French under Rochambeau are on the left, with Washington and his officers at the right. Alexander Hamilton is third from the right.

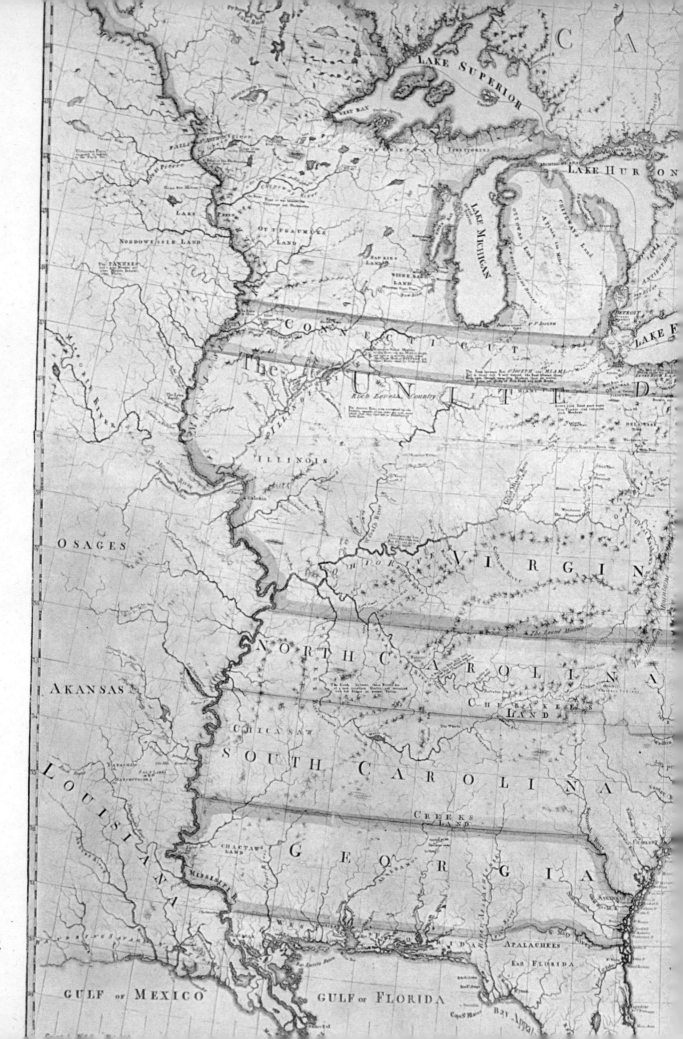

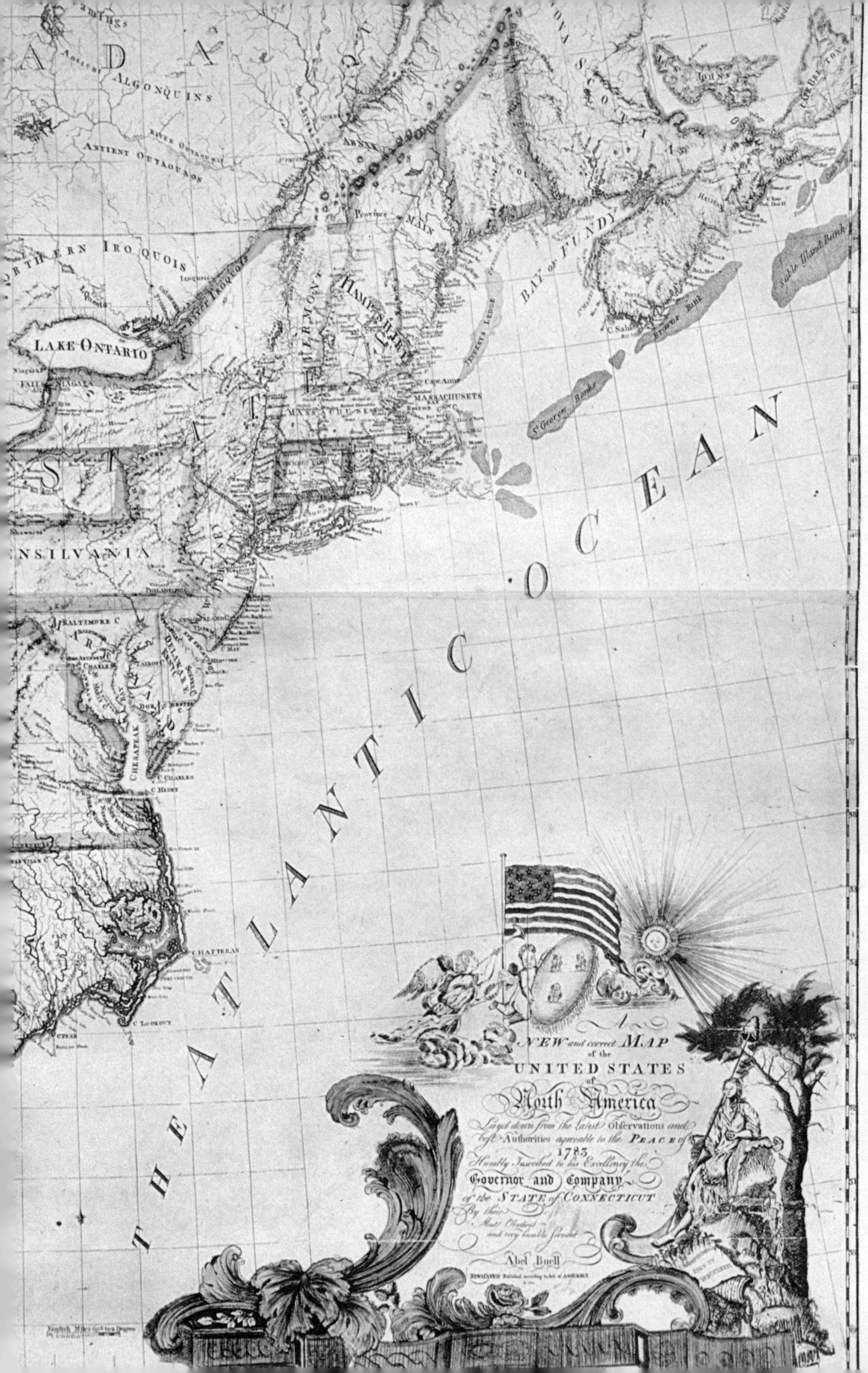

THE NEW JERSEY HISTORICAL SOCIETY

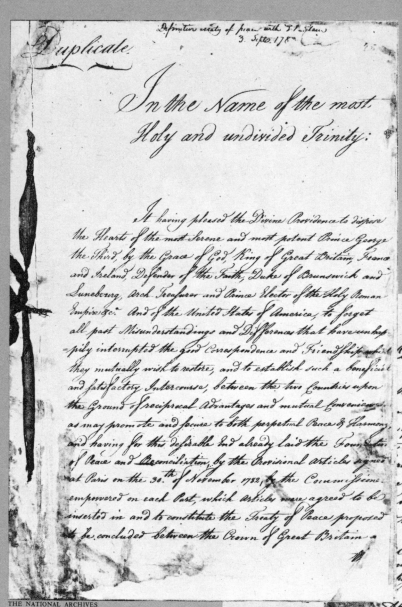

Duplicate

Definitive treaty of peace with B.P. States
3 Sept. 178

In the Name of the most Holy and undivided Trinity:

It having pleased the Divine Providence to dispose the Hearts of the most Serene and most potent Prince George the Third, by the Grace of God, King of Great Britain, France and Ireland, Defender of the Faith, Duke of Brunswick and Luneburg, Arch Treasurer and Prince Elector of the Holy Roman Empire &c.ª And of the United States of America, to forget all past Misunderstandings and Differences that have unhappily interrupted the good Correspondence and Friendship which they mutually wish to restore, and to establish such a beneficial and satisfactory Intercourse, between the two Countries upon the Ground of Reciprocal Advantages and mutual Convenience, as may promote and secure to both perpetual Peace & Harmony, and having for this desirable End already laid the Foundation of Peace and Reconciliation, by the Provisional Articles agreed at Paris on the 30.th of November 1782, by the Commissioners empowered on each Part, which Articles were agreed to be inserted in and to constitute the Treaty of Peace proposed to be concluded between the Crown of Great Britain a

THE NATIONAL ARCHIVES

33

Article 10.

Ratifications of the present Treaty expedited in ... shall be exchanged between the contracting ... of six Months or sooner, if possible, to be ... Day of the Signature of the present Treaty. ... We the undersigned their ministers ... in their Name and in Virtue of our ... with our Hands the present Definitive ... the Seals of our Arms to be affixed thereto.

... at Paris, this third Day of September ... of our Lord, one thousand seven hundred ... ty three. —

D Hartley

John Adams.

B Franklin

John Jay

America's eight-year struggle for independence ended in Paris on September 3, 1783. David Hartley signed the Treaty of Paris for Great Britain, and Adams, Franklin and Jay signed for the United States.

Overleaf: Map of the United States by Abel Buell, 1784. This is the first map of the United States that was made in the new nation. An American flag tops an elaborate cartouche.

Chapter Four

Documents of Freedom

How the Declaration was Preserved

The ink was scarcely dry on the parchment after fifty-one of the fifty-six signers had put their names to it on August 2, 1776, before the question arose as to its safekeeping. At first it was placed in the custody of the Secretary of Congress, Charles Thomson, who had attested Hancock's signature on Jefferson's original draft. When Philadelphia was threatened by invasion, Congress adjourned on December 12, 1776, and moved to Baltimore. The Declaration was transported there, along with other government papers, in a horsedrawn wagon. After about two months in Baltimore, the document was taken back to Philadelphia. Then, in September 1777, the British advance forced Congress to move again. They took the Declaration to Lancaster, then to York, Pennsylvania, where it remained for a little over a year.

In 1779, Congress and the parchment were back in Philadelphia, but only four years later, in 1783, it was taken to Annapolis, then to Princeton in the same year. In 1784 it was in Trenton, and a year later when the seat of government was shifted to New York City, it was moved again. The document was stored in the old New York City Hall on Wall Street, a structure that was later remodeled into the Federal Building.

When Thomas Jefferson was appointed Secretary of State in 1790, he kept the Declaration in his temporary offices on lower Broadway. Shortly afterward, the document was taken back to Philadelphia where it was kept somewhere on Market Street, then in a building at Fifth and Chestnut Streets.

Not until 1800 was the Declaration moved to Washington, D.C. It was stored in the Treasury Building at 19th and Pennsylvania Avenue for a few months before it was transferred to the War Office Building on 17th Street. There it remained until 1814, when, during the War of 1812, a British force approached the capital. Within sound of rifle and cannon fire, Secretary of State James Monroe ordered the parchment removed for safekeeping. It was placed in a linen bag and transported by wagon to a barn on the farm of Edgar Patterson. After a night in the barn it was taken to Reverend Littlejohn's home in Leesburg, Virginia, where it was safely stored for a few weeks. When the British troops were withdrawn from Washington, it was brought back to the 17th Street War Office Building.

In 1823, Secretary of State John Quincy Adams requested that a facsimile of the Declaration be made by a transfer process, but in the course of making the transfer, a considerable amount of the original ink was removed. Meanwhile, since curious visitors were permitted to examine the parchment, the constant rolling and unrolling began to damage the surface seriously. Still, no one seemed to be greatly concerned. Secretary of State Daniel Webster decided to put the Declaration on public view in a glass-enclosed frame. It was placed on display on the second floor of the Patent Office at 7th and F Streets. Unfortunately, the frame hung opposite a window that allowed full sunlight to fall on the parchment for prolonged periods causing the aging ink to fade. After thirty-five years in this location, the Declaration was sent to the Philadelphia Centennial Exposition of 1876.

By this time the precious document was warped and cracked, the script was growing faint, and some of the signatures were all but indistinguishable. At a ceremony during the Centennial, Richard Henry Lee, grandson of the signer, read the document to a large crowd. Then the Declaration was placed in a glass-enclosed case to be viewed by thousands of visitors to the Exposition.

At the close of the fair, the parchment was taken back to the Patent Office in Washington. Concerned about deterioration of the

When the British burned Washington during the War of 1812 the Declaration was removed for safekeeping and for a time was hidden in the barn of a nearby farm.

paper and ink, Congress ordered a study to be made of methods of restoration and preservation, but none of the "experts" consulted was able to offer a practicable solution.

Shortly after the Declaration was moved to a new State Department Building in 1877, the Patent Office burned to the ground. A further effort at restoration of the parchment was made in 1880 when a committee asked William R. Rogers, president of the National Academy of Sciences, to conduct new studies. All that these studies produced was a recommendation to keep the Declaration in a dark place. Thirteen years later, in 1893, the document was put in a steel case and stored in the State Department basement. No one could see it without special permission of the Secretary of State.

A 1903 committee came up with the suggestion that the Declaration and the Constitution be placed between thick panes of glass and put on view at the Library of Congress, but no action was taken.

During the Harding administration in 1921, Librarian of Congress Herbert Putnam drove to the State Department in a Model T Ford mail truck, took the two documents to his own office and had them mounted between double sheets of glass, with a layer of special gelatin designed to screen out actinic rays. These invaluable "sandwiches" were then mounted in a marble and bronze display case.

During the Second World War, on December 23, 1941, the documents were carefully removed from the case, covered by acid-free manila paper, inserted into a container made of all-rag neutral millboard which was then sealed with tape. Next the millboard was put into a bronze container and this was heated to 90° F for several hours in order to remove moisture. Finally the container was sealed with lead, surrounded by rock wool, deposited in a heavy box and secretly

transported to Union Station. There it was carried into a Pullman compartment for a journey to Fort Knox. During its wartime stay there, experts repaired the Declaration by painstakingly filling microscopic holes and cracks in the parchment.

Returned to the Library of Congress on September 19, 1944, the documents were again put on display, protected by an armed guard twenty-four hours a day.

When the present National Archives Building was constructed, the plan included a special hall for valuable papers. Then on December 13, 1952, accompanied by an armed escort, the Declaration and the Constitution were taken in an armored truck to the new building. There they may be seen today, fully protected from light damage and magnificently encased for public view.

117

The Declaration of Independence

IN CONGRESS, JULY 4, 1776.

When, in the course of human events, it becomes necessary for one people to dissolve the political bands which have connected them with another, and to assume, among the powers of the earth, the separate and equal station to which the laws of nature and of nature's God entitle them, a decent respect to the opinions of mankind requires that they should declare the causes which impel them to the separation.

We hold these truths to be self-evident: — that all men are created equal; that they are endowed by their Creator with certain unalienable rights; that among these are life, liberty, and the pursuit of happiness. That, to secure these rights, governments are instituted among men, deriving their just powers from the consent of the governed; that whenever any form of government becomes destructive of these ends, it is the right of the people to alter or to abolish it, and to institute new government, laying its foundation on such principles, and organising its powers in such form, as to them shall seem most likely to effect their safety and happiness. Prudence, indeed, will dictate that governments long established should not be changed for light and transient causes; and, accordingly, all experience hath shown that mankind are more disposed to suffer, while evils are sufferable, than to right themselves by abolishing the forms to which they are accustomed. But, when a long train of abuses and usurpations, pursuing invariably the same object, evinces a design to reduce them under absolute despotism, it is their right, it is their duty, to throw off such government, and to provide new guards for their future security. Such has been the patient sufferance of these colonies; and such is now the necessity which constrains them to alter their former systems of government. The history of the present King of Great Britain is a history of repeated injuries and usurpations, all having, in direct object, the establishment of an absolute tyranny over these states. To prove this, let facts be submitted to a candid world.

He has refused his assent to laws the most wholesome and necessary for the public good.

He has forbidden his Governors to pass laws of immediate and pressing importance, unless suspended in their operation till his assent should be obtained; and, when so suspended, he has utterly neglected to attend to them.

He has refused to pass other laws for the accommodation of large districts of people, unless those people would relinquish the right of representation in the legislature — a right inestimable to them, and formidable to tyrants only.

He has called together legislative bodies at places unusual, uncomfortable, and distant from the depository of their public records, for the sole purpose of fatiguing them into compliance with his measures.

He has dissolved representative houses repeatedly, for opposing, with manly firmness, his invasions on the rights of the people.

He has refused, for a long time after such dissolutions, to cause others to be elected; whereby the legislative powers, incapable of annihilation, have returned to the people at large for their exercise; the State remaining, in the meantime, exposed to all dangers of invasion from without, and convulsions within.

He has endeavored to prevent the population of these states; for that purpose obstructing the laws for the naturalization of foreigners; refusing to pass others to encourage their migration hither, and raising the conditions of new appropriations of lands.

He has obstructed the administration of justice, by refusing his assent to laws for establishing judiciary powers.

He has made judges dependent on his will alone for the tenure of their offices, and the amount and payment of their salaries.

He has erected a multitude of new offices, and sent hither swarms of officers to harass our people and eat out their substance.

He has kept among us, in times of peace, standing armies, without the consent of our legislatures.

He has affected to render the military independent of, and superior to, the civil power.

He has combined with others to subject us to a jurisdiction foreign to our constitutions, and unacknowledged by our laws; giving his assent to their acts of pretended legislation:

For quartering large bodies of armed troops among us;

For protecting them, by a mock trial, from punishment for any murders which they should commit on the inhabitants of these states;

For cutting off our trade with all parts of the world;

For imposing taxes on us without our consent;

For depriving us, in many cases, of the benefits of trial by jury;

For transporting us beyond the seas, to be tried for pretended offences;

For abolishing the free system of English laws in a neighboring province, establishing therein an arbitrary government, and enlarging its boundaries, so as to render it at once an example and fit instrument for introducing the same absolute rule into these colonies;

For taking away our charters, abolishing our most valuable laws, and altering, fundamentally, the forms of our governments;

For suspending our own legislatures, and declaring themselves invested with power to legislate for us in all cases whatsoever.

He has abdicated government here, by declaring

us out of his protection, and waging war against us.

He has plundered our seas, ravaged our coasts, burnt our towns, and destroyed the lives of our people.

He is at this time transporting large armies of foreign mercenaries to complete the works of death, desolation, and tyranny, already begun with circumstances of cruelty and perfidy scarcely paralleled in the most barbarous ages, and totally unworthy the head of a civilized nation.

He has constrained our fellow-citizens, taken captive on the high seas, to bear arms against their country, to become the executioners of their friends and brethren, or to fall themselves by their hands.

He has excited domestic insurrections amongst us, and has endeavored to bring on the inhabitants of our frontiers the merciless Indian savages, whose known rule of warfare is an undistinguished destruction of all ages, sexes, and conditions.

In every stage of these oppressions we have petitioned for redress in the most humble terms; our repeated petitions have been answered only by repeated injury. A prince whose character is thus marked by every act which may define a tyrant is unfit to be the ruler of a free people.

Nor have we been wanting in attentions to our British brethren. We have warned them from time to time, of attempts by their legislature to extend an unwarrantable jurisdiction over us. We have reminded them of the circumstances of our emigration and settlement here. We have appealed to their native justice and magnanimity; and we have conjured them, by the ties of our common kindred, to disavow these usurpations, which would inevitably interrupt our connections and correspondence. They, too, have been deaf to the voice of justice and of consanguinity. We must, therefore, acquiesce in the necessity which denounces our separation; and hold them, as we hold the rest of mankind, enemies in war, in peace, friends.

We, therefore, the representatives of the United States of America, in General Congress assembled, appealing to the Supreme Judge of the world for the rectitude of our intentions, do, in the name and by the authority of the good people of these colonies, solemnly publish and declare, that these united colonies are, and of right ought to be, free and independent states; that they are absolved from all allegiance to the British Crown, and that all political connection between them and the state of Great Britain is, and ought to be, totally dissolved; and that, as free and independent states, they have full power to levy war, conclude peace, contract alliances, establish commerce, and to do all other acts and things which independent states may of right do. And, for the support of this Declaration, with a firm reliance on the protection of Divine Providence, we mutually pledge to each other our lives, our fortunes, and our sacred honor.

The foregoing Declaration was, by order of Congress, engrossed and signed by the following members: —

JOHN HANCOCK

NEW HAMPSHIRE
JOSIAH BARTLETT
WILLIAM WHIPPLE
MATTHEW THORNTON

MASSACHUSETTS
SAMUEL ADAMS
JOHN ADAMS
ROBERT TREAT PAINE
ELBRIDGE GERRY

RHODE ISLAND
STEPHEN HOPKINS
WILLIAM ELLERY

CONNECTICUT
ROGER SHERMAN
SAMUEL HUNTINGTON
WILLIAM WILLIAMS
OLIVER WOLCOTT

NEW YORK
WILLIAM FLOYD
PHILIP LIVINGSTON
FRANCIS LEWIS
LEWIS MORRIS

NEW JERSEY
RICHARD STOCKTON
JOHN WITHERSPOON
FRANCIS HOPKINSON
JOHN HART
ABRAHAM CLARK

PENNSYLVANIA
ROBERT MORRIS
BENJAMIN RUSH
BENJAMIN FRANKLIN
JOHN MORTON
GEORGE CLYMER
JAMES SMITH

GEORGE TAYLOR
JAMES WILSON
GEORGE ROSS

DELAWARE
CAESAR RODNEY
GEORGE READ
THOMAS MCKEAN

MARYLAND
SAMUEL CHASE
WILLIAM PACA
THOMAS STONE
CHARLES CARROLL
OF CARROLLTON

VIRGINIA
GEORGE WYTHE
RICHARD HENRY LEE
THOMAS JEFFERSON

BENJAMIN HARRISON
THOMAS NELSON, JR.
FRANCIS LIGHTFOOT LEE
CARTER BRAXTON

NORTH CAROLINA
WILLIAM HOOPER
JOSEPH HEWES
JOHN PENN

SOUTH CAROLINA
EDWARD RUTLEDGE
THOMAS HEYWARD, JR.
THOMAS LYNCH, JR.
ARTHUR MIDDLETON

GEORGIA
BUTTON GWINNETT
LYMAN HALL
GEORGE WALTON

The Forgotten Document

On the same June day in 1776 when the Continental Congress appointed a committee to draft a declaration of independence and another to prepare a plan of treaties, it also decided to appoint a committee to implement the third part of the Richard Henry Lee Resolution, "to prepare and digest the form of a confederation to be entered into between these colonies."

This was not the first time confederation had been proposed in the Continental Congress. A plan of union was put forth by Benjamin Franklin in July 1775. It provided for a temporary confederation until Britain's differences with the American colonies were reconciled. Congress, however, was unable to consider confederation for nearly a year.

Once independence was under serious consideration, however, a committee made up of one member from each of the thirteen colonies was named to determine the form of a confederation. John Dickinson, delegate for Delaware, headed the committee.

The Dickinson draft of the Articles of Confederation was ready for consideration on July 12. It provided for a congress in which each state was represented in proportion to its population, but the smaller states were strongly opposed to this system. There was also vigorous resistance to the clause of the Dickinson draft, which would have assigned to the national government all powers not specifically reserved to the states. Having just declared themselves independent of a distant centralized control by King and Parliament, the new states were not yet ready to create a strong central government in America.

It was not until July 9, 1778, that the final form of the Articles of Confederation was accepted and an engrossed copy was prepared for signature by the delegates. By 1779, when Delaware's delegates signed, all the states but Maryland had ratified the agreement for confederation.

Sometimes called "the first constitution of the United States," the Articles of Confederation were in many ways more like a treaty among a group of small nations than a true frame of government. Each state expressly retained

its sovereignty, freedom and independence, and every Power, Jurisdiction and right, . . . not by this confederation expressly delegated to the United States, in Congress assembled.

Every state had one vote in Congress, regardless of its geographic area or population. Congress was legally given the powers it had been exercising during its existence since 1775: the "United States in Congress assembled" could make war and peace, send and receive ambassadors, enter into treaties and alliances, coin money, regulate Indian affairs, and establish a post office. It could not levy taxes or regulate commerce. There was no national executive and no system of national courts. The Articles could be amended only by unanimous vote, and the confederation was not to come into being until all thirteen states had ratified.

Maryland's ratification was withheld until February 2, 1781. A small state cut off from expansion to the West by the territorial claims of Virginia and Pennsylvania, Maryland was apprehensive about joining a confederation in which some states claimed land extending to the Mississippi River, or even to the Pacific. Gradually other states bowed to Maryland's insistence that Congress control western lands.

Only after Virginia ceded her claims on January 2, 1781, was Maryland willing to ratify the Articles of Confederation. In its eight-year life span the Confederation was to achieve some solid accomplishments, but by 1787 new bonds of union were needed to replace the deliberately weak Confederation. Today the Articles are almost forgotten.

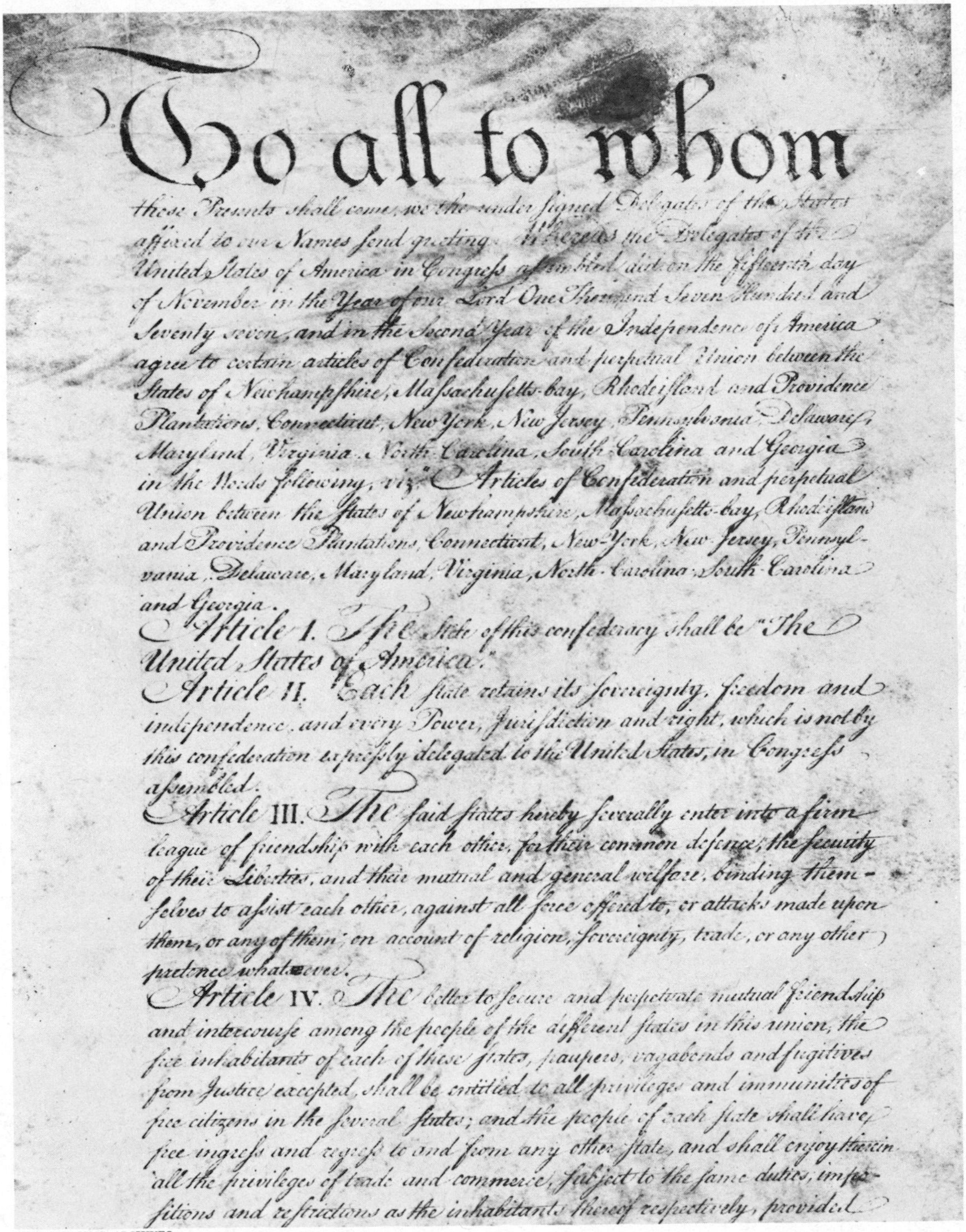

Last page of the Articles
of Confederation with the signatures
of the delegates from the thirteen states.

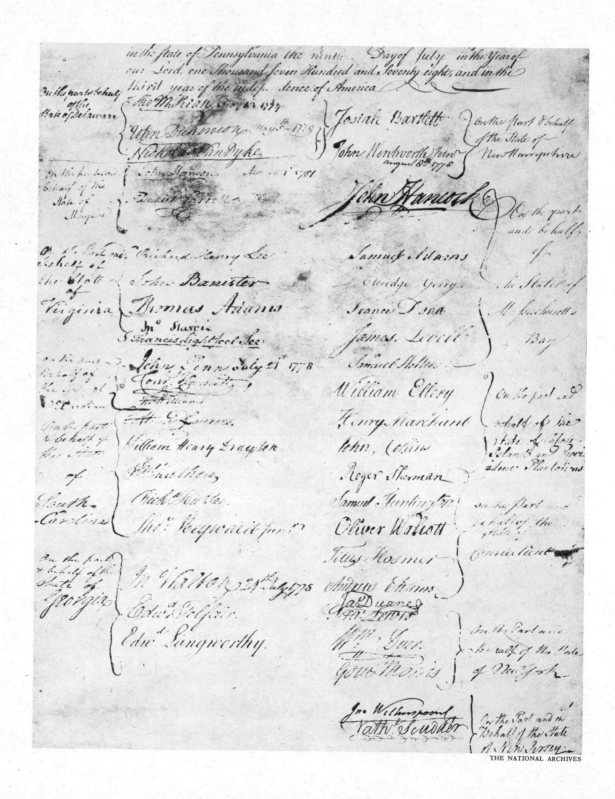

122

The Articles of Confederation

To all to whom these Presents shall come, we the under signed Delegates of the States affixed to our Names, send greeting.

Whereas the Delegates of the United States of America, in Congress assembled, did, on the 15th day of November, in the Year of Our Lord One thousand Seven Hundred and Seventy seven, and in the Second Year of the Independence of America, agree to certain articles of Confederation and perpetual Union between the States of Newhampshire, Massachusetts-bay, Rhodeisland and Providence Plantations, Connecticut, New York, New Jersey, Pennsylvania, Delaware, Maryland, Virginia, North-Carolina, South-Carolina, and Georgia in the words following, viz. "Articles of Confederation and perpetual Union between the states of Newhampshire, Massachusetts-bay, Rhodeisland and Providence Plantations, Connecticut, New-York, New-Jersey, Pennsylvania, Delaware, Maryland, Virginia, North-Carolina, South-Carolina and Georgia.

ARTICLE I. The Stile of this confederacy shall be "The United States of America."

ARTICLE II. Each state retains its sovereignty, freedom, and independence, and every Power, Jurisdiction and right, which is not by this confederation expressly delegated to the United States, in Congress assembled.

ARTICLE III. The said states hereby severally enter into a firm league of friendship with each other, for their common defence, the security of their Liberties, and their mutual and general welfare, binding themselves to assist each other, against all force offered to, or attacks made upon them, or any of them, on account of religion, sovereignty, trade, or any other pretence whatever.

ARTICLE IV. The better to secure and perpetuate mutual friendship and intercourse among the people of the different states in this union, the free inhabitants of each of these states, paupers, vagabonds and fugitives from justice excepted, shall be entitled to all privileges and immunities of free citizens in the several states; and the people of each state shall have free ingress and regress to and from any other state, and shall enjoy therein all the privileges of trade and commerce, subject to the same duties, impositions and restrictions as the inhabitants thereof respectively, provided that such restriction shall not extend so far as to prevent the removal of property imported into any state, to any other state, of which the Owner is an inhabitant; provided also that no imposition, duties or restriction shall be laid by any state, on the property of the united states, or either of them.

If any Person guilty of, or charged with treason, felony, or other high misdemeanor in any state, shall flee from Justice, and be found in any of the united states, he shall, upon demand of the Governor or executive power, of the state from which he fled, be delivered up and removed to the state having jurisdiction of his offence.

Full faith and credit shall be given in each of these states to the records, acts and judicial proceedings of the courts and magistrates of every other state.

ARTICLE V. For the more convenient management of the general interests of the united states, delegates shall be annually appointed in such manner as the legislature of each state shall direct, to meet in Congress on the first Monday in November, in every year, with a power reserved to each state, to recal its delegates, or any of them, at any time within the year, and to send others in their stead, for the remainder of the Year.

No state shall be represented in Congress by less than two, nor by more than seven Members; and no person shall be capable of being a delegate for more than three years in any term of six years; nor shall any person, being a delegate, be capable of holding any office under the united states, for which he, or another for his benefit receives any salary, fees or emolument of any kind.

Each state shall maintain its own delegates in a meeting of the states, and while they act as members of the committee of the states.

In determining questons in the united states in Congress assembled, each state shall have one vote.

Freedom of speech and debate in Congress shall not be impeached or questioned in any Court, or place out of Congress, and the members of congress shall be protected in their persons from arrests and imprisonments, during the time of their going to and from, and attendance on congress, except for treason, felony, or breach of the peace.

ARTICLE VI. No state, without the Consent of the united states in congress assembled, shall send any embassy to, or receive any embassy from, or enter into any conference, agreement, alliance or treaty with any King prince or state; nor shall any person holding any office of profit or trust under the united states, or any of them, accept of any present, emolument, office or title of any kind whatever from any king, prince or foreign state; nor shall the united states in congress assembled, or any of them, grant any title of nobility.

No two or more states shall enter into any treaty, confederation or alliance whatever between them, without the consent of the united states in congress assembled, specifying accurately the purposes for which the same is to be entered into, and how long it shall continue.

No state shall lay any imposts or duties, which may interfere with any stipulations in treaties, entered into by the united states in congress assembled, with any king, prince or state, in pursuance of any treaties already proposed by congress, to the courts of France and Spain.

No vessels of war shall be kept up in time of peace by any state, except such number only, as shall be deemed necessary by the united states in congress assembled, for the defence of such state, or its trade; nor shall any body of forces be kept up by any state, in time of peace, except such number only, as in the judgment of the united states, in congress assembled, shall be deemed requisite to garrison the forts necessary for the defence of such state; but every state shall always keep up a well regulated and disciplined militia, sufficiently armed and accoutred, and shall provide and constantly have ready for use, in public stores, a due number of field pieces and tents, and a proper quantity of arms, ammunition and camp equipage.

No state shall engage in any war without the consent of the united states in congress assembled, unless such state be actually invaded by enemies, or shall have received certain advice of a resolution being formed by some nation of Indians to invade such state, and the danger is so imminent as not to admit of a delay till the united states in congress assembled can be consulted: nor shall any state grant commissions to any ships or vessels of war, nor letters of marque or reprisal, except it be after a declaration of war by the united states in congress assembled, and then only against the kingdom or state and the subjects thereof, against which war has been so declared, and under such regulations as shall be established by the united states in congress assembled, unless such state be infested by pirates, in which

case vessels of war may be fitted out for that occasion, and kept so long as the danger shall continue, or until the united states in congress assembled, shall determine otherwise.

ARTICLE VII. When land-forces are raised by any state for the common defence, all officers of or under the rank of colonel, shall be appointed by the legislature of each state respectively, by whom such forces shall be raised, or in such manner as such state shall direct, and all vacancies shall be filled up by the State which first made the appointment.

ARTICLE VIII. All charges of war, and all other expences that shall be incurred for the common defence or general welfare, and allowed by the united states in congress assembled, shall be defrayed out of a common treasury, which shall be supplied by the several states in proportion to the value of all land within each state, granted to or surveyed for any Person, as such land and the buildings and improvements thereon shall be estimated according to such mode as the united states in congress assembled, shall from time to time direct and appoint.

The taxes for paying that proportion shall be laid and levied by the authority and direction of the legislatures of the several states within the time agreed upon by the united states in congress assembled.

ARTICLE IX. The united states in congress assembled, shall have the sole and exclusive right and power of determining on peace and war, except in the cases mentioned in the sixth article — of sending and receiving ambassadors — entering into treaties and alliances, provided that no treaty of commerce shall be made whereby the legislative power of the respective states shall be restrained from imposing such imposts and duties on foreigners as their own people are subjected to, or from prohibiting the exportation or importation of any species of goods or commodities, whatsoever — of establishing rules for deciding in all cases, what captures on land or water shall be legal, and in what manner prizes taken by land or naval forces in the service of the united states shall be divided or appropriated — of granting letters of marque and reprisal in times of peace — appointing courts for the trial of piracies and felonies committed on the high seas and establishing courts for receiving and determining finally appeals in all cases of captures, provided that no member of congress shall be appointed a judge of any of the said courts.

The united states in congress assembled shall also be the last resort on appeal in all disputes and differences now subsisting or that hereafter may arise between two or more states concerning boundary, jurisdiction or any other cause whatever; which authority shall always be exercised in the manner following. Whenever the legislative or executive authority or lawful agent of any state in controversy with another shall present a petition to congress stating the matter in question and praying for a hearing, notice thereof shall be given by order of congress to the legislative or executive authority of the other state in controversy, and a day assigned for the appearance of the parties by their lawful agents, who shall then be directed to appoint by joint consent, commissioners or judges to constitute a court for hearing and determining the matter in question: but if they cannot agree, congress shall name three persons out of each of the united states, and from the list of such persons each party shall alternately strike out one, the petitioners beginning, until the number shall be reduced to thirteen; and from that number not less then seven, nor more than nine names as congress shall direct, shall in the presence of congress be drawn out by lot, and the persons whose names shall be so drawn or any five of them, shall be commissioners or judges, to hear and finally determine the controversy, so always as a major part of the judges who shall hear the cause shall agree in the determination: and if either party shall neglect to attend at the day appointed, without showing reasons, which congress shall judge sufficient, or being present shall refuse to strike, the congress shall proceed to nominate three persons out of each state, and the secretary of congress shall strike in behalf of such party absent or refusing; and the judgment and sentence of the court to be appointed, in the manner before prescribed, shall be final and conclusive; and if any of the parties shall refuse to submit to the authority of such court, or to appear or defend their claim or cause, the court shall nevertheless proceed to pronounce sentence, or judgment, which shall in like manner be final and decisive, the judgment or sentence and other proceedings being in either case transmitted to congress, and lodged among the acts of congress for the security of the parties concerned: provided that every commissioner, before he sits in judgment, shall take an oath to be administered by one of the judges of the supreme or superior court of the state, where the cause shall be tried, "well and truly to hear and determine the matter in question, according to the best of his judgment, without favour, affection or hope of reward:" provided also, that no state shall be deprived of territory for the benefit of the united states.

All controversies concerning the private right of soil claimed under different grants of two or more states, whose jurisdictions as they may respect such lands, and the states which passed such grants are adjusted, the said grants or either of them being at the same time claimed to have originated antecedent to such settlement of jurisdiction, shall on the petition of either party to the congress of the united states, be finally determined as near as may be in the same manner as is before prescribed for deciding disputes respecting territorial jurisdiction between different states.

The united states in congress assembled shall also have the sole and exclusive right and power of regulating the alloy and value of coin struck by their own authority, or by that of the respective states — fixing the standard of weights and measures throughout the united states — regulating the trade and managing all affairs with the Indians, not members of any of the states, provided that the legislative right of any state within its own limits be not infringed or violated — establishing or regulating postoffices from one state to another, throughout all the united states, and exacting such postage on the papers passing thro' the same as may be requisite to defray the expences of the said office — appointing all officers of the land forces, in the service of the united states, excepting regimental officers — appointing all the officers of the naval forces, and commissioning all officers whatever in the service of the united states — making rules for the government and regulation of the said land and naval forces, and directing their operations.

The united states in congress assembled shall have authority to appoint a committee, to sit in the recess of congress, to be denominated "A Committee of the States," and to consist of one delegate from each state; and to appoint such other committees and civil officers as may be necessary for managing the general affairs of the united states under their direction — to appoint one of their number to preside, provided that no person be allowed to serve in the office of president more than one year in any term of three years; to ascertain the necessary sums of money to be raised for the service of the united states, and to appropriate and apply the same for defraying the public expences — to borrow money, or emit bills on the credit of the united states, transmitting every half year to the

125

respective states an account of the sums of money so borrowed or emitted, — to build and equip a navy — to agree upon the number of land forces, and to make requisitions from each state for its quota, in proportion to the number of white inhabitants in such state; which requisition shall be binding, and thereupon the legislature of each state shall appoint the regimental officers, raise the men and cloath, arm and equip them in a soldier like manner, at the expence of the united states; and the officers and men so cloathed, armed and equipped shall march to the place appointed, and within the time agreed on by the united states in congress assembled: But if the united states in congress assembled shall, on consideration of circumstances judge proper that any state should not raise men, or should raise a smaller number than its quota, and that any other state should raise a greater number of men than the quota thereof, such extra number shall be raised, officered, cloathed, armed and equipped in the same manner as the quota of such state, unless the legislature of such state shall judge that such extra number cannot be safely spared out of the same, in which case they shall raise officer, cloath, arm and equip as many of such extra number as they judge can be safely spared. And the officers and men so cloathed, armed and equipped, shall march to the place appointed, and within the time agreed on by the united states in congress assembled.

The united states in congress assembled shall never engage in a war, nor grant letters of marque and reprisal in time of peace, nor enter into any treaties or alliances, nor coin money, nor regulate the value thereof, nor ascertain the sums and expences necessary for the defence and welfare of the united states, or any of them, nor emit bills, nor borrow money on the credit of the united states, nor appropriate money, nor agree upon the number of vessels of war, to be built or purchased, or the number of land or sea forces to be raised, nor appoint a commander in chief of the army or navy, unless nine states assent to the same: nor shall a question on any other point, except for adjourning from day to day be determined, unless by the votes of a majority of the united states in congress assembled.

The congress of the united states shall have power to adjourn to any time within the year, and to any place within the united states, so that no period of adjournment be for a longer duration than the space of six Months, and shall publish the Journal of their proceedings monthly, except such parts thereof relating to treaties, alliances or military operations, as in their judgment require secrecy; and the yeas and nays of the delegates of each state on any question shall be entered on the Journal, when it is desired by any delegate; and the delegates of a state, or any of them, at his or their request shall be furnished with a transcript of the said Journal, except such parts as are above excepted, to lay before the legislatures of the several states.

ARTICLE X. The committee of the states, or any nine of them, shall be authorized to execute, in the recess of congress, such of the powers of congress as the united states in congress assembled, by the consent of nine states, shall from time to time think expedient to vest them with; provided that no power be delegated to the said committee, for the exercise of which, by the articles of confederation, the voice of nine states in the congress of the united states assembled is requisite.

ARTICLE XI. Canada acceding to this confederation, and joining in the measures of the united states, shall be admitted into, and entitled to all the advantages of this union: but no other colony shall be admitted into the same, unless such admission be agreed to by nine states.

ARTICLE XII. All bills of credit emitted, monies borrowed and debts contracted by, or under the authority of congress, before the assembling of the united states, in pursuance of the present confederation, shall be deemed and considered as a charge against the united states, for payment and satisfaction whereof the said united states, and the public faith are hereby solemnly pledged.

ARTICLE XIII. Every state shall abide by the determinations of the united states in congress assembled, on all questions which by this confederation are submitted to them. And the Articles of this confederation shall be inviolably observed by every state, and the union shall be perpetual; nor shall any alteration at any time hereafter be made in any of them; unless such alteration be agreed to in a congress of the united states, and be afterwards confirmed by the legislatures of every state.

And Whereas it hath pleased the Great Governor of the World to incline the hearts of the legislatures we respectively represent in congress, to approve of, and to authorize us to ratify the said articles of confederation and perpetual union. Know Ye that we the undersigned delegates, by virtue of the power and authority to us given for that purpose, do by these presents, in the name and in behalf of our respective constituents, fully and entirely ratify and confirm each and every of the said articles of confederation and perpetual union, and all and singular the matters and things therein contained: And we do further solemnly plight and engage the faith of our respective constituents, that they shall abide by the determinations of the united states in congress assembled, on all questions, which by the said confederation are submitted to them. And that the articles thereof shall be inviolably observed by the states we respectively represent, and that the union shall be perpetual. In Witness whereof we have hereunto set our hands in Congress. Done at Philadelphia in the state of Pennsylvania the ninth day of July, in the Year of our Lord one Thousand seven Hundred and Seventy-eight, and in the third year of the independence of America.

JOSIAH BARTLETT
JOHN WENTWORTH
  Junr August 8th 1778
On the part & behalf of the State of New Hampshire

JOHN HANCOCK
SAMUEL ADAMS
ELBRIDGE GERRY
FRANCIS DANA
JAMES LOVELL
SAMUEL HOLTEN
On the part and behalf of The State of Massachusetts Bay

WILLIAM ELLERY
HENRY MARCHANT
JOHN COLLINS
On the part and behalf of the State of Rhode-Island and Providence Plantations

ROGER SHERMAN
SAMUEL HUNTINGTON
OLIVER WOLCOTT
TITUS HOSMER
ANDREW ADAMS
on the part and behalf of the State of Connecticut

JA^S DUANE
FRA^S LEWIS
W^M DUER.
GOUV MORRIS
On the Part and Behalf of the State of New York

JNO WITHERSPOON
NATH^L SCUDDER
On the Part and in Behalf of the State of New Jersey. Novr 26, 1778.—

ROB^T MORRIS
DANIEL ROBERDEAU
JON^A BAYARD SMITH.
WILLIAM CLINGAN
JOSEPH REED 22^d July 1778
On the part and behalf of the State of Pennsylvania

THO^S MCKEAN FEBY 12 1779
JOHN DICKINSON MAY 5th 1779
NICHOLAS VAN DYKE,
On the part & behalf of the State of Delaware

JOHN HANSON
  March 1 1781
DANIEL CARROLL d^O
On the part and behalf of the State of Maryland

RICHARD HENRY LEE
JOHN BANISTER
THOMAS ADAMS
JN^O HARVIE
FRANCIS LIGHTFOOT LEE
On the Part and Behalf of the State of Virginia

JOHN PENN July 21St 1778
CORN^S HARNETT
JN^O WILLIAMS
On the part and Behalf of the State of North Carolina

HENRY LAURENS
WILLIAM HENRY DRAYTON
JN^O MATHEWS
RICH^D HUTSON.
THO^S HEYWARD JUN^r
On the part & behalf of the State of South-Carolina

JN^O WALTON 24th July 1778
EDW^D TELFAIR.
EDW^D LANGWORTHY.
On the part & behalf of the State of Georgia

PART II

"... to form a

nore perfect union ...''

"We the People of the States of New-Hampshire, Massachusetts, Rhode-Island and Providence Plantations, Connecticut, New-York, New-Jersey, Pennsylvania, Delaware, Maryland, Virginia, North-Carolina, South-Carolina, and Georgia, do ordain, declare and establish the following Constitution for the Government of Ourselves and our Posterity. . . . The title of this Government shall be 'the United States of America.' . . ."

First Printed Draft of the Constitution
August 6, 1787

Overleaf: Early engraving
reflected confidence in the Constitution.

The Story of Our Constitution

The Declaration of Independence stated a fundamental concept of human rights and freedom, but it did not provide a governmental system to ensure those rights. Soon after the Revolution it became clear that free men could not rule themselves without some formal instrument of government, and a genuine national crisis drove the founders to assemble in a Constitutional Convention. The result of this epic meeting was the Constitution of the United States.

Although it has been frequently referred to as an "immortal document," and although men have stood in awe of it since the time of its framing, the Constitution is essentially a human document. The astonishing debate that took place at Independence Hall in Philadelphia during the hot months of 1787 brought forth a living, breathing concept of government. There is in it surprisingly little legalistic rhetoric, few complicated or high-sounding phrases, and its overriding concerns are for human rights and human values.

Unlike most architects of governmental systems, the framers of the Constitution did not think of themselves as infallible god-like creatures who knew what was best for the lowly populace. In fact they were so acutely aware of their own shortcomings as well as of everyday human failings that much of their debate was concerned with how to prevent human frailty from bringing disaster to the United States. So well did they understand human greed and man's eternal desire for power that they spent hours debating how they might keep such evils in check without diluting federal power to the point where it would be ineffectual.

The Constitutional Convention itself was torn by such opposite points of view that many delegates feared for the country as a whole. Individual states were jealous of their authority; the small states feared the power of the large ones. Some influential Southern delegates fought to retain slavery, while most Northern members sought to abolish this inhuman practice at the outset.

Despite such serious rifts and despite the fact that the Convention was made up of strong-willed, opinionated men, the result of their meetings in Philadelphia was a document that stands to this day as one of mankind's greatest achievements. In the last analysis, a spirit of compromise prevailed, and because the majority of the delegates were reasonable men, they reached a conclusion that revealed above all else their essential humanity.

Even today, after many decades of amending and refining the basic document, the United States Constitution, like the American people who live by its guidance, has its weaknesses and its contradictions. But its overall wisdom endures.

The story of the men and their debates that led to the final creation of this document is one of the great human dramas of all time. From it we can learn much, not only about the Founding Fathers but about ourselves, for although the times and technology have changed greatly, fundamental human nature has not.

D.E.C.
Wayne, Pa.

In 1787 the thirteen original states
were loosely bound together
under the Articles of Confederation.
Conflicting state claims to
the old northwest had been resolved,
but Britain and Spain refused to accept
national boundaries and other provisions agreed to
in the Treaty of Paris.

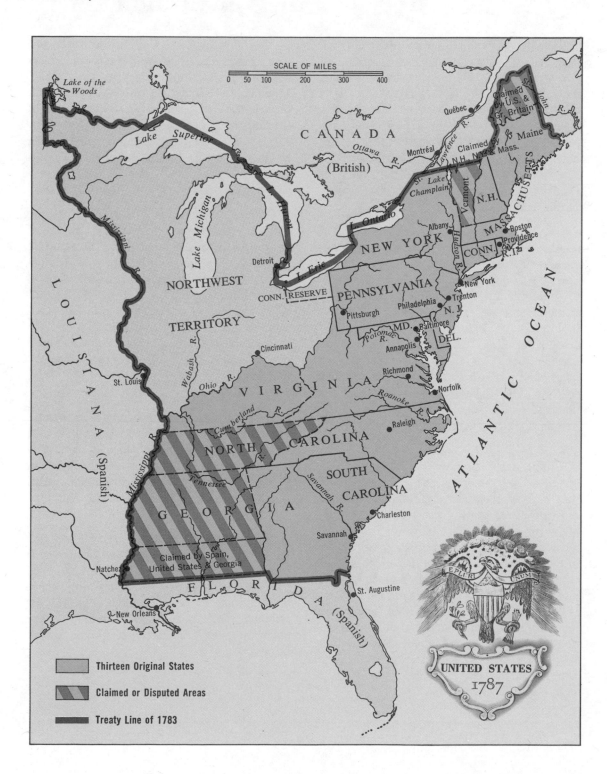

Chapter Five

The Dilemma

Bloody Rebellion

The question was whether thirteen independent states, united in war by a common determination to be free of foreign tyranny, could remain united in peace. Only five years had passed since the war with England ended, and already Americans were fighting Americans. Violence, born of frustration and want, was erupting in the very places where rebellion against British rule had been spawned, and angry men like Daniel Shays and Luke Day were threatening to overthrow the government they had formed with their own sweat and blood.

It had been ten years since 56 courageous revolutionaries had met at the State House in Philadelphia to declare independence from Great Britain. Somehow the thirteen states had stood up to British military power, and under the astonishing leadership of George Washington they had forced Lord Cornwallis to surrender at Yorktown in 1781. Now, in the summer of 1786, the infant United States was in grave danger of strangulation.

There was no lack of patriotic fervor. Since the end of the war Fourth of July celebrations had become increasingly festive. Flags were popular, and the Stars and Stripes could be seen fluttering from the window sills of private homes and flying proudly from the flagpoles in front of taverns from Maine to Georgia. Men bragged of their service in the Continental Army; many still liked to wear their uniform tunics on holidays. But under the surface a muttering of dissatisfaction was increasing to an ominous rumble. It was difficult to say exactly where it all began. Actually, complaints about the Congress had been voiced as much as three years before the conclusion of the war. Alexander Hamilton, who in 1778 was one of General Washington's staff officers, had expressed this dissatisfaction by saying that the delegates who were being sent to the Congress were inferior men. Leading citizens, he said, "have been fonder of the emoluments and conveniences of being employed at home; and local attachment, falsely operating has made them more provident for the particular interests of the States to which they belonged, than for the common interests of the Confederacy." As a result, Hamilton complained, "the Congress is feeble, indecisive, and improvident."

After the war the condition became even worse. Without real statesmen at the helm of such a loosely organized central government a serious financial crisis developed. Continental banknotes, some issued in denominations of the old British pounds, shillings and pence, and others in Spanish dollars, were received with varying degrees of contempt in the several states. For example, a Spanish dollar was considered to be worth eight shillings in New York, seven shillings in Pennsylvania, 32 shillings in South Carolina, and only six shil-

Foreclosure was faced by craftsmen and farmers.

A promissory note issued in 1780 by the State of Massachusetts for $255. Massachusetts refused to issue paper money and instead went ahead with tax levies to support the state's debt.

lings in most parts of New England. It wasn't long before most United States "continental" currency was virtually worthless. Disgusted citizens coined the phrase "not worth a Continental," which has persisted as an expression of contempt to this day.

Of course the war had piled huge debts upon the struggling young government, but, as popular confidence in Congress waned, the central body lost what little power it ever had to raise funds, either through taxation or by means of further loans. While more and more worthless paper money flooded the country, inflation spiraled and counterfeiting of valuable foreign currencies added to the hazards of doing business. Farmers who had prospered even during the trying days of the war now found themselves going heavily into debt—debts they were unable to pay with anything but gold or silver, which was now almost unobtainable.

Local governments heaped fuel on the smoldering fire by ordering stiff jail sentences for debtors. In order to raise needed funds for government operations some of the states began to impose import and export duties on farm products. New York aroused the ire of New Jersey and Connecticut farmers by such legislation, and angry words were exchanged between the various state houses. Pennsylvania added to New Jersey's difficulties by imposing duties on imports which passed through the port of Philadelphia.

As with the Revolution itself, the most violent expressions of discontent occurred in Massachusetts. Perhaps the earlier spirit of rebellion was still hot in the veins of those Yankee farmers, but whatever the reason, several armed bands of dissenters began to gather in and around Concord, Cambridge and Springfield, Mass., and were threatening insurrection against the state and federal authorities. There were riots in Pennsylvania and New Hampshire, but these seemed to be isolated disturbances with no real leadership. Massachusetts was different. A fellow named Job Shattuck organized a mob in Concord. In the summer of 1786 they camped on the village green, carousing for a few days until a troop of Massachusetts militia started out from Cambridge to disperse them. Shattuck and some of his men made a run for it, but when they were trapped in the woods outside of Groton, Shattuck was wounded in the fight.

Meanwhile in West Springfield, other self-appointed leaders were organizing "mobbers," as the rebels were called. Luke Day, a young brevet major of the Continental Army, began drilling his followers in the squares. Between drills he made fiery speeches, urging all honest citizens to throw out the rascals who were running the government. Another outspoken leader was Daniel Shays, who had gathered and drilled a formidable force of about a thousand men. Governor of Massachusetts James Bowdoin called up all the militia he could muster. At the same time he asked the legislature to hold an emergency session. Driven by a sense of panic, the legislature voted for a law to confiscate the "lands, goods and chattels" of anyone who participated in a "riotous assembly." This act also called for the convicted culprit to be whipped at the public whipping post and imprisoned for a term of six to twelve months, with additional whippings at intervals during the time of his imprisonment. Such severe punishment gives some idea of the temper of the times.

Yet Daniel Shays and Luke Day were by no means intimidated by drastic laws. Shays kept his force intact during the fall and winter of 1786. He threatened to march on Boston, but in December, as a large contingent of militia became organized at Boston under General Benjamin Lincoln, Shays moved farther away from the city. The rebels stopped near Springfield where the situation was approaching a showdown. Major General Wil-

Daniel Shays, former Revolutionary War officer, led the debtors' revolt in Massachusetts in 1786.

liam Shepard was waiting in Springfield with some 1,200 militiamen. Shays had about a thousand of his mobbers spread out to the east along the Boston Post Road, while rebels Luke Day and Eli Parsons each had four or five hundred men from Berkshire County stationed across the river north of Springfield.

There were few uniforms to be seen in these motley armies. Even General Shepard's militia came straight from their farms for the most part, and the only identification of opposing forces were sprigs of hemlock in the hats of the rebels and strips of white paper worn by the Loyalists. To play safe, travelers at that time often stuck both of these symbols in their three-cornered hats.

On January 25, 1787, Shays decided to attack the federal arsenal in Springfield, where he knew that tons of military equipment were stored—gunpowder, shot and several thousand muskets. If he could get his hands on this materiel he could equip a formidable army. The arsenal was housed in a recently constructed brick building as solid as a fortress. Before he launched the assault he sent a messenger across the frozen river to ask Luke Day for help. For some reason Day wanted more time—he proposed to join in an attack on the following day, but Shays had already ordered his men to advance.

Seeing the approaching waves of rebellious citizens, Shepard was appalled, unable to believe that the mobbers would defy militia. He held his fire, trying to warn off the attackers, but they came on in the face of several cannon. Finally Shepard directed his gunners to fire a volley over the heads of the rebels. Some of Shays' men hesitated, but only for an instant. On they trudged, determined to overwhelm the arsenal. Then Shepard fired point-blank into the rebel ranks. The volley killed four of the attackers; the rest turned and ran. Though he tried to rally his men, Shays found that they had no stomach for further blood-

shed. He had no choice, therefore, but to retreat from Springfield. After he joined with the Berkshire men of Eli Parsons, the two leaders tried to map out a new course of strategy.

By this time General Lincoln had arrived in Springfield with his militia. After chasing Luke Day from his position along the river, Lincoln set out to smash Shays. In bitter cold weather and deep snow, the rebels were growing desperate. They had already raided some of the small communities and had loaded several sleighs with provisions. Outraged villagers informed Lincoln of the route Shays had taken. At Middlefield, one of Lincoln's officers, a General Tupper, surrounded a force of rebels and persuaded their leader to surrender. Since the two officers had served together in the Revolution, the rebel lieutenant Luddington could not find it in his heart to carry on the fight. It became more of a reunion than a surrender.

On January 29, Lincoln's scouts reported that Shays' main force had broken camp and was moving along the road between Pelham and Petersham. In a raging snowstorm, the militia covered 30 miles and surprised Shays at Petersham. Without firing a shot, they surrounded the rebels and took most of them prisoner. Although Shays escaped to New Hampshire, his rebellion was crushed, and the members of Shays' army swore allegiance to Massachusetts. Some of the ringleaders were fined or sentenced to prison terms, but for the most part, both sides were relieved at having the hostilities ended, and a spirit of amnesty prevailed.

Nevertheless, the Shays' rebellion alarmed the entire country. As it was obvious to everybody that a strong and just federal government was needed, a number of the men who had been the architects of American independence were now determined to bring order to the thirteen disorganized states.

Anxious Men at Annapolis

With the people in turmoil and the state governments bickering over trade agreements, men like James Madison and George Washington grew seriously concerned. The master of Mount Vernon had hoped to spend the rest of his days as a country gentleman. Washington was not in the best of health. He suffered from attacks of rheumatism and his ill-fitting false teeth irritated him. On top of this he still owed debts from Revolutionary days, and he had hoped to get his plantation operating profitably enough to erase his obligations. On the other hand, the conflicting trade arrangements between the states were hurting business generally, and of course any large scale civil disorder would mean the ruination of all Virginia planters.

So, despite his reluctance to return to public life, George Washington had been willing to help when James Madison suggested calling a trade conference between Maryland and Virginia. The immediate purpose was to reach an agreement for free trade on the Potomac River. This was in 1784, and though the only accomplishment at this meeting was the opening of the Potomac to unrestricted commerce, this limited success led the delegates to consider inviting all the states to a major convention for the formation of a more effective federation.

Again Madison was in the forefront of the efforts to strengthen federal authority. In the Virginia legislature he spoke eloquently in favor of giving Congress full authority to regulate interstate commerce as well as foreign trade. When his proposal was voted down he tried another approach, asking the Virginia lawmakers to call a convention of all the states to discuss "how far a uniform system in their commercial relations may be necessary to their common interest and their permanent harmony."

After some heated debate a call went out for a meeting of state delegations to be opened in Annapolis on the first Monday of September 1786. There was considerable doubt that this proposed convention would be well attended. Even though all the states finally agreed, before the Annapolis meeting, to give Congress authority over commerce, New York demanded a number of conditions that killed the plan before it could be put into operation. New York insisted that revenue collectors be kept under state control and that duties be paid in state, not federal, currencies. Other states, such as New Jersey and Connecticut, immediately abolished duties to attract trade away from New York, and the commerce war between the states grew hotter than ever.

By the time of the Annapolis convention only nine of the thirteen states had elected delegates. Madison arrived early on the opening day, but his enthusiasm chilled when only a handful of men showed up. For New York there were two delegates—Alexander Hamilton and Egbert Benson. One man by the name of Tench Coxe arrived from Pennsylvania. After several days only New Jersey, Delaware and Virginia had complete delegations. Yet the dozen or so men who took the trouble to go to Annapolis were not enough dismayed to abandon their purpose. It was Abraham Clark of New Jersey, a signer of the Declaration of Independence, who came to the meeting with the most authority to act for his state, and it was he who proposed calling another convention, this time to "effectually provide for the exigencies of the union."

In the telling of history it is difficult to depart from the cold, recorded facts, but in any age when violence and dissent seem to be the order of the day, it is well to reflect upon what must have been the feelings and emotions of men who lived before us. As a group, the signers of the Declaration of Independence and the authors of the United

THE GRANGER COLLECTION

States Constitution were by no means violent or emotional men. They were hardheaded lawyers, businessmen and plantation owners who were as concerned about the value of a pound or a dollar as any modern business leader. But beyond that, they had the vision of men who recognized that every individual requires two things: personal security and personal dignity. It is the second of these two requirements that makes the difference between the security provided by a supreme authority and that offered by the founding fathers of the United States. These men— these "'pillars of society" of their day—were faced with an explosive situation. Americans who had recently fought for liberty and economic survival against Great Britain were now ready to fight for liberty and survival against a corrupt and weak American Congress.

What motivated James Madison, George Washington and Edmund Randolph of Virginia to work so tirelessly for a union of the states that would be just and at the same time strong? It could be attributed to greed, but greed has more often than not resulted in the seizure of absolute power over other men. Somehow the combination of English pride and Yankee determination produced a unique class of politicians who not only worked to protect their self-interests but who at the same time understood that the lowliest man among them deserved an equal opportunity.

At Annapolis in 1786 a handful of men who had utterly failed to organize a national convention nevertheless formed a committee to inform the state legislatures that their cause was so urgent that a second convention, representing all the states, would have to be held. In a resolution and report drawn up by Alexander Hamilton, the time and place were

Proclamation of Governor Bowdoin
of Massachusetts offering amnesty
after Shays' rebellion was suppressed.

Commonwealth of Massachusetts.

By His EXCELLENCY

JamesBowdoin, Esq.

GOVERNOUR OF THE COMMONWEALTH OF

MASSACHUSETTS.

A Proclamation.

WHEREAS by an Act passed the sixteenth of February instant, entitled, " An Act describing the disqualifications, to which persons shall be subjected, which have been, or may be guilty of Treason, or giving aid or support to the present Rebellion, and to whom a pardon may be extended," the General Court have established and made known the conditions and disqualifications, upon which pardon and indemnity to certain offenders, described in the said Act, shall be offered and given ; and have authorized and empowered the Governour, in the name of the General Court, to promise to such offenders such conditional pardon and indemnity :

I HAVE thought fit, by virtue of the authority vested in me by the said Act, to issue this Proclamation, hereby premising pardon and indemnity to all offenders within the description aforesaid, who are citizens of this State ; under such restrictions, conditions and disqualifications, as are mentioned in the said Act : provided they comply with the terms and conditions thereof, on or before the twenty-first day of March next.

GIVEN at the Council Chamber in Boston, this Seventeenth Day of February, in the Year of our LORD One Thousand Seven Hundred and Eighty Seven, and in the Eleventh Year of the Independence of the United States of AMERICA.

JAMES BOWDOIN.

By His Excellency's Command,

JOHN AVERY, jun. Secretary.

BOSTON : Printed by ADAMS & NOURSE, Printers to the GENERAL COURT.

set for Philadelphia on the second Monday in May 1787.

It might be said that Daniel Shays played one of the key roles in the creation of the Constitution. But for his violent rebellion in Massachusetts which genuinely shocked leaders in every other state, the Constitutional Convention in Philadelphia might have been as poorly attended as the Annapolis meeting. It is a sad fact of history that in generation after generation, sober men who have the knowledge and ability for wise leadership will rarely act on vitally needed change until a violent catastrophe forces them to do so.

The men who met in Annapolis in 1786 were nervous. They were clearly worried, not only about the condition of their own business interests but about the future of personal freedom under the new and revolutionary form of government they had tried to establish ten years earlier. Months before most of their contemporaries, who did not even bother to attend the conference, they knew that the fledgling United States had reached a crucial turning point where men would either advance toward self-government or go back in political history to the easy solution of a supreme ruler.

Since the date set for the Philadelphia Convention provided time for reflection, James Madison made good use of the interim period. He was determined to go to Philadelphia with far more than a few suggestions for improving trade relations between the states. He would have a plan of government that would at the same time strengthen the union and free citizens from debt and economic disaster. While attending a session of the Continental Congress in New York, he read everything he could find about federations of states and the problems that had brought them together or destroyed them. His studies ranged from ancient Greece to renaissance Italy and contemporary European duchies. From these readings Madison reached the conclusion that a powerful central government was needed, exercising authority beyond that of the individual state legislatures.

Fired with an almost fanatical desire to make the Philadelphia Convention a success, Madison saw to it that his own State of Virginia promptly agreed to sending a distinguished delegation. He wrote an enthusiastic letter to George Washington, suggesting that in order to "Give this subject a very solemn dress," Virginia should send her most prominent men "with your name at the head of them."

139

The presence of George Washington, hero of Yorktown, was needed to give stature to the proposed convention at Philadelphia.

INDEPENDENCE NATIONAL HISTORICAL PARK COLLECTION, PHILADELPHIA

However, Washington was not immediately persuaded. His chief worry was that the Philadelphia Convention would be no more successful than the one at Annapolis, and he shuddered at the thought of lending his prestige to a dismal failure. At Madison's urging, Governor Randolph also spoke to Washington, pointing out that it was the duty of all prominent Americans to seek solutions to the country's dilemma. At last, after several states announced their selection of distinguished delegates, Washington agreed to attend. This was the signal for more states and more leading citizens to fall in line.

Although the Congress never formally acknowledged Hamilton's call for a convention, they eventually announced that there would be a general meeting of state delegations at the same time and place as the Annapolis Committee had proposed. This, they said, would be "for the sole . . . purpose of revising the articles of confederation."

Chapter Six

The Great Debate

The Opening Sessions

The State House in Philadelphia was already a historic landmark when the first arrivals to the Constitutional Convention crossed the threshold. Many of the men who were to engage in the debate over how to govern the new nation recalled the tense days a decade earlier when, in the same hall, they were preparing to break with England. The atmosphere in May 1787 was charged with anxieties similar to those in the spring of 1776, but the political problems were now internal ones, not involving a government three thousand miles away. Idealists among the delegates were learning that political problems are not solved by a stroke of a pen, or even by substituting one governing body for another. They now saw in the current upheaval that no government will be accepted by a people simply because it is their own. Before all other considerations, justice and equality must be the ruling order, and whether a nation is ruled by democratically-elected representatives or by "divinely ordained" kings, injustice will spawn rebellion.

Philadelphia had not changed a great deal since Revolutionary days. It had continued to grow, and it was still looked upon as the major metropolis of the United States. The cobbled streets resounded to the clatter of horses' hooves and to the rumble of cart and carriage wheels. Along the riverfront, noisy markets did a brisk trade in produce from the surrounding farms; the fish markets were redolent of the sea and of a wide variety of glassy-eyed merchandise. Within view of Independence Hall were livery stables and blacksmith shops which clanged more cheerfully and far more steadily than the great bell in the Hall tower. Bewigged gentlemen in richly colored frock coats strolled along the sidewalks with their long-skirted ladies, protected from passing carriages by rows of iron hitching posts, some of which can be seen to this day along the narrower back streets of old Philadelphia.

On the opening day of the Convention, Monday, May 14, 1787, about a dozen delegates appeared at the State House. Among them was General Washington, whose arrival in Philadelphia the day previous was heralded by clanging bells and gun salutes. Despite the previous disappointing showing at Annapolis, none of those early arrivals was in any way dismayed by their small number. Travel in those days was arduous and slow—no one expected a full complement of delegates on the very first day. However, since only Virginia and Pennsylvania were fully represented at the opening of the Convention, the first formal business to be voted was merely an agreement to reconvene each morning until a quorum was assembled.

Two weeks passed before such a quorum could be counted. By Tuesday, May 29, with seven states represented, the Convention was ready to start its work.

On that portentous occasion, the men who gathered in the State House were sober, determined, and aware that they were playing an important role in history. Few of them, however, looked upon themselves as great innovators. They came as representatives of several sovereign states, instructed to protect the interests of those states while they endeavored to construct a more workable central government. They were even then referred to as "that august body." Indeed they were a distinguished group, though many of the delegates were yet to perform their greatest accomplishments.

As he had been during the turbulent days leading to signing the Declaration of Independence, Dr. Benjamin Franklin was the revered senior delegate. He was there with the Pennsylvania representatives, leaning on his cane, his hair white and his step uncertain. But his eyes still sparkled with the old irrepressible humor, and his wise counsel fre-

The cobbled streets of Philadelphia
resounded to the clatter of horses' hooves
and the rumble of carriage wheels as the
first delegates began arriving in the
early weeks of May 1787.

143

quently cooled the hot tempers that sometimes
flared during debates.

While Thomas Jefferson had been the author of that other great document, the Declaration, James Madison emerged as the
prime mover in the creation of the Constitution. Not only had his insistence upon holding
the Convention brought the delegates to Philadelphia, but once the formal business began,
his voice and his pen were most active in the
Hall. He was only thirty-six when the Constitutional Convention met, yet his knowledge
of historic governments, his vision and keen
insight shone as a constant beacon throughout the sessions, which were often stormy,
and he became known as the "master builder
of the Constitution." While the dignified
Washington was to officially preside over the
Convention, it was Madison's enthusiasm
and logic that actually led the meetings day
after day.

By contrast to Madison's youth, quick wit
and intense dedication, George Washington
moved through the distinguished gathering
with quiet authority. One of the tallest men
of his time, he towered above the others as a
physical symbol of leadership. His presence
alone gave importance to the proceedings.

When on May 29 it was agreed that the
seven states represented constituted a quorum,
Robert Morris of Pennsylvania proposed that
George Washington be appointed President
of the Convention. Morris, whose prosperous
shipping firm had made it possible for him
to issue huge sums of credit to the Revolutionary cause, had been in serious financial
difficulties immediately after the war. But before long Willing, Morris and Company developed profitable trade with China and
France, and Robert Morris once again became
one of America's wealthiest citizens. As a close
friend and admirer of Washington, he was a
logical choice to put the famous Virginian's
name in nomination. Actually it was a mere

INDEPENDENCE NATIONAL HISTORICAL PARK COLLECTION, PHILADELPHIA

formality, since it was a foregone conclusion
among the delegates that Washington would
preside, and the vote for him was unanimous.
He took the speaker's chair on the dais at the
front of the assembly room. Here he would
sit for four months in quiet dignity.

With the presiding officer elected and pro-
cedural rules adopted, Edmund Randolph of
Virginia was called upon to deliver the
opening speech of the Convention.

"I regret," he said, "that it should fall to
me rather than to those who are older and
more experienced to open the great subject of
our mission." But as the Convention had originated from Virginia, Randolph pointed out,
the Virginia delegates had asked him to speak
first. "It is absolutely necessary in this difficult crisis," he went on, "to prevent America's downfall."

Randolph then asked a series of pointed
questions. What properties ought a federal

government to possess? What are the defects of the Confederation? What is our present danger, and what is the remedy? He then proceeded to answer his own questions by stating that the government should first secure the nation against foreign invasion and second, against dissensions between members of the Union or against sedition within the various states. On the other hand, said Randolph, the Confederation had produced no security against foreign invasion since Congress was not permitted to prevent nor to support a war on its own authority. At the same time an individual state could provoke a war without being restrained by other members of the Confederation. The present federal government had no power to check a quarrel between states. Such a situation invited insurrection, anarchy and the piecemeal dismemberment of America by foreign powers.

This was strong language, but most of the delegates at the Convention felt strongly about the need for positive action. While there were a few men who were not prepared to go as far as the Virginians were about to propose, none of them was surprised by the resolution Edmund Randolph now put forward:

1. Resolved, that the Articles of Confederation ought to be so corrected. . . . as to accomplish the objects proposed by their institution; namely, "common defense, security of liberty, and general welfare."

2. Resolved, therefore, that the rights of suffrage in the National Legislature ought to be proportioned to the quotas of contribution, or to the number of free inhabitants.

3. Resolved, that the National Legislature ought to consist of two branches.

4. Resolved, that the members of the first branch of the National Legislature ought to be elected by the people of the several States. . .

5. Resolved, that members of the second branch of the National Legislature ought to be elected by those of the first, out of a proper number of persons nominated by the individual Legislatures, to hold their offices for a term sufficient to ensure their independency . . .

6. Resolved, that each branch ought to have the right of originating Acts; that the National Legislature ought to be empowered to . . . negate all laws passed by the States contravening, in the opinion of the National Legislature, the Articles of Union. . . ; to call forth the force of the Union against any member failing to fulfill its duty under the Articles thereof.

7. Resolved, that a National Executive be instituted to be chosen by the National Legislature, with authority to execute national laws.

8. Resolved, that the Executive and a convenient number of a National Judiciary ought to compose a Council of Revision, with authority to examine every act of the National Legislature before a negative thereon shall be final.

9. Resolved, that a National Judiciary be established, to consist of one or more supreme tribunals and of inferior tribunals to be chosen by the National Legislature.

10. Resolved, that provision ought to be made for admission of States lawfully arising within limits of the United States. . .

11. Resolved, that a republican government and territory of each State ought to be guaranteed by the United States. . .

12. Resolved, that provision be made for continuance of Congress until a given day after new Articles of Union shall be adopted.

13. Resolved, that provision be made for amendment of the Articles of Union. . .

14. Resolved, that legislative, executive and judiciary powers within the several States be bound by oath to support the Articles of Union.

15. Resolved, that amendments which shall be offered to the Confederation by the Con-

Edmund Randolph, Governor of Virginia,
presented Madison's plan for a
new government.

vention, after approval of Congress, be submitted to an assembly or assemblies of representatives recommended by the several State Legislatures, to be expressly chosen by the people to consider and decide thereon.

————

The man who presented these resolutions, Edmund Randolph, was a member of a distinguished Virginia family and a man who had already established an enviable reputation. A graduate of William and Mary College, he had studied law with his father and had established a successful practice in Williamsburg about 1772. In 1775 his father fled from Williamsburg with the deposed Royal Governor, and Edmund chose to side with his uncle, the eminent patriot, Peyton Randolph. For a brief period Edmund served on Washington's military staff at Cambridge, Mass., but the death of his uncle caused him to return to Virginia where he became the youngest delegate to the Convention of 1776. There he helped to draft the Virginia Constitution. During the next ten years he served

his state as Attorney General, at the same time going to Congress for a term (1779 to 1782), and making a name for himself in Philadelphia as a colorful speaker.

Randolph succeeded Patrick Henry as Governor of Virginia in 1786, winning this exalted position at the age of thirty-three. He once said of himself, "I am a child of the revolution . . . I feel the highest . . . attachment to my country; her felicity is the most fervent prayer of my heart . . . The unwearied study of my life shall be to promote her happiness."

Despite his shining record as a patriot and his professed desire for a strong central government, he was not so enamored of the federal concept as to forget entirely his interests as a Virginia politician. During the debates that were to develop in the next few weeks he was often inclined to protest that his resolutions were meant to provide a base for discussion and not to be taken as his own absolute conviction. His friend and associate, James Madison, was much more determined than he to see real power built into the new framework of government. Randolph was destined to become United States Attorney General in Washington's first administration and was appointed Secretary of State when Jefferson resigned.

Madison had chosen a seat at the Convention in front of the presiding member. From this vantage point he diligently made notes of everything that took place. Being familiar with most of the prominent delegates, he was able, he said, to record accurately "the style and the train of observation and reasoning which characterized the principal speakers." His enthusiasm, not only for the purpose of the meetings but for the men who attended them, is reflected in his notation, "There never was an assembly of men, charged with a great and arduous trust, who were more devoted to the object committed to them, than were the members of the Fed-

146

James Madison, a bachelor of thirty-six, emerged as the prime mover in the creation of the Constitution.

Charles Pinckney of South Carolina
was eager to be in the forefront
of the new government.

eral Convention of 1787." He was well qualified to judge, for even at that early age he was an experienced legislator.

Madison's birth was in Port Conway, Virginia, in 1751. His parents were well-to-do (but not wealthy) farmers who saw to it that their son received the best education available. He received a B.A. degree at Princeton in 1771, then spent a year studying Hebrew and ethics with John Witherspoon, the great Scottish president of the college. As the Revolution broke, Madison espoused the patriot cause with great enthusiasm. He was chairman of his local Committee of Safety, attended the 1776 Convention and served in the Virginia legislature. Always in the forefront of debates, he won many eminent friends who supported him throughout his political career. Soon after he returned to Virginia from Congress he was elected to the Virginia lower house, where he helped to bring about the Annapolis Convention, and where he led the debates for separation of church and state, for establishing the new State of Kentucky, and for free public education.

Meanwhile he had begun his campaign for a stronger federal constitution, writing letters to George Washington, Edmund Randolph and Thomas Jefferson, and taking every opportunity to press for reform in speeches before the Virginia legislature, and later, before Congress which was assembled in New York in 1787. Consistently he urged that federal authority be extended to include regulation of trade, appointment of a national judiciary, and full control over national defense.

Madison was slight, neat and fastidious in his person — a bachelor whose sole passion seemed to be the study of books, particularly those concerning government and law. He was labeled a "political monk" by some of his contemporaries.

After Randolph's resolutions had been formally referred to the Committee of the Whole, Charles Pinckney of South Carolina came forward with a proposal for the form of a federal government. Like Randolph's plan, Pinckney's called for the establishment of supreme executive, legislative and judicial branches. It also would establish two houses of the legislature, with a "House of Delegates" to be chosen by the people of the several states and a "Senate" to be elected by the lower house. Differing from the Randolph resolutions was Pinckney's proposal that there be three classes of senators, each with different times of service. As a given class retired, the vacancies would be filled, thus assuring a continuity of service and avoiding a complete change in the legislative body at any given election. Pinckney also suggested a method of overriding an executive veto of legislation by a two-thirds majority, at which point the bill in question would become law. He spelled out in detail the specific authority to be allotted to each branch of government and provided for amendment of the Con-

148

WORCESTER ART MUSEUM

stitution on approval of two-thirds of the state legislatures.

Charles Pinckney was handsome, vain and eager to be in the forefront of the new government. Only twenty-nine at the time of the Convention, he took pains to inform his colleagues that his "promising talents and polite learning" had been acquired in only a little more than twenty years! His family had hoped to send him to London to study law, but the Revolution had spoiled these plans and had forced Pinckney to pursue his own study of law in Charleston. He began to prac-

tice in 1779 and was elected to the state legislature about the same time. During the war he served as an officer in the defense of Charleston, was captured by the British and lost most of his property. But by 1784 he had rebuilt his fortune and was sent to Congress where he pressed for strengthening of the federal government.

Pinckney's second cousin, General Charles Cotesworth Pinckney, had also been sent to the Philadelphia Convention. General Pinckney was born in Charleston, South Carolina, in 1746, but he received his education in Eng-

land, since his father became the colony's agent in London when Charles was a young boy. After completing studies at Westminster and Oxford, Charles Cotesworth Pinckney attended the famed Middle Temple in London. Then in 1770 he returned to Charleston where he established a highly successful law practice. In public affairs, the older Pinckney was a staunch patriot. He served on the State Council of Safety, took part in framing the Constitution of 1776 and was an active military commander during the Revolution. He was on Washington's staff during the battles of Brandywine and Germantown. He fought in the field in bloody campaigns through South Carolina and other parts of the South. Like his cousin, he was captured by the British at Charleston in 1780, and all his property was confiscated at the time. Pleasant-mannered, cultured and of a distinguished bearing, he commanded the respect of his colleagues and was greatly admired by the people of his own state.

The submission of the two major constitutional plans—Randolph's and Pinckney's—had occupied all of Tuesday, May 29, and on the following morning the points of contention immediately became evident. Wednesday's session had scarcely opened when a heated argument developed over the degree of federal power implied by the terms "national" and "supreme."

Charles Pinckney pointedly asked Randolph if it was his intention to abolish state governments altogether.

In reply, Edmund Randolph showed his customary noncommittal restraint. "I meant by these general propositions merely to introduce the particular ones which explained the outlines of the system we had in view." Seeing that an angry discussion was in the making, Pierce Butler of South Carolina attempted to inject a soothing note. He had not yet made up his mind, he said, but was open to full discussion as to the extent of central government authority. Previously he had opposed granting additional power to Congress since this would put the entire authority into the hands of a single body. However, the proposal to distribute the powers between two houses of Congress and between separate executive and judicial branches was much more to his liking.

————

Butler, a native of Ireland, was born in County Carlow in 1744. His father was a member of the House of Commons, and young Butler received an excellent education. After some study of law, he entered the British army and was sent with his regiment to Boston, which was then seething with rebellion. There he married a Miss Middleton, wealthy heiress from South Carolina. Butler resigned his commission in 1773 and moved to Charleston where he assumed the life of a landed gentleman. By 1778 he was serving in the state legislature, was appointed adjutant general of the South Carolina militia, and in the course of the war lost most of his property. Still in financial difficulties in 1787, Butler was appointed a delegate to the Constitutional Convention. He accepted the appointment proudly. Although Butler was not wholly committed to the "States' Rights" point of view, he approached the idea of federalism cautiously, seeking as many safeguards as possible for the protection of the state governments.

In the course of the debate over the extent of "national" power Gouverneur Morris of Pennsylvania rose to remind the delegates that there was a great difference between the terms federal and national in regard to a supreme government. "The former," he explained "is a mere compact, dependent upon the good faith of the parties; whereas the latter consists of a complete and *compulsive* operation."

Gouverneur Morris, delegate for
Pennsylvania and spokesman for a strong
central government, had a special talent
for public debate and majestic prose.

Morris himself believed in having one and only one ultimate authority. The youngest of the Pennsylvania delegation, Morris had come originally from New York. He was the fourth son of Lewis Morris, signer of the Declaration and lord of the famous Morrisania estate in the Bronx area of New York City. Young Morris had moved to Philadelphia after a heated argument with New York's Governor Clinton and a political defeat for re-election to the Continental Congress in 1779. Morris was born at the family manor in 1752. He received his early education at a Huguenot school in New Rochelle and he graduated from King's College, where Loyalist sympathies were strong. Yet he was a staunch patriot with liberal ideas. At 19 he was admitted to the bar, launched a successful law practice and was soon a popular, respected member of his community. A sportsman who loved fast horses, Morris led a rather wild life until a riding accident resulted in the loss of a leg. Friends said the artificial limb he acquired was "the only wooden thing about him." In 1776, when Gouverneur Morris took part in drafting a constitution for New York, he attempted in vain to make slavery illegal. The disagreement with col-

151

leagues over this issue and fights with his own family about their Loyalist tendencies probably led to his ultimate abandonment of his native state.

Morris was a devout believer in strong central government. Many of his views were similar to those of James Madison, but of the two, his was a far more dynamic and vocative personality. He entertained lavishly, was a brilliant conversationalist, and had a flair for oratory which had aided his political career. William Pierce once said of him, "He winds through all the mazes of rhetoric and throws around him such a glare that he charms, captivates, and leads away the senses of all who hear him." He is credited with having spoken to the Convention more often than any other delegate. After the new government became established, Morris spent ten years in Europe, part of the time attending to business interests and later as Minister to France.

The debate over the question of national authority soon led to a consideration of another burning question: on what basis of proportional representation should the legislature be made up? The second of Edmund Randolph's resolutions had called for "the rights of suffrage in the National Legislature to be proportioned to the quotas of contribution, *or to the number of free inhabitants.*"

Madison argued that this last phrase should be removed, as it could clearly become the subject of endless debate between advocates and opponents of slavery. As the debate grew more and more heated, the Delaware delegates threw a verbal bombshell by announcing that if any change were to be made in the rule of suffrage they might be forced to withdraw from the Convention.

A chill settled over the Hall. Every delegate was aware that the future of America might rest on the solution of this delicate point, for the small states feared that proportional representation would overwhelm them in the proposed new Congress.

Gouverneur Morris rose slowly from his seat and, in carefully chosen words, he attempted to soothe the Delaware deputies. He hoped to express the concern of all that no delegates should be forced to withdraw. Yet, Morris emphasized, the rule of suffrage was so fundamental an article that it could not be put aside without discussion. To this statement Madison added his voice, pleading with the members from small states to realize that the situation had changed since the days of the Revolution and that some form of proportional representation might have to be worked out by a drafting committee.

That day's session ended with a general feeling of dissatisfaction on the part of the smaller states and with a general sense of uneasiness hanging over the entire Convention.

On the following day Edmund Randolph's third resolution that the national legislature should consist of two houses was easily agreed to, but when the Convention took up the next resolution concerning the method of electing representatives, the storm broke again. Voicing vigorous opposition to popular election was the Mayor of New Haven, Connecticut, Roger Sherman. It was wrong, he insisted, to entrust the selection of leaders to the people, "who lack information and are liable to be misled." He felt that national representatives should be appointed by the various state legislatures.

———————

Roger Sherman was a stubborn, pious, and thoroughly honest Yankee who typified many New England attributes of that time. He was born in Massachusetts in 1721, the son of a farmer in modest circumstances. Young Roger began to earn his living as a Jack-of-all-trades, walking from town to town with a bag of tools. He split rails for fences, repaired shoes, helped farmers with their plowing and storekeepers with their inven-

Roger Sherman, prominent businessman, politician, ex-shoemaker and former Yale treasurer was stubborn, pious and thoroughly honest — a true "Yankee."

tories. Meanwhile he managed to teach himself law, did some surveying, and published a number of reasonably successful almanacs. Eventually he established his home in New Haven, about 1761, and there he became treasurer of Yale University. For his services in this capacity, as well as for his handling of the college bookstore, he was later given an honorary M.A. Sent as a delegate to the first and second Continental Congresses, Sherman was appointed to the drafting committee for the Declaration of Independence, which he signed with enthusiasm. He also took part in drawing up the Articles of Confederation. Still, Sherman's fierce patriotism did not fill him with any zeal for a liberal interpretation of democracy. Actually his views were somewhat antinationalist. Possibly his defense of the Articles of Confederation stemmed from pride in having assisted in their creation. In any case, he was a formidable opponent of popular elections for national offices.

Another severe critic of the democratic concept was Elbridge Gerry of Massachusetts. The lean Harvard graduate had acquired a wide reputation throughout the states for his active role in state as well as national government. He was a signer of the Declaration of Independence, an esteemed legislator and a man of considerable wealth which he had acquired through West Indies trade that had been established by his father. Despite his prestige, he frequently confused his colleagues by his inconsistencies and his unpredictable changes of mind. At one time he seemed to support the ideas of James Madison. At another, he spoke unfavorably of strong national government. Now, following Sherman's attack on popular elections, Gerry likewise lashed out at what he termed "an excess of democracy." He told the Convention, "The evils we experience flow from the excess of democracy. The people do not want virtue, but they are the dupes of pre-

153

INDEPENDENCE NATIONAL HISTORICAL PARK COLLECTION, PHILADELPHIA

VIRGINIA MUSEUM, COURTESY BOARD OF REGENTS OF GUNSTON HALL

tended patriots. In Massachusetts it has been fully confirmed by experience that they are daily misled into the most baneful measures and opinions, by the false reports circulated by designing men."

Fortunately for the country, this was not the prevailing view of the Convention. Following Gerry's outburst, George Mason of Virginia rose quickly to his feet to defend popular voting, and Mason was strongly supported by James Wilson of Pennsylvania.

Mason, the affluent owner of Gunston Hall in Fairfax County, Virginia, was born in 1725 on his father's great plantation. He was educated by the best tutors money could hire, and was brought up to the life of a landowning private gentleman, with a plantation of about 5,000 acres not far from George Washington's estate. Although he owned slaves, he continually spoke out against the practice; he had formulated a plan for freeing and resettling slaves in western territories. Mason's political career had not, up to this time, been extensive. While he had served briefly in the Virginia House of Burgesses, most of his earlier life had been devoted to growing wheat and tobacco, some study of law, and to speculation in western land. But in 1775 he had emerged as an active patriot. He served on the Committee of Safety and at the Virginia convention, taking a leading role in drafting the state constitution in 1776. It was his pen that produced the Virginia Declaration of Rights, guaranteeing freedom and equality to all men, though he still held some 300 Negroes in slavery at the time.

In this respect, George Mason was not alone. Many great Southern leaders of that time, including George Washington, owned slaves. These men cannot be wholly condemned for not immediately abandoning a system that had been built up for generations and which they had inherited from their forefathers. It is to their credit that they spoke

154

James Wilson of Pennsylvania
fought for the Electoral College system
of choosing our chief executive.

INDEPENDENCE NATIONAL HISTORICAL PARK COLLECTION, PHILADELPHIA

and wrote in condemnation of slavery, urging the adoption of some plan that would undo the wrong without bringing about economic disaster. They recognized, too, that most of the slaves themselves were unprepared for a sudden plunge into the responsibilities and the insecurity of freedom.

It was Mason's close association with James Madison, Thomas Jefferson, Edmund Randolph and James Monroe that led to his election to the Philadelphia Convention.

In his defense of popular elections as he addressed the Constitutional Convention, George Mason said, "The National House of Representatives should be the grand depository of the democratic principle of government. . . Every selfish motive, every family attachment, ought to recommend such a system of policy as would provide no less carefully for the rights and happiness of the lowest, than of the highest order of citizens."

To this ringing statement James Wilson added, "I would raise the federal pyramid to a considerable altitude, and for that reason I would give it as broad a basis as possible."

———

Wilson at forty-four was, next to Franklin, the oldest Pennsylvania delegate to the Convention. Born in Scotland in 1742 and educated at the universities of Glasgow, St. Andrews and Edinburgh, he sailed to America in 1765. He was then a young man, fired with ambition and eager to make a name for himself in the new world. For a time Wilson taught Latin at the College of Philadelphia, meanwhile studying law in John Dickinson's prestigious law firm. Wilson began his practice of law in Carlisle, Pennsylvania, and it was there that he emerged as a defender of the patriot cause. His writings condemning Britain's rulers were widely circulated. Yet he was not by nature a compelling person. Despite his courageous stand in the Revolu-

tion and his signing of the Declaration he remained quiet and diffident. In debates his was generally a moderating voice. Nevertheless Wilson was firm in his convictions and did not waver in his support for a popularly elected and strong central government. Even as a delegate to the Continental Congress he had urged strengthening of federal powers. Since he had a number of wealthy Loyalists among his clients prior to the Revolution, public sentiment had turned against him, and in the early days of the war he was forced to barricade his house against the attacks of an angry mob. But in the long run people recognized him as a staunch patriot.

Despite the vociferous objections of Elbridge Gerry and a small minority of delegates, the Convention voted in favor of having a House of Representatives elected by the people. Consideration was then given to the manner of choosing members of the

155

Gunning Bedford, Jr., of Delaware favored a three-year term for President with a limit on the number of reelections.

Senate. Randolph was asked to clarify his ideas concerning the makeup of the upper house. In his resolutions he had called for members to be selected by the House of Representatives out of lists furnished by the various state legislatures. As usual Randolph pointed out that his suggestions were "general in nature" and were meant simply to provide a basis of discussion. At that time no definite decision was reached as to the Senate's composition, and the Convention moved on to other questions. Whether by design on the part of Washington and Madison or by fortuitous circumstance, the delegates next discussed matters on which there was general agreement. By unanimous votes the Convention passed on Randolph's 6th resolution that both houses of Congress should have the power to originate laws and that all powers vested in the existing Congress should be transferred to the proposed new national legislature.

Although Pierce Butler again expressed his fear that too much power was being taken from the states, the Convention delegates refused to be drawn into a serious argument on this point for the time being, and the day ended on a note of restrained optimism. Most members felt that genuine progress was being made. Still, there was a host of major obstacles to be overcome.

As the Convention sessions continued into the month of June, one of the most critical matters came under discussion. This was the question of how a chief executive should be chosen and what powers this executive should enjoy.

While citizens of old Philadelphia strolled through the tree-lined streets and squares in the pleasant June weather they gained little information about the proceedings inside Independence Hall. The discussions were conducted with the utmost secrecy, and at this stage of the Convention it was probably just

as well. Old fears and current prejudices were being aired by the delegates as they attempted to resolve the differences of the various state delegations. One overriding fear was common to all the members, however. They had not yet forgotten the tyranny of a British king, and the suggestion of setting up a powerful federal executive opened up a Pandora's box of alarming possibilities. None of the delegates to the Constitutional Convention wanted any part of a plan that could result in the establishment of a supreme ruler.

There were some who wanted the executive branch to be in the hands of more than one man, thus dividing the power and the responsibility and minimizing the possibility of producing a monarchy. When James Wilson moved that the executive be a single person Charles Pinckney seconded the motion. Before the motion could be carried Roger Sherman expressed his belief that the chief executive should be a mere figurehead for carrying out the will of the legislature. Therefore, he told the assemblage, the executive should be appointed by and be accountable to the legislature. Further, he felt that the executive department ought to be flexible as to number. Congress should be allowed to appoint one or more persons as experience might dictate.

Randolph expressed similar views, opposing a one-man executive as being too much in the pattern of the British system.

The pendulum of this debate swung back and forth as one delegate after another argued for or against the single-executive concept. They debated, too, the matter of a term of office, suggestions running from three to seven or eight years. Among those favoring a single executive but strongly opposed to a long term of office was Gunning Bedford, Jr., Attorney General of Delaware.

Bedford was born in Philadelphia in 1747. He had been a classmate of James Madison at Princeton and had studied law in the firm of Joseph Reed. Although he saw some service in the army during the Revolution he did nothing spectacular to distinguish himself. Soon Bedford was engaged in a quiet law practice in the towns of Dover and Wilmington, Delaware. He was elected to Congress in 1783, then to the Annapolis Convention which he never bothered to attend. Apparently one of his most notable qualities was his great size. According to contemporaries he was warm and impetuous by nature and "very corpulent." Whenever he did speak Bedford's commanding figure and bold manner drew attention. His views were generally conservative. At the Constitutional Convention he often favored the limiting of government powers. In the matter of the executive he cautioned the delegates to consider what would be the situation if, after a short period in office, the executive was found to be unqualified or incompetent. He therefore favored a maximum term of three years and a definite limit on the number of re-elections.

It was James Wilson who first proposed a method of choosing the chief executive by means of "electors" who would represent various districts. He reasoned that this would do more to win public confidence than a system of election through the legislature. Although this suggestion was initially voted down a number of other delegates found the idea intriguing. In the midst of all this discussion the aged Benjamin Franklin asked for the floor, and as always, the Convention was hushed in deference to the old man's experience and wisdom.

Sometimes Franklin would have his words read for him by a younger delegate, but in this case, he rose, and leaning on his cane, expressed his belief that a chief executive should receive no salary for his services and be reimbursed only for necessary out-of-pocket expenses.

INDEPENDENCE NATIONAL HISTORICAL PARK COLLECTION, PHILADELPHIA

"There are two passions," said Franklin, "which have a powerful influence on the affairs of men. These are ambition and avarice; the love of power, and the love of money. Separately, each of these has great force in prompting men to action; but when united in view of the same object, they have in many minds the most violent effects. . . . There is a natural inclination in mankind to kingly government. It sometimes relieves them from aristocratic domination. They had rather have one tyrant than five hundred. I am apprehensive, therefore . . . that the government of these States may in future times end in a monarchy."

In his record of the Convention Madison wrote concerning Franklin's proposal that the executive receive no salary, "The motion was seconded by Colonel Hamilton. It was treated with great respect, but rather for the author of it than from any apparent conviction of its expediency or practicability."

At the time of the Constitutional Convention the eighty-one-year-old Franklin was President of Pennsylvania, a post that he had held for the past two years. He had been elected head of the State upon his return from France in 1785 after having negotiated a final treaty of peace with England. Arrival of the great Doctor Franklin in Philadelphia had been celebrated with a wild ringing of church bells, the lighting of bonfires and the firing of cannon. No man in America, including George Washington, had achieved the international fame and respect that had been bestowed upon Benjamin Franklin. His writings were read throughout the world; his inventions, such as the Franklin stove, the lightning rod and bifocal spectacles were benefiting people everywhere. At considerable personal risk he had experimented with electrical power and was the first oceanographer to chart the flow of the Gulf Stream with reasonable accuracy. So many and varied were his talents that it is almost impossible to exaggerate Franklin's contribution to mankind. Yet, in keeping with his views concerning greed which he had voiced at the Constitutional Convention, he refused to take out patents on his inventions, explaining that he wished them to be used without restraint wherever they could be helpful in making life more comfortable.

Franklin's efforts to enlist military and financial aid from France during the Revolution had been a major factor in America's success. A signer of the Declaration and an unwavering patriot, his mere presence gave strength and prestige to the Convention. Despite his infirmity he took an active part in the discussions. When the question was raised as to whether or not a chief executive should have absolute veto power over laws passed by Congress, Franklin voiced his misgivings, citing the example of Pennsylvania where the president, or governor, had been bribed with salary increases in order to win his approval of legislation.

Franklin frequently entertained the delegates with anecdotes from his vast store of knowledge and experience. During a discussion of how judges should be appointed he told about the Scottish practice of having attorneys choose judges from their own ranks. "The nomination proceeded from the lawyers," said Franklin, "who always selected the ablest of the profession in order to get rid of him and share his practice among themselves."

For several days debate swirled around the question of popular election of representatives and other government officials. While Charles Pinckney and Elbridge Gerry led the fight against voting by the people, James Wilson, George Mason and James Madison were among those who argued powerfully for it. In one celebrated speech Madison eloquently defended the overall wisdom of the electorate.

"In all cases," he said, "where a majority are united by a common interest or passion, the rights of the minority are in danger. What motives are to restrain them? A prudent regard to the maxim that honesty is the best policy, is found by experience to be as little regarded by bodies of men as by individuals. Respect for character is always diminished in proportion to the number among whom the blame or praise is to be divided. Religion itself may become a motive to persecution and oppression.

"In Greece and Rome, the rich and poor as well as the patricians and plebeians alternately oppressed each other with equal unmercifulness. . . Why was America so justly apprehensive of parliamentary injustice? Because Great Britain had a separate

John Dickinson, the leader of the Delaware delegation, wanted a Senate patterned after the British House of Lords.

interest, and, if her authority had been admitted, could have pursued that interest at our expense. We have seen the mere distinction of color made, in the most enlightened period of time, a ground of the most oppressive dominion ever exercised by man over man. What has been the source of those unjust laws complained of among ourselves? Has it not been the real or supposed interest of the major number?

"The lesson we are to draw from the whole is, that where a majority are united by a common sentiment, and have an opportunity, the rights of the minor party become insecure. . . *The only remedy is to enlarge the sphere,* and thereby divide the community into so great a number of interests and parties, that, in the first place, a majority will not be likely at the same moment to have a common interest separate from that of the whole, or of the minority; and in the second place, that in

case they should have such an interest, they may not be so apt to unite in pursuit of it.

"It is incumbent on us, then, to try this remedy, and to frame a republican system on such a scale and in such a form as will control all the evils which have been experienced."

John Dickinson of Delaware immediately expressed his approval of Madison's view. Although he represented the smallest state in the union, his delegation was far more disposed toward strengthening the federal power than were the members from Rhode Island. As leader of the Delaware group Dickinson often expressed the point of view for his state and was frequently on his feet during the deliberations. He felt it was essential that at least one branch of Congress should be elected by the people, but he favored having the other chosen by state legislatures. While he believed in the principle of popular suffrage, at the same time he wanted the states to play an important role in the system. Why not, he suggested, have the Senate patterned after the British House of Lords?

This view was not surprising from a man who had grown up in an aristocratic environment. John Dickinson was born in Maryland in 1732, the son of a wealthy and prestigious family. His early education was given to him by a private tutor. Later he studied law at the Middle Temple in London, then returned to America in 1757 to set up a law practice in Philadelphia. So successful was he in his profession that when he married the wealthy Miss Norris he persuaded her to turn her inheritance over to a relative, since the couple had no need of her money.

Dickinson entered politics in the 1760's by serving in the Pennsylvania legislature. There he frequently debated with Benjamin Franklin, whom he opposed politically. During this period he wrote a series of essays on British

George Read, although from a small state, looked for a strong national government unhampered by state governments.

taxation of the colonies under the title, *Letters from a Farmer in Pennsylvania.* These writings focused public attention on the author, and he was soon sent as a delegate to the Continental Congress where he did much important work. Dickinson drafted the original version of the Articles of Confederation and was the author of several major resolutions that led up to the break with England. Yet in the final analysis his legalistic mind kept him from signing the Declaration of Independence. At the moment of the crucial vote on breaking ties with Great Britain he and Robert Morris stayed away. It was said that this was their way of giving tacit agreement to the action without their having to commit themselves to an actual affirmative vote. Morris later signed the document, but Dickinson could never bring himself to do so. He later moved to Delaware where he became a Congressional delegate and then served as President of the State in 1781. He was also elected President of Pennsylvania from 1782 to 1785. As a major contributor

to a new college established in Carlisle, he was destined to have his name immortalized when the institution was named Dickinson College.

More radical in his views than his associate, Dickinson, was George Read of New Castle, Delaware, who was ready to discard completely the old plan of confederation. There was too much attachment to state governments, he told the Convention. Some form of national authority, he felt, must of necessity swallow them. To many of the delegates from small states, such a view was heresy. But it was consistent with his background and reputation.

During the debates on independence at the second Continental Congress Read had opposed a break with England. He was a believer in constituted authority, and a loosely organized confederation rankled in his basically conservative soul. Read was born in Maryland in 1734, one of six sons in a well-to-do family. After studying law in Philadelphia he moved to New Castle, Delaware, set up a successful law practice and bought a small farm. During the turbulent times leading up to the Revolution he had become Attorney General of Delaware and served in the state assembly. From there he was sent to the Continental Congress where his opposition to independence threatened to prevent a unanimous vote for the Declaration.

Although the two other members of the Delaware delegation, Thomas McKean and Caesar Rodney, favored the break with England, Rodney was absent on business in Delaware when the crucial vote was about to be taken. It was then that McKean dispatched a rider to summon Rodney, and after a wild night ride in stormy weather, Rodney arrived just in time to break the tie and place Delaware on the side of Independence. Later, however, Read signed the Declaration without the slightest hesitation.

George Read was dignified, cool and remote. Few people felt that they knew him. Yet he served his state well and was elected to many important offices. When John McKinley, President of Delaware during the Revolution, was captured by British troops, Read served as acting president from 1777 to 1778. He was a judge of the Court of Appeals, and as a commissioner to the Annapolis Convention he signed the report recommending the formation of a strong national government.

While many of the delegates who were anxious to establish a strong central government were pleased to have Read's support, few of them went so far as he in their denunciation of state authority. Most of them remained loyal to their own states and hoped that a system could be devised whereby the local governments might retain their identity without seriously weakening the federal power. James Wilson and Madison both argued strongly that both levels of government could be compatible provided the states were limited to control over certain local matters. Wilson pointed out, however, that most confederated systems in the ancient world as well as in modern times had fallen apart as individual governments seized power belonging to the whole.

Like Madison, Franklin and many other distinguished delegates to the Convention, Wilson showed an extraordinary knowledge of historical government. Frequently these men quoted Greek philosophers and writers of ancient Rome. They discussed in detail the performance of the Roman lawmaking bodies —their successes and failures. They were thorough scholars of the British parliamentary system and were also conversant with the rise and fall of governments in renaissance and contemporary Europe.

In an attempt to solve the problem of unequal state representation in the proposed new Congress, David Brearly, Chief Justice of New Jersey, proposed that the United States be redivided into thirteen equal parts. Then each state could have one vote and there could be no argument over proportional representation. Brearly's idea, though interesting, was clearly impracticable when considered in depth since there was no way of guaranteeing, even if an equal division could be made, that the redivided states could remain equal from a standpoint of population. And it would be impossible to carve out territories that would be equal *both* as to population and area.

David Brearly was forty-one when he attended the Constitutional Convention. Known as a good and honest public servant, he was by no means one of the more brilliant delegates. His career, like his character, had been a quiet, decent one, consisting mainly of rural law practice in the Trenton area and a period as a lieutenant colonel of militia during the Revolution. While his war service had not been marked by any great exploits he had served the patriot cause honorably. Brearly resigned his commission in 1779 to become a justice of the New Jersey Supreme Court. One of the few delegates in modest circumstances, he apparently had no income other than his salary.

One of Brearly's associates, William Paterson, vigorously opposed any notion of setting up a national government that would swallow up the states or that might change the existing state boundaries. The Convention, he pointed out, had been called under the authority of the existing Congress, and therefore he believed it should act within strict limits set by the Articles of Confederation. New Jersey would never submit to a plan that would give a large state more votes than a small one. This, he reasoned, was no more fair

Top: William Paterson, diminutive
but vigorous champion of the smaller
states, countered the Virginia Resolves
with the New Jersey Plan.

Bottom: John Rutledge, planter from
Charleston, South Carolina, was called
"Dictator John" by his detractors.

than giving a rich man more votes than a poor one.

Paterson, who happened to be the same age as Brearly, was born in Ireland. When his father brought him to America he was only two years old, and he therefore had little knowledge of his native country. Raised in Princeton, he attended the College of New Jersey, received a B.A. in 1763 and an M.A. three years later. After studying law with Richard Stockton, Paterson began to practice in Hunterdon County about 1768. During the Revolution Paterson served on the Committee of Safety, the Provincial Congress, and the New Jersey militia. For a period from 1779 to 1783 he was State Attorney General, then he again took up private law practice.

It is interesting to consider whether his opposition to a strong federal government might have been traced to his personal financial interest, since at the end of the war he had purchased the confiscated estate of a Loyalist sympathizer. Under the Treaty of Paris which called for return of Loyalist properties to their former owners, a strong central government would be in a position to enforce this and other provisions which up to that time had been largely ignored by Americans.

The debates in the Convention continued for the first few days of June without resolving any major points. The matter of proportional representation remained a bone of contention between large and small states. On June 11 Benjamin Franklin was moved to prepare a paper which, because of his own infirmity, he asked James Wilson to read for him. In his opening statement Franklin commented that he was pleased by the coolness of the delegates' tempers until the question of state representation arose. "We were sent here," he reminded them, "to consult, not to contend with each other." It was Franklin's hope that the members would carry on the deliberations without contention. He remarked that when a union between Scotland and England was formed early in the eighteenth century, Scotland feared being overwhelmed by superior representation of England, the northern country having only 40 members in the House of Commons and 16 members in the House of Lords. Yet in practice the Scots' fears were not borne out. Actually, if in America the smaller states were given equal representation with the large ones, the former could swallow up the latter, since their combined vote could defeat that of the more populous states.

Franklin went on to propose that, if the weakest state were to say what proportion of money or arms it was able and willing to furnish the union, all others could be obliged to furnish equal proportions. In this event Congress could be composed of an equal number of representatives from each state.

Franklin's logical and calm approach to the problem succeeded in putting the delegates in a more reasonable frame of mind, and they voted overwhelmingly to have the House of Representatives based upon some type of equitable ratio. There was some debate as to what an "equitable ratio" between the states should be. John Rutledge of South Carolina believed it should be according to quotas of contributions. In other words, wealth should be the basis of representation. On a number of occasions this conservative viewpoint was raised by Rutledge.

John Rutledge, 48 years of age, was well known to his fellow delegates since he had distinguished himself in the first Congress. A brilliant attorney whose practice had been so successful that in fifteen years he had acquired five plantations, Rutledge exemplified the Southern aristocrat. During the Revolutionary War he was Governor of South Carolina and when the British invaded the South he vigorously directed the defense of his state. For his devotion to the patriot cause the British retaliated by seizing his properties and burning his home.

After the delegates had approved the motion to base the first or lower branch of Congress on proportional representation they turned to consider the second branch or Senate. A motion by Roger Sherman to allow each state one vote in the Senate was defeated. The Convention delegates then voted by states, 6 to 5, to have the Senate representation based upon the same rule as that of the lower house, namely population. This close vote on the composition of the Senate once more left the small states unsatisfied. A national legislature with both houses apportioned according to taxes paid or according to free citizens was unacceptable to them. The bitter debate was not over.

While arguments swirled around many issues during the warm days of late May and early June 1787 more and more delegates continued to arrive in Philadelphia, so that the Hall was becoming filled and the proceedings took on an ever-greater air of national importance.

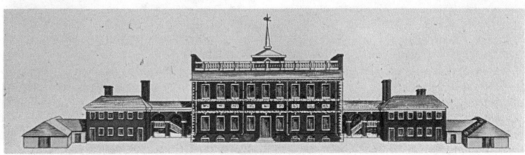

INDEPENDENCE NATIONAL HISTORICAL PARK COLLECTION, PHILADELPHIA

163

Competing Proposals

As cool spring gave way to the heat of summer new faces had been added to the proceedings. For Massachusetts there were Rufus King, Nathaniel Gorham, and Caleb Strong; for Connecticut, Oliver Ellsworth and William Samuel Johnson. Three more Pennsylvanians arrived together: George Clymer, Thomas Mifflin and Jared Ingersoll. New York sent John Lansing, Robert Yates and the great federalist, Alexander Hamilton. And from Maryland came James McHenry, Luther Martin, Daniel Carroll and John Francis Mercer.

The Massachusetts delegation was dominated by Elbridge Gerry, though it is difficult to say what direction his influence took since he himself wavered on so many issues. Like him, Rufus King had difficulty making up his mind. King had joined with Gerry in 1785, warning the Massachusetts legislature against any "hasty" moves to alter the Confederation. Yet they both attended the Convention with enthusiasm in the hope of establishing a strong central government.

King was born on a farm in Maine in 1755. His family was not wealthy but was well enough off to send Rufus to Harvard. As he attended college during the Revolution his studies were occasionally interrupted by military service. He nevertheless managed to read law with Theophilus Parsons and to establish a reasonably successful practice in Newburyport, Massachusetts. In 1784, when he was barely 29, King was sent to Congress in New York. There he worked diligently on various committees and spoke before the lawmaking body with enough eloquence that his friendship was cultivated by such brilliant leaders as Madison, Monroe and Hamilton. Despite his earlier doubts about a strong federal government, his association with Madison and Hamilton evidently contributed to his change of heart, for early in 1787 he wrote to Elbridge Gerry that

"Prudent and sagacious men should be ready to seize the most favorable circumstances to establish a more permanent and vigorous government."

Nathaniel Gorham, the oldest member of the Massachusetts delegation, was the son of a well-to-do packet-boat owner and operator. Apprenticed to a New London mechanic when he was fifteen, his formal education was somewhat limited; yet by the time of the Revolution he had emerged as a successful merchant and politician. Early in the war British forces destroyed the bulk of his property, but like many another Yankee trader of that period Gorham turned to privateering and blockade running. By canny management mixed with an element of good fortune, he was able to survive the Revolution in a strong financial position. He also learned much about politics and government while serving on a host of emergency committees, local councils and town meetings. He was elected to the United States Congress after serving in

Left: Rufus King of Massachusetts was at first in favor of a weak federal government but ended up an advocate of a strong one.

Below: Nathaniel Gorham, well-to-do merchant of Boston, had been president of the Continental Congress.

Connecticut's delegation included the fine legal mind of Oliver Ellsworth. Besides his efforts in achieving the Connecticut Compromise, he is credited with coining the phrase "United States."

the provincial legislature and provincial congresses before and during the war. As a delegate to the Constitutional Convention he came as a supporter of Massachusetts Governor Bowdoin's belief in strong nationalism.

Another Massachusetts delegate endorsing the federal concept, Caleb Strong of Northampton was a sober, quiet, highly respected lawyer with deep convictions.

As it was later to turn out one of the key delegates to propose a practical compromise at the Convention was Oliver Ellsworth of Connecticut. Ellsworth, born in Windsor, Connecticut, in 1745, studied at Yale and Princeton and was tutored in theology. But before completing his formal education he decided to switch to law. There is little question that his real talents were in that direction, for after establishing a law practice in Hartford, he acquired a considerable fortune as one of the outstanding legal minds of his time. During the Revolution he served in various state judicial posts, then became a delegate to the Continental Congress. In later years,

after working hard to gain Connecticut's ratification of the Constitution, he was elected to the United States Senate and still later was appointed Chief Justice of the United States. Tall, restrained and imposing in his manner, Ellsworth was widely respected and admired.

Dr. William Samuel Johnson, an aristocratic gentleman from Stratford, was another of the Connecticut delegates destined to play an important role in reaching a compromise on the thorny issue of state representation. He was the son of a scholarly clergyman who was the first president of Columbia University (known as King's College in those early days). With such parental background it was not surprising that William should have an academic schooling. He earned a B.A. degree at Yale in 1744 and his M.A. at Harvard three years later. In keeping with his father's wishes he studied theology, but he chose to become a lawyer and was admitted to the Connecticut bar at an early age. Although he proved himself to be a brilliant attorney, more often than not he turned his cases over to

INDEPENDENCE NATIONAL HISTORICAL PARK COLLECTION, PHILADELPHIA

other lawyers since he found it unnecessary to earn his living by his profession. His large inheritance and a wealthy wife combined to make him financially independent. Much of his time was devoted to social affairs at his magnificent estate. It seemed unlikely that such a man should have joined the patriot cause prior to the Revolution, yet he broke with many of his conservative friends and participated in the Stamp Act Congress of 1765. As Connecticut's agent in England, Johnson became a close friend of Benjamin Franklin during the years between 1766 and 1770. At the same time he made the acquaintance of the more famous Samuel Johnson of England.

On his return to the colonies he found the mood of rebellion running so strongly that he felt he could no longer support the patriots, and he refused an appointment to the Continental Congress. During the war, he was torn between his loyalty to England and his intellectual belief in the Colonial cause. On a number of occasions he took part in local government. Since much of his property was

seized or destroyed by British troops he was forced to increase his activity as a practicing lawyer. He made friends easily, was an able legislator in Congress and was appointed president of Columbia College at the time of the Constitutional Convention.

The newly arrived Pennsylvanians were a welcome addition to the Convention. George Clymer, a distinguished signer of the Declaration of Independence, had been an outspoken patriot since the 1760's. Born in 1739, Clymer became an orphan only a year after his birth. He was raised by William Coleman, a friend of the Clymers and a wealthy merchant. Young George showed an early interest in the shipping and importing business. Immediately after his graduation from the College of Philadelphia he joined Coleman's firm. Clymer was himself a prosperous merchant before he was 30, having become a partner in his father-in-law's company. Meanwhile he was taking a very active part in the growing protests against England. He gained a captain's commission in the militia, was elected to the Pennsylvania Committee of Safety and to the Continental Congress. As treasurer, charged with raising funds for Washington's army, he exchanged his personal assets for Continental paper money. Not long after he signed the Declaration, in 1777, Clymer's fine home in Chester County was sacked and burned by the British. During the severe winter of 1778, he had made a hazardous trip to Fort Pitt to investigate the cause of a series of Indian massacres. Clymer reported to Congress that the raids had been instigated by the British. As a result, a force of 500 men was organized to attack Detroit.

When the Revolution's finances were at their lowest ebb George Clymer worked closely with Robert Morris. The two men courageously stayed in Philadelphia during the British occupation of the city. Risking

Left to right: George Clymer, Thomas
Mifflin and Jared Ingersoll of the
Pennsylvania delegation.

THE GRANGER COLLECTION

their lives day after day, they continued, right under the British noses, to raise money for the war, meeting secretly with wealthy Philadelphians and with agents from European countries.

When he came to the Constitutional Convention, Clymer was one of the four largest holders of public securities to attend the deliberations. He therefore had a strong personal desire to see the central government strengthened.

No less a celebrity was Thomas Mifflin, speaker of the Pennsylvania legislature. Mifflin, a wealthy Philadelphia Quaker, was born in that city in 1744. He, too, had graduated from the College of Philadelphia and had spent the following year, 1761, studying and traveling in Europe. He then became a successful merchant and one of the youngest delegates to the First Continental Congress. During the Revolution he saw action at the battles of Long Island, Princeton and Trenton; ultimately he was raised to the rank of major general. After the war, he returned to politics. As a delegate to Congress in 1783 he was chosen president, succeeding Richard Henry Lee.

The other Pennsylvanian, with the intriguing name of Jared Ingersoll, was a man who had cast aside most of his background and upbringing in order to support the Revolutionary movement. Not a native of Pennsylvania, he had been born in New Haven in 1749. At the age of seventeen he graduated from Yale, then moved with his family to Philadelphia. His father, a prominent judge, was highly respected by the British government, which he wholeheartedly supported.

Jared Ingersoll followed in his eminent father's footsteps, studying law for three years at the Middle Temple in London. When the Revolution broke out he was traveling in Europe. Despite his father's Loyalist stand, Jared returned to America to practice law and to work quietly for the patriot cause. In 1780 he was elected to Congress. It could not be said, however, that Ingersoll's views were either radical or revolutionary. He was by nature and by training a conservative who distrusted rapid change. When he was selected as a delegate to the Constitutional Convention, it was evidently hoped by his constituents that he would be a restraining influence in the deliberations, since he had always supported the Articles of Confederation and had generally opposed an all-powerful central government.

The dominating figure in the New York delegation when he was present was Alexander Hamilton. Hamilton's views were a

167

Alexander Hamilton was influential in calling the Constitutional Convention, but he was irregular in attendance and unpersuasive in debate. His real contribution came after adjournment

strange political mixture of strong federalism and an unswerving belief in democracy. When arguments developed over the makeup of the Senate, he invariably spoke vigorously for proportionate representation and for popular election of the delegates. At the same time, he favored a more powerful central authority than most of the members were willing to concede. He was an eloquent speaker, a forceful, handsome man who knew how to dramatize a political argument to sway an audience toward his viewpoint.

This brilliant statesman was born on Nevis, an island in the British West Indies—probably in 1755, although the exact date has never been established. His early education was apparently a sometime thing. At the age of 16, after working for a time as a clerk in a St. Croix trading post, he came to America where he attended a school in Elizabeth, New Jersey. While he was at King's College in 1776 the war was spreading rapidly, and

Luther Martin, "a rollicking . . . reprobate genius," whose primary interest lay in the sovereignty of the State of Maryland.

Hamilton left his studies to command an artillery company. Having distinguished himself in the Long Island and New Jersey campaigns, he was appointed an aide on Washington's staff and promoted to the rank of lieutenant colonel. In 1781, ambitious for a combat assignment, he persuaded Washington to give him a field command. As a result he won further laurels for himself by leading troops in the final assault on Yorktown.

The war over, Hamilton turned his remarkable energies to the study of law. Soon he was the recognized leader of the New York bar, which was generally considered to have the most brilliant legal minds in the United States. He served in Congress in 1782-1783. There he quickly became known for his positive views on strengthening the national government. It was no surprise to anyone when he was sent to the Annapolis Convention in 1786 to discuss the problems of the Confederation, and it was there that he drew up the report to Congress calling for a national convention in Philadelphia to consider the drafting of a completely new constitution. Naturally he became a New York delegate to the Constitutional Convention.

Ironically, as the most outspoken proponent of federalism at the Convention, Hamilton was outvoted by a New York delegation of antinationalists. His battle for a strong document was not only with the Convention as a whole, but with his own delegation as well.

John Lansing, Jr., for example, was a wealthy landowner who had friends among the most influential people of New York, most of whom wished to guard the state's sovereignty with the utmost jealousy. Lansing was a pleasant-mannered aristocrat who was more interested in riding to the hounds on his forty-thousand acre estate than he was in debating the great issues of a burgeoning nation. He had studied law with his associate,

Robert Yates, and during the Revolution he had served as General Schuyler's military secretary, a post similar to the one Hamilton had held with General Washington. His gracious home in Lansingburgh was a center for social gatherings, and he extended his hospitality to people of varied political leanings as long as he considered them "gentlemen." Governor Clinton, himself an antinationalist, had handpicked Lansing and Yates as two men he could trust to defend the state's independent power.

Robert Yates, a jurist who served as judge of the New York Supreme Court, was born in 1738 near Albany. His well-to-do family had provided him with an excellent education at schools in New York City. After reading law in William Livingston's law office Yates embarked on a mediocre career as an attorney. Never a particularly colorful personality, he worked hard and served his community and state well. He had helped to draft the Constitution of New York in 1777. His views, like Lansing's, were conservative, anti-federalist, and largely echoes of Lansing's and Governor George Clinton's convictions.

Yates and Lansing were among the men who, in the final analysis, refused to sign the completed draft of the Constitution. Another member who would not put his name to the document was Maryland delegate Luther Martin. Martin, the State Attorney General and a brilliant lawyer, had been an ardent patriot during the Revolution. He had worked closely with Samuel Chase, a signer of the Declaration who had been a leader of mob protests against the British Stamp Act and who had spoken passionately for independence at the First Continental Congress. When Governor Chase appointed Luther Martin to the post of Attorney General in 1778, Martin took great delight in prosecuting Maryland Loyalists and in meting out to them the most severe punishments. Martin

Left to right: John Francis Mercer,
Daniel Carroll and Daniel of St. Thomas
Jenifer, delegates from Maryland.

was born in New Jersey in 1747, the son of a struggling farmer. Somehow he managed to scrape up enough money to go to Princeton. He graduated in 1766 with high honors. It was shortly after this that he moved to Maryland to accept a teaching job, but tiring of pedagogy he took up law and was soon highly successful. His associates were amazed at his capacity for heavy drinking. Though he was frequently "in his cups," he could sober up quickly if occasion demanded it and could then conduct a courtroom case with consummate skill. He earned and spent money with ease; he never owned a great deal of property, but neither did he ever seem to want for anything. Elected to Congress in 1784, Martin made it clear to his colleagues that his primary interest lay in the sovereignty of the State of Maryland. Thus, as a delegate to the Constitutional Convention, he opposed every move that might reduce the powers of the individual states.

Like Martin, young John Francis Mercer was another of Maryland's antinationalists. Mercer, who had just turned twenty-nine,

came to the Convention determined to protect his state's interests. He, too, was a close friend of Samuel Chase, and he moved in the wealthiest circles of prosperous planters, most of whom feared that a strong central government would threaten their power and affluence. Mercer had been sent by his well-to-do family to William and Mary in 1775. But he had little time for studies, for he was soon fighting with the Third Virginia Regiment. He was wounded at Brandywine and was cited for conspicuous gallantry at Yorktown. Following the war he practiced law, was elected to the Virginia legislature and then to Congress. When he married a wealthy Maryland girl in 1785 he took up residence on her estate. Soon afterward he was playing an active part in Maryland politics.

Of the Maryland delegates, Daniel Carroll was probably the most dedicated to nationalism. Although he was a wealthy landowner with a tobacco plantation worked by about sixty slaves, he nevertheless disagreed with others of his group and generally supported those who sought to strengthen the nation.

Daniel's second cousin was the distinguished Charles Carroll of Carrollton, the only Roman Catholic signer of the Declaration. Born in 1730, Daniel Carroll was educated at a Jesuit school at St. Omer, Flanders. He toured Europe for a time, then returned to Maryland where he assumed his family responsibilities, taking part in the management of the Carroll estates. In 1781 he was elected to Congress. There he worked quietly for strengthening the federal government before being sent to the Constitutional Convention.

Carroll was supported in his nationalist views by the senior Maryland delegate, sixty-four-year-old Daniel of St. Thomas Jenifer. Jenifer, a close friend of George Washington, had supported the patriots prior to the Revolution, much to the surprise of many of his Loyalist neighbors. He was the first president of the Maryland Council of Safety and was a delegate to Congress from 1778 to 1782. As one of Maryland's elder statesmen he wielded a powerful influence in his state and was highly respected by the delegates to the Convention.

By mid-June opposing points of view were reaching a stage of confrontation. Many of the heated debates that had been temporarily cooled by the moderating words of Franklin and of Oliver Ellsworth were ready to break out again in force. Most of the delegates sensed that a violent storm of dissension was in the making.

On June 13 Nathaniel Gorham of Massachusetts, Chairman of the Committee of the Whole, submitted a report to the Convention consisting of 19 resolutions summarizing the various points on which there had been general agreement. In essence this was a modified version of Edmund Randolph's original resolutions, but it added at the end, "Resolved, that the amendments which shall be offered to the confederation by the convention ought, at a proper time . . . be submitted to an assembly or assemblies recommended by the several Legislatures, to be expressly chosen by the people to consider and decide thereon."

At William Paterson's suggestion, the delegates adjourned for a day in order to study the report. In the meantime Paterson's New Jersey delegation prepared an alternative plan which contained some startling differences from those put forward up to that time. Basically the New Jersey plan would merely enlarge somewhat the powers of the existing federation. Each state was to have equal representation in a Congress which consisted of only one house. It called for Congress to elect a Federal Executive who in turn would appoint all federal officers "not otherwise provided for." At the same time the authority of the national judiciary was much more strictly defined and limited than in the Randolph outline.

The submission of the New Jersey proposal came as a shock to many delegates who saw in this action a threat to the progress of the entire Convention. Some expressed a genuine fear that the members opposing a national

While delegates debated at the Convention,
artist Charles W. Peale recorded
a minor tragedy on Lombard Street.
A dropped "pye from the Bake-House"
provided amusement for sooty chimney sweeps.

THE GRANGER COLLECTION

government would destroy the Convention.

John Dickinson of Delaware confided in Madison, "You see the consequence of pushing things too far. Some of the members from the small States wish for two branches in the General Legislature, and are friends to a good National Government; but we would sooner submit to a foreign power, than submit to be deprived in both branches of the legislature of an equality of suffrage, and thereby be thrown under the domination of the larger States."

Dickinson was himself a proponent of nationalism even though his was the smallest of the states. As leader of the Delaware delegation he played an important role and had become an advocate of sensible compromise.

No sooner had the New Jersey plan been submitted than antinationalist John Lansing was on his feet supporting it, claiming that

Paterson was sustaining the sovereignty of the states whereas Randolph's proposal would destroy them.

There were cries that proportional representation based on population would be fair to all the states.

"Is it so?" demanded Paterson. "If a proportional representation be right, why do we not vote so here?"

Randolph then made a final plea to the Convention before that day's adjournment. "A National Government alone, properly constituted, will answer the purpose," he said. "I beg it to be considered that the present is the last moment for establishing one."

On the following Monday, June 18, Alexander Hamilton spoke to the Convention. Up to this point he had been silent during most of the discussions, partly because of his delicate position in respect to his own delegation,

172

with whom he disagreed. But he now stated that he was opposed to both the Virginia and New Jersey plans, though he was especially antagonistic to the latter. He flatly denied that the Convention had limited authority. They had been sent, he declared, to handle a national emergency. "To rely on and propose any plan not adequate to these exigencies, merely because it is not clearly within our powers would be to sacrifice the means to the end."

Hamilton pointed out the weaknesses in both plans and praised the British government which, he said, "is the only government in the world which unites public strength with individual security."

He then proceeded to outline some of his own ideas of what the American government should be. Probably his strong views came as a shock, not only to the Anti-Federalists, but to Madison himself. Hamilton envisioned a Congress of two houses empowered to pass any laws whatsoever. His concept of a chief executive was a national governor, to be elected for life and to hold the power of absolute veto over Congressional legislation.

It seems likely that Hamilton consciously exaggerated his plan for an all-powerful central authority in order to make the propositions of the milder Federalists more palatable to their opponents. In any case, his speech had the effect of interrupting the efforts of the Anti-Federalists for a day and of giving the delegates a pause for reflection.

Debate continued over the alternative plans for the next few days, yet nothing seemed to be resolved. Finally Dr. Johnson suggested to the Convention that if it could be shown under Randolph's plan how the states would retain a reasonable degree of authority, the objections of the New Jersey delegation as well as those of other smaller states could be overcome. Unless this could be done he saw no end to the bickering and dissension.

Madison and Wilson countered that there was more danger of encroachment of the states upon a central government than the other way around.

In the course of these arguments Charles Pinckney delivered a significant address in which he spoke of the people of the United States as the most remarkable in the world. "Among them," he said, "there are fewer distinctions of fortune and less of rank, than among the inhabitants of any other nation. And this equality is likely to continue; because in a new country, possessing immense tracts of uncultivated lands, where every temptation is offered to emigration, and where industry must be rewarded with competency, there will be few poor and few dependent . . . None will be excluded by birth, and few by fortune, from voting for proper persons to fill the offices of government."

Pinckney further stated a point which America seems to have lost sight of in more recent years. He said, "We mistake the object of our Government, if we hope or wish that it is to make us respectable abroad. *Conquest or superiority among other powers is not, or ought never to be the object of republican systems.*"

With astonishing foresight many of these founding fathers recognized how the government they were forming should provide for the future. "In framing a system which we wish to last for ages," said James Madison, "we should not lose sight of the changes which ages will produce. An increase of population will of necessity increase the proportion of those who will labor under all the hardships of life, and secretly sigh for a more equal distribution of its blessings. These may in time outnumber those who are placed above the feelings of indigence . . . The power will then slide into the hands of the former. How is the danger, in all cases of interested coalitions, to oppress the minority, to be guarded against?"

Madison answered his question by insisting that they form a body in the government with sufficient wisdom and virtue to aid justice by throwing its weight into the scale. This was how he conceived of the Senate, and he hoped that the method of choosing and composing the upper house would bring about such a result.

Although Hamilton and Madison strove to keep the minds of the delegates on high principles, and though Benjamin Franklin, observing the rising temperature of the debates, entered a motion to start each day's session with prayers, the determined anti-nationalists continued to hammer on the theme of states' rights. Luther Martin expressed the belief that a general government for America should be constructed to preserve the state governments and not to govern individuals. "Power," he insisted, "should be held within narrow limits. Too little power could be added to; too much could never be curtailed."

Alexander Hamilton roundly criticized the states for having different qualifications for voting rights. The contest in Philadelphia, he felt, had become one for power, not for liberty. He acknowledged that the State of Delaware with a population of 40,000 would lose power if she had only one-tenth of the votes of Pennsylvania with her 400,000 citizens. "But will the *people* of Delaware *be less free,* if each citizen has an equal vote with each citizen of Pennsylvania?" asked Hamilton.

It was at this point that Oliver Ellsworth injected the all-important word, "compromise."

"The proportional representation in the first branch," said Ellsworth, "is conformable to the national principle and will secure the large States against the small. An equality of voices in the second branch (Senate) is conformable to the federal principle, and is necessary to secure the small States against the large. I trust that on this middle ground, *a compromise will take place.*"

But many of the delegates were still in no mood for compromise. On the last day of June, while several members continued to plead for an accommodation, others angrily denounced the plans thus far submitted. As there were still no delegates from New Hampshire, David Brearly asked Washington if he would dispatch a letter to the governor of that New England state, emphasizing the urgency of the matters being discussed and the need for a complete representation of the states.

It should be recalled that Brearly, a New Jersey delegate, favored the equal rights of states, and he believed that New Hampshire would support the smaller states in opposing proportional representation.

James Wilson, immediately sensible of the intent of Brearly's request, asked the Convention, "Can we forget for whom we are forming a government? Is it for *men,* or for the imaginary beings called States?"

"We are running from one extreme to another," Ellsworth told them. "We are razing the foundations of the building, when we need only repair the roof."

And Benjamin Franklin once more begged for sanity, saying, "When a broad table is to be made, and the edges of two planks do not fit, the artist takes a little from both and makes a good joint. In like manner, here, both sides must part from some of their demands in order that they may join in some accommodating proposition." He then proposed a compromise plan similar to Ellsworth's, giving equal suffrage to states in all cases where their sovereignty might be affected and proportional representation in all bills concerning expenditures from the general Treasury.

With the Fourth of July holiday approaching it was decided that a committee

174

Whether slaves were to be counted in establishing
a fair distribution of representatives in Congress
was a crucial issue at the Convention.
It was not until the Census of 1790 that accurate
data on the slave population was available.

should be established to study and report on how the Senate should be composed. Madison then suggested that the Convention recess for two days "that time may be given to the committee and to such as choose to attend the celebrations on the anniversary of Independence."

When the Convention reconvened on July 5, the Committee, composed of Gerry, Ellsworth, Yates, Paterson, Franklin, Bedford, Martin, Mason, Rutledge and Baldwin, made their recommendation: that the first branch of the legislature be allowed one member for every 40,000 inhabitants, and that the second branch have an equal vote for each state.

If the moderate members had hoped that the brief holiday would serve to cool tempers and to provide time for a sobering review of what had transpired they were due for a shock. Debate following the Committee report grew in intensity and bitterness. The question of how the states should be represented spilled over into the murky depths of the slavery issue. It started with fears being expressed that the concept of an exclusive Senate, composed of men of property, would encourage an aristocracy. To this Gouverneur Morris replied, "My creed is that there never was, nor ever will be, a civilized society without an aristocracy. My endeavor is to keep it as much as possible from doing mischief."

William Paterson then asked what position slaves would occupy in the voting of Southern states. He regarded slaves as property. Not being free agents, they had no faculty for acquiring property of their own and were entirely at the will of the master. Had a man in Virginia, he asked, a number of votes in proportion to the number of his slaves?

This was an explosive question which had been scrupulously avoided by most delegates, but now the whole ugly issue came to the

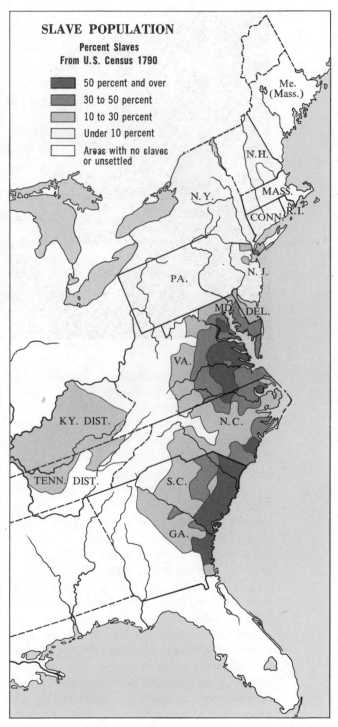

SLAVE POPULATION

Percent Slaves
From U.S. Census 1790

50 percent and over

30 to 50 percent

10 to 30 percent

Under 10 percent

Areas with no slaves
or unsettled

Me.
(Mass.)

N.H.

N.Y.

MASS.

CONN. R.I.

N.J.

PA.

MD. DEL.

VA.

KY. DIST.

N.C.

TENN. DIST.

S.C.

GA.

The walls of the now restored Assembly Room of the old Pennsylvania State House once echoed to heated debates on the Constitution.

forefront of the discussions. When Randolph made the interesting proposal that a national census be required in order to establish a fair distribution of representatives in the House, James Wilson wanted to know if slaves would be counted as citizens in such a census.

Even as the nation's cornerstone was being laid, the seeds of the Civil War were embedded with it. It is often forgotten that many of the "founding fathers" clearly recognized the fundamental evil of slavery and made strong efforts to kill it at the outset. There were numbers of men who agreed with Gouverneur Morris when he cried out to the Convention, "I will never concur in upholding domestic slavery. Slavery is a nefarious institution. It is the curse of Heaven on the States where it prevails . . . The vassalage of the poor has ever been the favorite offspring of aristocracy. And what is the proposed compensation to the Northern States, for a sacrifice of every principle of right, of every impulse of humanity? They are to bind themselves to march their militia for the defence of the Southern States, for their defence against those very slaves of whom they complain. On the other side the Southern States are not to be restrained from importing fresh supplies of wretched Africans. I would sooner submit myself to a tax for paying for all the Negroes in the United States, than saddle posterity with such a Constitution."

The Northern delegates, combined with those Southerners who opposed slavery in principle, outnumbered the real believers in slavery. Yet everyone at the Convention knew that unless debate on this subject were dropped their efforts would end in disaster. The large and powerful slave states would not be moved. Without accommodation on this issue there would be no Constitution—no nation at all.

Chapter Seven

Masters of Compromise

The Rough Draft

A solution for the issues in debate was finally reached on July 16. This major break in the deadlock over representation came in the form of a resolution assigning a specific number of representatives to each state: New Hampshire was to send three; Massachusetts, eight; Rhode Island, one; and so forth. The "Great Compromise," as it was called, further stated that, as the current situation of the states would undoubtedly change as to the number of inhabitants, the legislature of the United States would be authorized from time to time to apportion the number of representatives, provided always that the representation would be proportioned to the amount of direct taxation. Further, in order to determine the extent of such changes, a census would be taken within six years from the first meeting of Congress and once every ten years thereafter.

All bills for raising money were to originate in the House of Representatives, not to be altered by the Senate. It was also resolved that in the second branch of the legislature each state should have an equal vote.

It is interesting to observe that this resolution, which became known as the Great Compromise and sometimes as the Connecticut Compromise because it was proposed by that state, was by no means a clear-cut agreement by all members of the Convention. The vote in favor of it narrowly passed, five to four, and debates pro and con the various elements of the resolution continued for some days. But it was from that point forward that most of the discussion became narrowed to details rather than to broad general principles. Still undetermined was the method of choosing a Chief Executive, and again there was the division between those who wanted popular election and those who favored some type of legislative appointment.

An indication of how widely separated were opinions on this subject is given in the statements made by two delegates, the one following the other.

Gouverneur Morris argued, "It is said that the multitude will be uninformed. It is true they would be uninformed of what passed in the Legislative conclave, if the election were to be made there, but they will not be uninformed of those great and illustrious characters which have merited their esteem and confidence. If the Executive be chosen by the national Legislature, he will not be independent of it; and if not independent, usurpation and tyranny on the part of the Legislature will be the consequence."

To this, Colonel Mason replied, "It would be as unnatural to refer the choice of a proper character for Chief Magistrate to the people, as it would be to refer a trial of colors to a blind man. The extent of the country renders it impossible that the people can have the requisite capacity to judge of the respective pretensions of the candidates."

The proceedings became increasingly tedious. Sixty ballots were taken before a method of selecting a President could be agreed upon. Instead of having the national legislature appoint the Chief Executive the Convention adopted James Wilson's earlier suggestion for a system of presidential electors. Left unresolved was the term of office for the President. A seven-year term was favored but it was later changed to four years without limiting the President's right to run again.

At last, on July 26 the Convention had forged a set of resolutions which it referred to a Committee of Detail. This was the beginning of a real draft for the Constitution, and in less than a week, on August 6, the Committee furnished all delegates with a printed report, summarizing by "Articles" the proposed structure of legislative, executive, and judicial government. The report went into greater detail than any previous plan. It explained how a presidential veto

Late eighteenth-century printshop.
From a shop such as this came printed
copies of the Constitution as drafted
by the Committee of Detail.

could be overridden by a two-thirds majority in both houses of the legislature; spelled out legislative powers to impose and collect taxes, to regulate commerce, to issue money and to establish standard weights and measures. Congress would be empowered to establish post offices, to borrow, to subdue rebellion in any state, to raise armies and to build fleets. It defined treason as making war against the United States or any state, or "adhering to the enemies of the United States."

A remarkable detail in the writing and publishing of this report is the speed with which it was accomplished. In this later day of high-speed printing presses and automated, even computerized typesetting it is difficult to conceive of so complex and extensive a document being written, printed, bound and distributed all in the space of four or five days. At that time every letter of every word was hand set, and copies of each page were laboriously imprinted on a hand-inked, hand-operated press. That such a task could be carried out almost overnight not only shows the dedication of those involved but demonstrates that human determination often counts for more than electronically automated machinery. Perhaps the most astonishing aspect of the drafters' work was the writing itself, which in today's lawmaking bodies would surely have required weeks "in committee."

On Tuesday, August 7, the preamble to the draft was accepted by the Convention along with the first two articles. In the detailed discussion of other portions of the committee report Madison once more demonstrated his uncanny foresight.

Said Madison, "In future times, a great majority of the people will not only be without landed, but any other sort of property."

It must be remembered that at the time of Madison's statement America was largely an agrarian country with a very large proportion of the population owning farms or plantations. Madison continued, "These people (those without property) will either combine, under the influence of their common situation —in which case the rights of property and the public liberty will not be secure in their hands—or, what is more probable, they will become the tools of opulence and ambition; in which case, there will be equal danger on the other side."

While he did not disagree with Madison's forecast of conditions in America, Franklin was more optimistic concerning the public's overall wisdom. "It is of great consequence," he said, "that we do not depress the virtue and public spirit of our common people; of which they displayed a great deal during the war, and which contributed principally to the favorable issue of it. . . . Some of the greatest

As chairman of the Convention, Washington received a copy of the printed draft of the Constitution. This document with its unwieldy preamble is marked with corrections in Washington's firm handwriting.

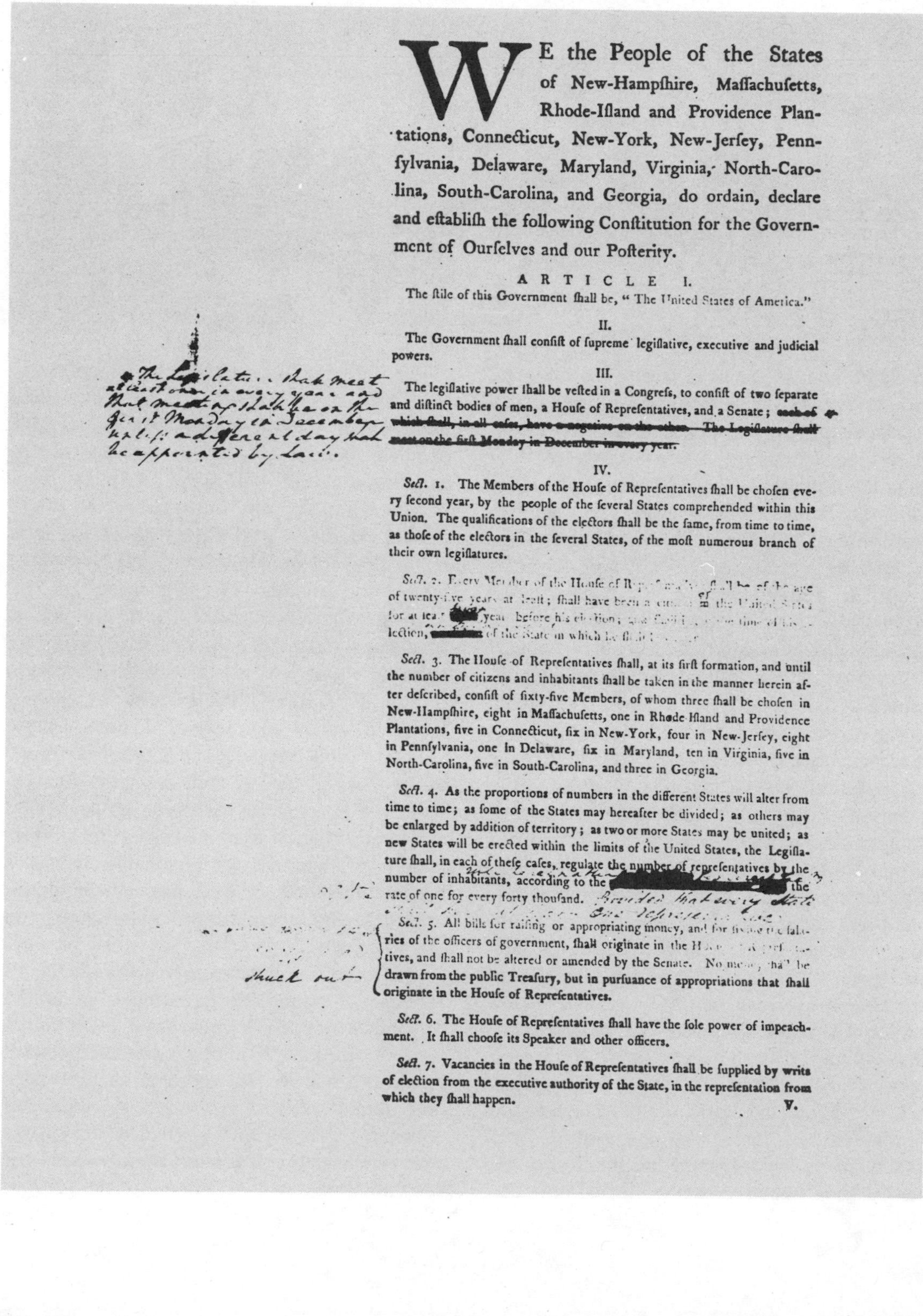

WE the People of the States of New-Hampfhire, Maffachufetts, Rhode-Ifland and Providence Plantations, Connecticut, New-York, New-Jerfey, Pennfylvania, Delaware, Maryland, Virginia, North-Carolina, South-Carolina, and Georgia, do ordain, declare and eftablifh the following Conftitution for the Government of Ourfelves and our Pofterity.

ARTICLE I.

The ftile of this Government fhall be, " The United States of America."

II.

The Government fhall confift of fupreme legiflative, executive and judicial powers.

III.

The legiflative power fhall be vefted in a Congrefs, to confift of two feparate and diftinct bodies of men, a Houfe of Reprefentatives, and a Senate; ~~each of which fhall, in all cafes, have a negative on the other. The Legiflature fhall meet on the firft Monday in December in every year.~~

[handwritten marginal note:] The Legiflature fhall meet at leaft once in every year, and fuch meeting fhall be on the firft Monday in December unlefs a different day fhall be appointed by Law.

IV.

Sect. 1. The Members of the Houfe of Reprefentatives fhall be chofen every fecond year, by the people of the feveral States comprehended within this Union. The qualifications of the electors fhall be the fame, from time to time, as thofe of the electors in the feveral States, of the moft numerous branch of their own legiflatures.

Sect. 2. Every Member of the Houfe of Reprefentatives fhall be of the age of twenty-five years at leaft; fhall have been a citizen of the United States for at leaft year before his election; and fhall be, at the time of his election, of the State in which he fhall be chofen.

Sect. 3. The Houfe of Reprefentatives fhall, at its firft formation, and until the number of citizens and inhabitants fhall be taken in the manner herein after defcribed, confift of fixty-five Members, of whom three fhall be chofen in New-Hampfhire, eight in Maffachufetts, one in Rhode-Ifland and Providence Plantations, five in Connecticut, fix in New-York, four in New-Jerfey, eight in Pennfylvania, one in Delaware, fix in Maryland, ten in Virginia, five in North-Carolina, five in South-Carolina, and three in Georgia.

Sect. 4. As the proportions of numbers in the different States will alter from time to time; as fome of the States may hereafter be divided; as others may be enlarged by addition of territory; as two or more States may be united; as new States will be erected within the limits of the United States, the Legiflature fhall, in each of thefe cafes, regulate the number of reprefentatives by the number of inhabitants, according to the ~~~~ the rate of one for every forty thoufand. *Provided that every State fhall have at leaft One Reprefentative.*

Sect. 5. All bills for raifing or appropriating money, and for fixing the falaries of the officers of government, fhall originate in the Houfe of Reprefentatives, and fhall not be altered or amended by the Senate. No money fhall be drawn from the public Treafury, but in purfuance of appropriations that fhall originate in the Houfe of Reprefentatives.

[handwritten marginal note:] ftruck out

Sect. 6. The Houfe of Reprefentatives fhall have the fole power of impeachment. It fhall choofe its Speaker and other officers.

Sect. 7. Vacancies in the Houfe of Reprefentatives fhall be fupplied by writs of election from the executive authority of the State, in the reprefentation from which they fhall happen.

V.

The Great Seal of the United States in two early versions used prior to 1877.

DEPT. OF STATE

rogues I was ever acquainted with were the richest rogues."

When Madison pointed out that the rule of one representative for 40,000 inhabitants would in the future make the number of representatives excessive as populations grew, Nathaniel Gorham showed his lack of foresight in this remarkable statement:

"It is not to be supposed that the government will last so long as to produce this effect. Can it be supposed that this vast country, including the western territory, will, one hundred and fifty years hence, remain one nation?"

Fortunately for America, Gorham's failure to grasp the import of his own work as a Convention delegate was the exception rather than the rule. Most of the representatives were consciously striving to create a government that would endure the rigors of time and future generations.

The hot days of August dragged on in seemingly interminable arguments over small points. One such argument developed over the government's power to issue paper money. George Mason had a "mortal hatred" of paper money. John Francis Mercer, on the other hand, liked the use of paper money but admitted that, at the moment, people were suspicious of the various worthless currencies that had been printed by the states. Ellsworth and Butler wanted no part of paper notes as legal tender, while Wilson and Randolph felt that at least the door should be left open for the government to print banknotes, since no one could foresee exactly what future circumstances might require. Because of the general dissatisfaction with existing unsound currencies the majority of delegates voted against federal power to issue paper money.

Now the Convention was getting down to debates over phrases, even individual words in the draft of the Constitution. For example, the delegates finally agreed to change a sentence in the section on legislative authority from "the power to *make* war" to "the power to *declare* war." As Mason put it, "I am for clogging, rather than facilitating war; but I am definitely for facilitating peace."

Meanwhile, Charles Pinckney submitted a series of important proposals which he wanted included somewhere in the Constitution. These were seeds of a Bill of Rights, over which there would later be much controversy:

"The liberty of the press shall be inviolably preserved;

"The military shall always be subordinate to civil power;

"No soldier shall be quartered in any house, in time of peace, without the consent of the owner;

"No religious test or qualification shall ever be annexed to any oath of office."

Pinckney at the same time suggested that the United States legislature should be authorized to make a Great Seal, which should be kept by the President, to be used as occasion might require. It would be called the Great Seal of the United States and would be affixed to all laws.

Other proposals were submitted by Gouverneur Morris. These included the establishment of cabinet members to assist the President—a Secretary of Domestic Affairs, Secretary of Commerce and Finance, Secretary of War and Secretary of State, all to be appointed by the Chief Executive.

In the last days of August, there was a final flurry of argument over slavery. The issue was too serious and too deep a one to be cast aside easily. But by this time the debate was more academic than purposeful and it was concluded without serious impairment of the progress being made in other areas. The issue was brought forward over a proposed clause in the draft to prohibit further importation of slaves.

181

Charles Pinckney was instantly on his feet to protest. He told the delegates that South Carolina could never receive the Constitution if it prohibited the slave trade. If, on the other hand, the states were all left at liberty to set their own policies in this matter, he believed that South Carolina would ultimately abolish the trade just as Virginia and Maryland had already done.

Less optimistic was Colonel Mason who delivered his last denunciation of the system to the Convention.

"This infernal traffic originated in the avarice of British merchants," said Mason. Further, he reminded the delegates that the British government had constantly interfered with attempts of Virginia to end the slave trade. "The present question," he went on, "concerns not the importing States alone, but the whole Union. Western people are already calling out for slaves in their new lands. Every master of slaves is born a petty tyrant. They bring the judgment of Heaven on a country. As nations cannot be rewarded or punished in the next world, they must be in this. By an inevitable chain of causes and effects, *Providence punishes national sins by national calamities.*"

The full import of these prophetic words would not be felt for another seventy years.

In Oliver Ellsworth's view, the national government should free the slaves already in the country. He argued that there would be enough poor laborers in the nation to make slavery unnecessary.

"If slavery be wrong," retorted the elder Pinckney, "it is justified by the example of all the world. Sanction for slavery has been given by France, England, Holland and other modern States. In all ages one half of mankind have been slaves."

John Dickinson, thoroughly aroused by Pinckney's words, told the delegates that he considered it inadmissable, "on every principle of honor and safety, that the importation of slaves should be authorized to the States by the Constitution."

Finally Randolph brought the explosive issue to a close. He pointed out that by agreeing to a clause allowing free importation of slaves, it would revolt Quakers, Methodists and many others in states having no slaves. On the other hand, two states might be lost to the Union. He therefore urged the convention to "try the chance of a commitment."

Later, a time limitation extending to the year 1800 was established for the importation of slaves. This restriction came in the form of a resolution introduced by William Livingston, Governor of New Jersey and leader of that state's delegation. He had seldom entered into debates on the floor of the Convention though he had worked actively on committees and had applied his influence in many important votes. As Governor of New Jersey his word had carried considerable weight not only with his own delegation but with all the members.

Livingston was born in Albany, New York, in 1723, and as the son of a powerful and wealthy family he received an excellent education largely through expert tutoring at home. He then went to Yale, where he received a B.A. degree in 1741; from there he took up the study of law in the office of attorney James Alexander in New York City. A highly successful lawyer, Livingston soon gained a reputation for a sharp tongue and fearless stands in political questions, but in 1772 he seemed to become tired of controversy. He retired to a large estate in New Jersey, hoping to become a gentleman farmer. But the outbreak of the Revolution decreed otherwise. In a short time he was once more engrossed in politics. He was sent to both Continental Congresses, took command of the New Jersey Militia and then was elected governor of the state. His attendance at the Philadelphia Convention

was spotty, since his duties as governor kept him away on several occasions. His most important contribution to the Constitutional Convention had been his chairmanship of the committee that finally came up with the formula on slavery, acceptable to the Southern States, calling for the slave trade to continue until the year 1800; meanwhile Congress was permitted to levy a tax on such trade as a means of slowing it until a prohibition could be authorized.

After some further discussion of refinements in the draft, most of the delegates were now ready to approve its submission to the states. But on September 10, the very man who had opened the Convention with his Constitutional outline now rose to voice his objections to the plan that was nearing completion.

Edmund Randolph felt that the number of representatives would be too small; there was no limitation established for a standing army; and there was not enough definition between national and state legislatures. "Am I," he asked, "to promote the establishment of a plan which, I verily believe, will end in tyranny?" In any case, he urged that the plan be submitted first to Congress, then to state conventions which would have the power to adopt, reject or amend the draft, and finally another General Convention with power to adopt or reject the alterations proposed by the various states.

Although Franklin seconded this motion it was tabled until a committee could have time to see if Randolph's objections might be overcome.

On the twelfth, William Samuel Johnson reported back to the Convention with printed copies of a revised draft together with a letter to the United States, in Congress assembled, stating that the Convention was submitting a Constitution "which has appeared to us the most advisable."

"It is obviously impracticable," the letter read, "in the federal government of these States, to secure all rights of independent sovereignty to each, and yet provide for the interest and safety of all. Individuals entering into society must give up a share of liberty, to preserve the rest . . .

"In all our deliberations on this subject, we kept steadily in our view that which appeared to us the greatest interest of every true American, the consolidation of our Union, in which is involved our prosperity, felicity, safety, perhaps our national existence. This important consideration, seriously and deeply impressed on our minds, led each State in the Convention to be less rigid in points of inferior magnitude, than might have been otherwise expected. And thus the Constitution which we now present is the result of a spirit of amity, and of that mutual deference and concession . . .

". . . that it may promote the lasting welfare of that country so dear to us all; and secure her freedom and happiness, is our most ardent wish."

183

Final Agreement

A vote of approval was close at hand. Only one other major point was raised by George Mason, who expressed a wish that a Bill of Rights be incorporated into the Constitution. Elbridge Gerry concurred and moved that a committee be formed to prepare such a Bill of Rights, but the motion was defeated.

Now the great day of decision had come. On Monday, September 17, Benjamin Franklin rose with a speech in his hand. He began to read it, but his voice failed him and he passed the paper over to James Wilson, who continued for him. Franklin admitted that there were parts of the Constitution of which he did not approve, but he added, "the older I grow, the more I am apt to doubt my own judgment and to pay more respect to the judgment of others." He therefore hoped that all who dissented would join with him in a unanimity of approval for the document.

"On the whole," said Franklin, "I cannot help expressing a wish that every member of the Convention who may still have objections to it, would with me, on this occasion, doubt a little of his own infallibility, and to

Painting by Thomas Rossiter of the
signing of the Constitution. Rossiter
took artistic license in showing
a sunburst tapestry behind Washington;
actually the wall was paneled.

make manifest our unanimity, put his name to this instrument."

When Nathaniel Gorham expressed a desire to change the number of representatives from one for every 40,000 inhabitants to one for every 30,000, George Washington rose for the purpose of putting the question to the Convention:

"Although my situation has hitherto restrained me from offering my sentiments on questions, yet I cannot forbear expressing my wish that the proposed alteration may take place." Washington said that it was de-sirable that objections to the plan recommended should be as few as possible. Yet the smallness of the proportion of representatives had been considered by many members of the Convention to be an insufficient security for the rights and interests of the people. He urged that the amendment be adopted.

This was the only occasion on which the president of the Convention entered into a discussion of the merits or shortcomings of any proposal, and the delegates voted unanimously in favor of the Gorham proposal.

It had been hoped by the majority that Franklin's gentle admonitions and the favorable vote on Gorham's motion might persuade Randolph to go along with the Constitution. They were disappointed. He told the assemblage that he appreciated Franklin's remarks and then apologized for his refusal to sign the document, because he felt that the object of the Convention would be thwarted by the plan they were about to present to the people. He predicted that nine states would fail to ratify the Constitution.

Gouverneur Morris and Alexander Hamilton both expressed deep concern over any delegate's refusal to sign. Morris, too, had objections to the plan, but since the majority had voted in its favor, he would abide by the result. "The moment this plan goes forth," said Morris, "all other considerations will be laid aside, and the great question will be, shall there be a National Government, or not? And this must take place, or a general anarchy will be the alternative." The pleas for unanimity won a favorable response from at least one delegate. William Blount, of North Carolina, had said earlier that he would not sign the Constitution. Now he expressed relief at the final form of the document and declared that he wished to attest the fact that the plan was the unanimous act of the states in Convention.

Blount, a native Carolinian, was the son

Rising sun (sketch left) was carved on the back of Washington's chair.

INDEPENDENCE NATIONAL HISTORICAL PARK COLLECTION, PHILADELPHIA

of a wealthy planter. He was born on his father's plantation in 1749. During the war he had served the state militia as a paymaster, then at the war's end he became a member of the state legislature. A recognized force in North Carolina politics, he was a member of Congress when the Constitutional Convention began. He was one of the few Convention delegates who had the knowledge and foresight to speak authoritatively about western expansion. Although as a Southern planter his views were generally in the direction of states' rights, he was an intelligent patriot, open to reason and compromise.

Unfortunately, Blount's conversion did nothing to sway Randolph. "Even though this is a step which might be the most awful of my life, I cannot sign," he told the delegates.

And now Elbridge Gerry, the perennial prevaricator, joined with Randolph in his refusal to sign. He feared that the proposed document would only deepen the current crisis in the United States. In his own state of Massachusetts he observed that there were two parties, one of which was devoted to Democracy, "the worst," he felt, "of all political evils," the other as violent in the opposite extreme. From the collision of these parties in debate over the Constitution, Gerry could see nothing but confusion and possibly civil war.

Despite the chilling effect of these observations, delegates prepared to sign the document. George Washington was asked to hold all records of the proceedings, subject to further instructions from a new Congress if it should be formed under the Constitution.

Only 42 of the 55 framers were in their seats at this historic moment.

The engrossed Constitution was placed upon the table in front of Washington, and once again, the stately, paneled room in Independence Hall became the scene of a turning point in history. The men in their frock coats, knee breeches and buckled shoes came forward and inscribed their names, by states, on the last page under George Washington's signature. Only three delegates refused to sign: Edmund Randolph, Elbridge Gerry and George Mason.

While the last members were affixing their signatures the venerable Franklin glanced at the President's chair, on the back of which a rising sun was painted. He observed to a few members near him that painters had always found it difficult in their art to distinguish a rising from a setting sun. "I have," he said, "often and often, in the course of the session, and the vicissitude of my hopes and fears as to its issue, looked at that behind the President without being able to tell whether it was rising or setting; but now at length, I have the happiness to know that it is a rising, and not a setting sun."

Chapter Eight

Launching the New Government

The Campaign for Ratification

We the people of the United States, in order to form a more perfect Union, establish Justice, insure domestic Tranquility, provide for the common defence, promote the general Welfare, and secure the Blessings of Liberty to ourselves and our Posterity, do ordain and establish this Constitution for the United States of America.

The great Preamble to the Constitution was soon to become familiar to nearly every citizen of a young and troubled nation, and would, ultimately, be committed to memory by every American school child. But days of domestic tranquility were a long way off. The document itself was about to be launched into a sea of turbulent politics.

After all the attending delegates except Randolph, Mason and Gerry had signed the Constitution, they left the Hall and strolled in small groups to the City Tavern on Walnut Street. There, according to George Washington's diary, they "dined together and took a cordial leave of each other."

Undoubtedly their relief at having completed a difficult task led many of them to make merry at the tavern and to drink quite a few toasts to the new Constitution. Yet underlying their satisfaction must have been doubt concerning public acceptance of their work. The more thoughtful among them probably discussed at length how the document would be received and what steps might be taken to help speed its adoption. In any case, they left the Philadelphia tavern for their respective homes, knowing that the great test of their accomplishment was yet to come, and that the future of the nation depended upon a successful outcome of the deliberations about to take place. The 55 men who had lived and breathed the Constitution for four months now scattered to all parts of the country, traveling by horseback, stage coach and packet boat. Most of them looked back with pride on the work they had done in Philadelphia.

But these were not men who rested on self-awarded laurels. They knew there were still two great tasks ahead of them: first, to persuade the people to adopt the Constitution; second, to implement the document and make it work.

Despite the times, with only the crudest of communications available, the new Constitution became public knowledge in a surprisingly short time. Newspapers in Philadelphia and Lancaster had printed the complete text by September 19, two days after the Convention ended. The Constitution had been read in the State House to the Pennsylvania Assembly on the 18th, and a courier arrived in New York on the 20th to lay the document before the United States Congress. German translations were available in Pennsylvania Dutch regions the same week, the Preamble leading off with "Wir das Volk. . ." In the course of the next two weeks, and by the first days of October, printed copies were being circulated all over America. According to newspaper accounts of the time, virtually every adult American had read the new Constitution by the end of October. Visitors from France and other countries were amazed to hear backwoodsmen heatedly discussing some of the more controversial provisions of the document. In village squares from Maine to Georgia and from the city of Richmond to frontier forts in Kentucky, the people buzzed with excitement over the proposed new national government.

The remarkable thing about the document was its strict adherence to essential principles. It did not attempt to spell out in detail such laws as would restrict human conduct. Primarily it established the means for creating and administering fair laws, and most of its prohibitions were written to restrict the powers of government itself. Above all, the wisdom of the framers had allowed for change, which would be made necessary by changing times and changing ways.

The new Constitution was
submitted to conventions elected
in each state. Approval by nine
states was required to put it into effect.

Surprisingly, in spite of the fact that the new Constitution would do away with the existing government, it was the old Congress that made the first move toward ratification, and they did it promptly. On September 28, 1787, driven by the persuasive arguments of several framers who had returned to their seats, Congress sent copies of the Constitution to each of the state legislatures which were asked to take whatever steps were necessary to vote on its adoption.

Ratification by nine states was required to put the Constitution into effect, and at the outset it appeared that there would be less difficulty than many people had anticipated. First of the states to ratify was Delaware, whose legislature voted solidly to adopt the Constitution on December 7, 1787. It thus became the "First State" under the new Consitutional government. Pennsylvania, New Jersey, Connecticut and Georgia followed suit within a few weeks, so that in January 1788 five states had ratified the Constitution.

However, this rash of approval created an illusion of quick success among many Federalists (those in favor of the Constitution), who envisioned even doubtful states falling in line. Instead of snowballing, the movement now faltered and ground to a virtual halt, while bitter debate raged in several areas of the country.

The beginnings of political parties could be seen as the Federalist and the Anti-Federalists gathered their forces for a battle that would not be resolved for almost a year.

In New York, Federalist Alexander Hamilton, who had been outvoted in his own delegation to the Convention, was now writing a series of papers urging adoption of the Constitution. Hamilton had been for the most part strangely silent in Philadelphia, but back in his home state he began to take a positive role. In letters which were later known under the title of *The Federalist* he poured forth

RATIFICATION of the CONSTITUTION		
State	**Date**	**Vote**
Delaware	Dec. 7, 1787	Unanimous
Pennsylvania	Dec. 12, 1787	46-23
New Jersey	Dec. 18, 1787	Unanimous
Georgia	Jan. 2, 1788	Unanimous
Connecticut	Jan. 9, 1788	128-40
Massachusetts	Feb. 6, 1788	187-168
Maryland	Apr. 26, 1788	63-11
South Carolina	May 23, 1788	149-73
New Hampshire	June 21, 1788	57-47
Virginia	June 25, 1788	89-79
New York	July 26, 1788	30-27
North Carolina	Nov. 21, 1789	195-77
Rhode Island	May 29, 1790	34-32

some of the country's most potent arguments for ratification. Hamilton's skillful pen was sorely needed in New York, for here two-thirds of the members of the state legislature were opposed to the Constitution.

Meanwhile, word had leaked across the border from Pennsylvania that some of the tactics used in the Pennsylvania legislature had been politically ruthless. Some opposition members who had tried to block ratification by staying away from the State House had been dragged bodily from their homes and forced to take their seats in order to assure a quorum when a vote was called. The Constitution was approved by a vote of 46-23.

Such reports were seized by New York's Anti-Federalists and used to illustrate what they called the tyrannical tendencies of Federalists. News spread rapidly through New York that when Pennsylvania's ratification was announced, residents of Carlisle had rioted in the town square and had burned Pennsylvania framer James Wilson in effigy.

Another crucial vote was taking place in Massachusetts. The state's Constitutional Convention met in Boston on January 9, 1788, with a majority of the 355 delegates opposed to ratification. Among the doubtful delegates were Samuel Adams and John Hancock, both of whom were finally persuaded to vote for the Constitution when a rally of Federalists, led by Paul Revere, was called, resulting in such enthusiasm on the part of the populace that even some out-and-out Anti-Federalists were swayed. It is said that the egotistical Hancock was bribed to vote for the Constitution with promises of support for the Presidency. The Massachusetts vote came on February 6, 1788. It favored ratification 187-168 and carried with it recommendations that certain amendments to the Constitution should be made at the earliest opportunity. These recommendations included some of the elements that were later to become "The Bill of Rights."

Still the powerful anti-federalist contingent in New York was blocking ratification in that state. But *The Federalist* papers were beginning to have their effect on public sentiment. Hamilton, with the help of James Madison and John Jay, was publishing in rapid succession the brilliant essays addressed "to the People of the State of New York." They appeared in such widely-read publications as *The Independent Journal* and the *New York Packet*. In his first paper, which appeared some time in the fall of 1787, Hamilton pointed out that, "among the most formidable of the obstacles which the new Constitution will have to encounter may be the obvious interest of a certain class of men in every State to resist all changes which may hazard a diminution of the power. . .they hold under the State establishments." He warned the public to consider the motivations of those who opposed the Constitution, though he added, "Candor will oblige us to admit that such men may be actuated by upright intentions; and it cannot be doubted that much of the opposition. . .will spring from sources

blameless at least, if not respectable—the honest errors of minds led astray by preconceived jealousies and fears. So numerous indeed and so powerful are the causes which serve to give a false bias to the judgment, that we will see wise and good men on the wrong as well as on the right side of questions of the first magnitude to society. This . . . would furnish a lesson of moderation to those who are ever so much persuaded of their being right in any controversy."

Hamilton signed his essay "Publius," and this pseudonym was used for the authorship of the entire series.

THE
FEDERALIST:
ADDRESSED TO THE
PEOPLE OF THE STATE OF NEW-YORK.

NUMBER I.
Introduction.

AFTER an unequivocal experience of the inefficacy of the subsisting federal government, you are called upon to deliberate on a new constitution for the United States of America. The subject speaks its own importance; comprehending in its consequences, nothing less than the existence of the UNION, the safety and welfare of the parts of which it is composed, the fate of an empire, in many respects, the most interesting in the world. It has been frequently remarked, that it seems to have been reserved to the people of this country, by their conduct and example, to decide the important question, whether societies of men are really capable or not, of establishing good government from reflection and choice, or whether they are forever destined to depend, for their political constitutions, on accident and force. If there be any truth in the remark, the crisis, at which we are arrived, may with propriety be regarded as the æra in which

A   that

One paper written by Madison also touched on the question of controversy and faction. "Among the numerous advantages promised by a well-constructed Union," he wrote, "none deserves to be more accurately developed than its tendency to break and control the violence of faction."

As to the causes of faction, Madison wrote, "The most common and durable source of factions has been the various and unequal distribution of property. Those who hold and those who are without property have ever formed distinct interests in society. . .The regulation of these various interfering interests forms the principal task of modern legislation."

Many of Hamilton's essays were devoted to analysis of individual sections of the Constitution and to the necessity for solidifying the Union. He dwelt at length upon the make-up of the Senate and House of Representatives, the proposed powers of the Executive and the functions of the Judiciary. In most of his essays he devoted considerable space to answering the arguments of Anti-Federalists.

One of the fundamental purposes of the Constitution was emphasized by Madison when he wrote, "In a confederacy founded on republican principles, and composed of republican members, the superintending government ought clearly to possess authority to defend the system against aristocratic or monarchical innovations . . . the (Constitution's) authority extends no further than to a *guaranty* of a republican form of government, which supposes a pre-existing government of the form which is to be guaranteed. As long, therefore, as the existing republican forms are continued by the States, they are guaranteed by the federal Constitution. The only restriction imposed on them is, that they shall not exchange republican for anti-republican Constitutions; a restriction which, it is presumed, will hardly be considered as a grievance."

This clearly and concisely spiked the guns of critics who argued that the new Constitution would abrogate the rights of individual states.

Hamilton pointed out that the document already guaranteed many of the rights that opponents sought to have included in a formal "Bill of Rights." He listed some of them as follows:

Article I, Section 9, Clause 2—The privilege of the writ of *habeas corpus* shall not be suspended, unless when in cases of rebellion or invasion the public safety may require it.

Clause 3—No bill of attainder or *ex-post-facto* law shall be passed.

Clause 8—No title of nobility shall be granted by the United States.

Article III, Section 2, Clause 3—The trial of all crimes, except in cases of impeachment, shall be by jury.

On the other hand, Hamilton argued, there was no need to guarantee rights where no restrictions had been established. "I go further," he said, "and affirm that bills of rights are not only unnecessary in the proposed Constitution, but would even be dangerous . . . For why declare that things shall not be done which there is no power to do? Why, for instance, should it be said that the liberty of the press shall not be restrained, when no power is given by which restrictions may be imposed? I will not contend that such a provision would confer a regulating power; but it is evident that it would furnish, to men disposed to usurp, a plausible pretence for claiming that power. They might urge with a semblance of reason, that the Constitution ought not to be charged with the absurdity of providing against the abuse of an authority which was not given, and that the provision against restraining the liberty of the press afforded a clear implication that a power to prescribe proper regulations concerning it was intended to be vested in the national government."

John Jay was not a delegate to the Constitutional Convention in Philadelphia, but his contribution to the *Federalist Papers* in behalf of ratification earns him a place with the other "Founding Fathers." Actually, Hamilton tried without success on several occasions to have Jay appointed as a delegate from New York to help bolster the Federalist forces from the Empire State. But John Jay like several other prominent New Yorkers favoring the Constitution was more highly esteemed outside of his state than within it. The ruling clique in New York, led by Governor Clinton, was strongly Anti-Federalist, yet it evidently represented a small but potent segment of the population.

Jay, who was born in New York City in 1745, was a graduate of King's College where he studied law. In 1768 he was admitted to the New York bar, and he was sent to represent his state in both the first and second Continental Congresses. In 1778, he was elected president of the Continental Congress. Later he served as Minister to Spain. He also went to Paris where he assisted Franklin in negotiating the Treaty with Britain. After working closely with

Hamilton in the effort to obtain New York's ratification of the Constitution, he was appointed first Chief Justice of the U.S. Supreme Court, and served in this important post from 1789 to 1795. He then was elected Governor of New York State.

Jay's dedication to the Constitution was reflected in his distinguished record on the Supreme Court, where he showed his courage and integrity by helping to make decisions that were sometimes politically unpopular.

While *The Federalist* papers were cajoling the populace in New York State, Hamilton succeeded in holding off a negative vote in the state legislature. "There are two to one against us," he wrote to a friend. "Tell the people of New York City the Convention shall never rise until the Constitution is adopted." During the summer of 1788 Hamilton, John Jay and a few other Federalists managed to keep debate going at the Convention in Poughkeepsie and to forestall a decision until more support could be mustered.

An even hotter debate was smouldering in Virginia. From Mount Vernon, George Washington wrote to the Marquis de Lafayette, "The plot thickens fast. A few short weeks will determine the political fate of America."

In Richmond, many of the framers and outspoken supporters of the Constitution attended the ratifying Convention. These included such great names as Washington, Madison, John Marshall and Henry "Lighthorse Harry" Lee. And to everyone's surprise Edmund Randolph agreed to support the Constitution even though he had refused to sign it. But the opposition, led by Patrick Henry, was equally powerful. Henry, the fiery orator of the Revolution, now loaned his talent to tirades against the new government. He referred to the proposed office of President as "an awful squinting towards monarchy."

"The Constitution is a threat to liberty," he thundered. "I would rather have a King, a House of Lords and Commons than the new government!"

During the course of this speech, Patrick Henry's rumbling was drowned in the crashing of real thunder. His warning that the happiness of half the human race was threatened by the proposed Constitution was punctuated by a violent storm. Lightning flashed in an ominously darkened sky and the proceedings were halted while Nature had her own say in the matter. After the weather cleared, James Madison patiently answered Henry's charges, and with his usual deliberate logic, won the support of many wavering delegates.

By this time, eight states had ratified the Constitution and it began to appear that dubious New Hampshire would soon throw in her lot with the Union. Yet everyone was well aware that without Virginia and New York, it would be a weak Union at best, and the crucial votes in those two important states were watched anxiously by the entire country.

Anti-Federalists in all parts of America were doing their best to bring about a negative vote in Virginia. They believed that failure in that state would result in a collapse of the entire Constitutional movement. At the very least, they hoped to force a second Constitutional Convention.

During the four-week debate at the State Convention in Richmond, the Constitution's weaknesses, as well as its strong points, were candidly exposed to public view. While others took an active part in the heated discussions the real debate narrowed to a confrontation of the two giants of rhetoric—Patrick Henry and James Madison. Yet toward the end of the debate, it was Randolph who summed up the situation and by doing so may have tipped the scales in favor of ratification when he said, "The accession of eight states has reduced our deliberations to the single question of *Union or no Union.*"

Fiery Patrick Henry (top) opposed the new Constitution. John Marshall defended its provisions in Virginia's ratifying convention.

When at last the vote was taken, even Patrick Henry's dire predictions of an American monarchy were softened by the realization that the first President would probably be a Virginian, the great George Washington, in whom the most nervous Anti-Federalist had utmost confidence.

Happily for the Union, Virginia's Convention voted 89-79 for ratification. At the same time they drafted a number of recommendations for amending the Constitution, calling particularly for some form of "bill of rights." This was on June 25, 1788.

Meanwhile, in Poughkeepsie, the New York Convention was still locked in debate, unaware of what had taken place in Richmond. Hamilton had shifted his attack on the Anti-Federalists from his written essays to masterful speeches on the floor of the Convention. He and John Jay led the fight for ratification day after day until the opposition was literally worn down and forced onto the defensive.

On July 2 word of Virginia's ratification reached the Congress in New York City. A

The news of Virginia's approval of the Constitution (broadside upper right) encouraged pro-Federalists at the deadlocked convention at Poughkeepsie. Celebrations which came later were as much in honor of Hamilton as the new Constitution.

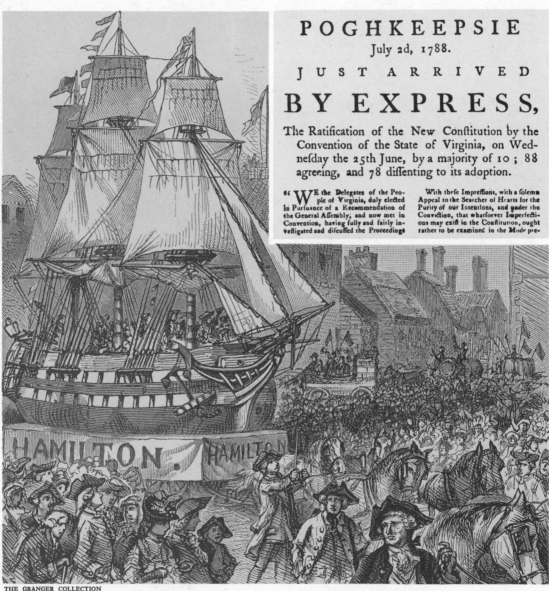

POGHKEEPSIE
July 2d, 1788.

JUST ARRIVED

BY EXPRESS,

The Ratification of the New Conftitution by the Convention of the State of Virginia, on Wednefday the 25th June, by a majority of 10 ; 88 agreeing, and 78 diffenting to its adoption.

"WE the Delegates of the People of Virginia, duly elected in Purfuance of a Recommendation of the General Affembly; and now met in Convention, having fully and fairly inveftigated and difcuffed the Proceedings

With thefe Impreffions, with a folemn Appeal to the Searcher of Hearts for the Purity of our Intentions, and under the Conviction, that whatfoever Imperfections may exift in the Conftitution, ought rather to be examined in the Mode pre-

Colonel Livingston volunteered to carry the important news to Poughkeepsie. He saddled a horse and set off on an eighty-four-mile ride, arriving in Poughkeepsie after a little less than eight hours in the saddle. His announcement that Virginia's final vote had favored the Constitution cheered the New York federation and helped turn the tide of the Convention.

The vote in Poughkeepsie came on July 26, 1788, 30-27 in favor of ratification. As in Massachusetts and Virginia, New York accompanied their ratification of the Constitution with recommendations for amend-

Approval by nine states was required
to make the Constitution binding.
Opposition came largely from rural areas
and was strongest in the crucial states
of New York and Virginia.

ments. Now eleven of the thirteen states, including the largest and most powerful, had adopted the new government. Even though a week later, on August 2, North Carolina's convention turned in an overwhelming negative vote of 184-84 and, although Rhode Island had not even called a ratifying convention, they could scarcely hold out against the swiftly-moving tide of nationalism. The Union was now secure.

The celebrations held to honor the ratification of the Constitution became a matter of civic pride as Boston, Philadelphia, Charleston, Richmond and New York tried to outdo one another in displays of patriotic ardor. Old accounts describe the mammoth parades and pageants of 1788. Stone masons, bricklayers, carpenters, wine merchants, brewers, and apprentices of every trade marched with tailors, hatters, wigmakers and other craftsmen behind banners and floats proclaiming support for the new government. In Philadelphia the city fathers selected the Fourth of July to honor the new Federal spirit. New York City celebrated on July 23, three days before its state convention ratified the Constitution. The New York celebration, although early, was as much in honor of Alexander Hamilton as it was in honor of the new Constitution. One of the floats which moved down Broadway to Bowling Green was a full-size frigate carrying 32 guns and emblazoned with the name *Hamilton*. A banquet followed in which 6,000 feasted and drank toasts.

With ratification assured it was time to set in motion the machinery of a new government. Congress had taken the first step on July 2, 1788, by appointing a committee to implement provisions of the Constitution. However, it was not until mid-September that a specific plan of action was approved. A presidential election was scheduled for March 4, 1789. Electors were chosen in the

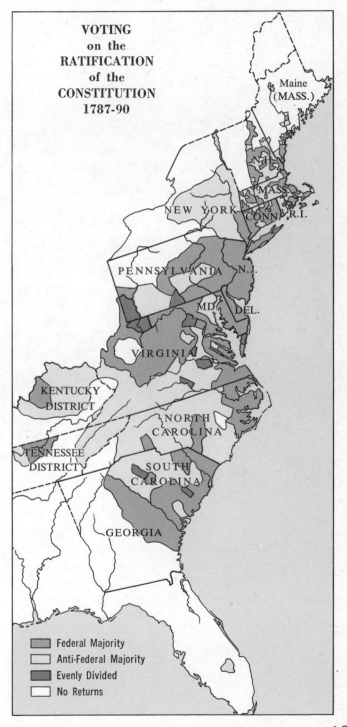

VOTING on the RATIFICATION of the CONSTITUTION 1787-90

Maine (MASS.)

N.H.
MASS.
NEW YORK
CONN. R.I.
PENNSYLVANIA
N.J.
MD. DEL.
VIRGINIA
KENTUCKY DISTRICT
NORTH CAROLINA
TENNESSEE DISTRICT
SOUTH CAROLINA
GEORGIA

Federal Majority
Anti-Federal Majority
Evenly Divided
No Returns

George Washington took the oath of office
and swore to uphold the Constitution on
the balcony of Federal Hall in New York City.

FEDERAL HALL NATIONAL MONUMENT

eleven states which had ratified the Constitution, and Congressional elections were
held so that, on the demise of the old
Congress under the Articles of Confederation,
a new one would be ready to take its place.
In those days the assembling of a Congress
was a slow process, since travel and communication were tedious. Though some members were at hand on March 4, it was not
until April 1789 that a quorum could be
reported in the House of Representatives
and in the Senate. They assembled in New

York City, where the old Congress still
officially resided but was in actuality already
defunct.

Meanwhile the electors had unanimously
picked George Washington to be the first
President. He arrived in New York on April
23, and the excited citizenry turned out in
force to cheer him. Washington's inaugura-
tion took place on April 30, when he was
sworn in by the Chancellor of New York,
Robert R. Livingston, on the balcony of
New York's Federal Hall.

196

The first inaugural address was given in the Senate chamber housed in Federal Hall. Shown here are the first and last pages of the address in Washington's own hand.

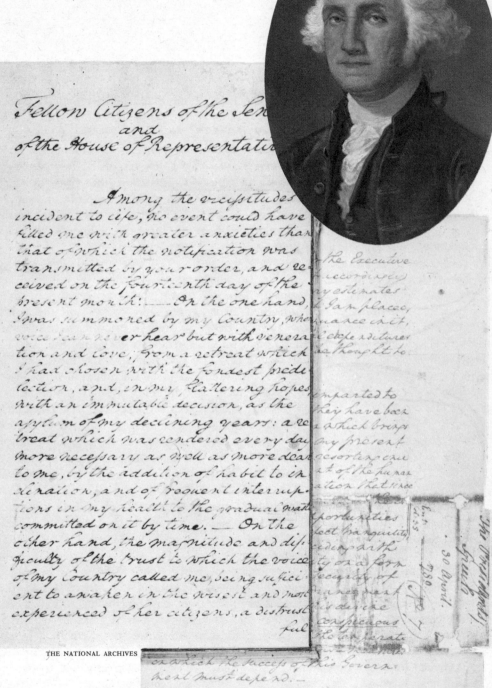

THE NATIONAL ARCHIVES

The Amending Process

Congress had scarcely opened its first formal session before the question of a Bill of Rights became the main order of business. Once again James Madison took the lead by introducing to Congress a proposal for amendments that would spell out a declaration of individual rights. Madison had been elected to the House of Representatives along with seven other framers of the Constitution: Roger Sherman, Thomas Fitzsimons, Nicholas Gilman, Daniel Carroll, Elbridge Gerry, George Clymer and Abraham Baldwin.

All the states recognized the need for a Bill of Rights in order to solidify support for the Constitution. Virginia and Massachusetts, in particular, had qualified their ratification with demands for such a bill, while Rhode Island and North Carolina were still holdouts, insisting that they would never join the Union until a satisfactory Bill of Rights was an integral part of the document.

Under Article V of the Constitution, which provided a routine for amendment, the Congress moved rapidly to draft a paper which could be sent to the states for approval. The draft was in the form of twelve proposals for amendment. The first two, which attempted to clarify the proportional representation in Congress and the size and composition of the House of Representatives, fell by the wayside and were never approved by the states. The other ten became law on December 15, 1791, after enough states had ratified them to make it official. Curiously, Virginia was one of the last of the states to approve the Bill of Rights, agreeing to it 18 months after Rhode Island had found it a satisfactory incentive to adopt the Constitution as a whole. This was in June 1790, and the action completed the union of all thirteen states, North Carolina having ratified the Constitution several months earlier.

Although the Bill of Rights consisted of ten amendments, only the first eight are genuinely concerned with fundamental rights of individuals. Amendments IX and X are more in the nature of further definitions of the powers of the federal government and of those reserved by the states and by the people. Despite Hamilton's earlier arguments that a Bill of Rights was superfluous to a Constitution that was designed to restrict and define the powers of government, most Federalists agreed that the specific provisions of these amendments were of the utmost importance.

The first amendment, in 45 words, guarantees freedom of religion, freedom of the press and the right of the people to assemble peaceably to petition the government for a redress of grievances. In one brief paragraph, Article I of the Bill of Rights assures Americans of the most vital ingredients for political freedom. Only recently, in the 1960's, Supreme Court interpretations have broadened the scope of the first amendment to include certain rights of privacy, freedom of association (as the right to join politically motivated organizations) and the right of expression through various forms of what has been termed "symbolic speech." These would include peaceful picketing and the wearing of armbands or buttons designed to promote causes or political ideas.

The second amendment, giving the people the right "to keep and bear Arms," has been a subject of controversy since the introduction of gun-control legislation. Those opposed to gun controls reason that the amendment guarantees the virtually unrestricted right of every citizen to own lethal weapons, yet the "right" is directly tied to the opening phrase of the amendment, "A well regulated Militia, being necessary to the security of a free State." It seems obvious that the framers had organized national defense in mind and not the right of individuals to carry arms indiscriminately or without restriction. At the

Interior view of Federal Hall
in New York where the House of
Representatives met. Here the
Bill of Rights was presented in 1789

FEDERAL HALL NATIONAL MONUMENT

The federal edifice was secure but not
complete until Rhode Island joined in 1790.

REDEUNT SATURNIA REGNA.
On the erection of the Eleventh PILLAR of the great National DOME, we beg leave most sincerely to felicitate " OUR DEAR COUNTRY."

The FEDERAL EDIFICE.

same time, it must be remembered that in the early days of the new nation a large proportion of the population lived in areas inhabited by hostile Indians, where the necessity to bear arms was unquestioned.

Concerned with the dangers of excessive military authority, the Congress included the third amendment, prohibiting soldiers in peacetime from occupying private dwellings without the consent of owners, or in wartime except "in a manner to be prescribed by law."

As a natural corollary to the third, the fourth amendment secures citizens against unreasonable searches of their persons or property. Here, the question has become what type of search is "unreasonable." There have been a great many legal cases which revolved around this question. Generally the courts have considered that search without a warrant is illegal, although warrantless searches have been upheld where they have been "incident to a valid arrest," where they have been proved necessary to protect an arresting officer, or to prevent destruction of important evidence. Recent police invasions of quarters occupied by militant groups have again raised controversy over application of the fourth amendment.

Finally, Amendments V, VI, VII and VIII deal with proper legal procedures to be followed in criminal and civil suits. These amendments are designed to protect Americans from arbitrary arrest or prosecution and to minimize the possibility of innocent persons being falsely convicted.

In 1963 an important case (Gideon vs. Wainwright) established the right of indigents to expert counsel. Since the sixth amendment guarantees a citizen's right to have "Assistance of Counsel for his defense," it seems obvious that this was meant to apply whether or not the defendant could afford a lawyer's fee. Yet many cases in the past went against poverty-stricken citizens and in favor of wealthy persons simply because the latter had the best legal talent available while the poor defendants had none.

The Bill of Rights, despite vagueness of some of its stipulations, has provided the Supreme Court with guidelines for their decisions in thousands of cases over the years.

As the nation has grown in area and in population it has become increasingly difficult for amendments to be passed through all the complex machinery of the many states. Because of this, and perhaps because previous amendments have rendered additional ones less necessary, the number of new amendments to the Constitution has decreased over the years.

Of all the amendments since the Bill of Rights probably the thirteenth was the most important and had the most far-reaching effects upon the nation. This brief statement was the culmination of bitter debates at the Constitutional Convention, of years of worsening relations between the Northern and the Southern states and of a terribly fratricidal war that nearly split the nation asunder:

"Neither slavery nor involuntary servitude, except as a punishment for crime whereof the party shall have been duly convicted, shall exist within the United States, or any place subject to their jurisdiction."

When the Civil War broke with all its fury in 1860, the animosities and the pent-up frustrations of a nation divided over a fundamental issue of freedom surfaced in all their ugliest forms. Abraham Lincoln, whose election had precipitated the South's secession, was a sworn opponent of slavery. Although technically the North fought over the illegality of secession, as the British publication *Spectator* put it in an 1861 editorial, "The quarrel, cover it with cotton as we may, is between freedom and slavery, right and wrong, the dominion of God and the dominion of the Devil . . ."

Beyond that the issue was whether or not the United States Constitution, for all its noble rhetoric and for all the magnificent words of the framers in its support, could endure when a gross injustice was being perpetrated under its aegis. Such an issue is not unknown in America today, though in the 1860's the problem was more specific and more concentrated geographically than any contemporary cause of dissension. With the Civil War at its bloody height in 1862, Lincoln yielded to the pressures of the public and of his own conscience, and on July 22 he presented his cabinet with a draft for the emancipation proclamation. Secretary of State Seward urged the President not to issue the proclamation at that time, arguing that foreign countries would view it as the last desperate gasp of a failing government. For the time being Lincoln let the matter rest, but after a major Union victory at Antietam the proclamation was formally issued on September 22. Contrary to what might have been supposed, Northern opinion on Lincoln's action was divided.

In order to establish Lincoln's proclamation as national law, the thirteenth amendment was proposed in Congress on February 1, 1865, and was finally adopted by the states and incorporated into the Constitution in December of that year.

Some three months later Congress passed a Civil Rights Act, which declared that all persons born in the United States and not subject to any foreign power, excluding Indians not taxed, were citizens of the United States and were to enjoy all the rights and privileges of full citizenship. The act was passed to protect freed slaves who, in some areas, were being restricted by discriminatory local laws. President Andrew Johnson vetoed the bill and, in his message to the Senate explaining his action, he pointed out that it seemed unnecessary to declare the freed men citizens.

Although Congress overrode the veto, doubts raised as to the act's constitutionality led to the inclusion of most of its provisions in another amendment — the fourteenth — which became a part of the Constitution on July 28, 1868. This and the brief fifteenth amendment finally gave all black Americans full citizenship and the right to vote. The fifteenth amendment, officially added to the Constitution on March 30, 1870, reads:

"The right of citizens of the United States to vote shall not be denied or abridged by the United States or by any State on account of race, color, or previous condition of servitude."

Although states in the South have attempted to circumvent this amendment by various "vote qualification" laws, the Supreme Court has consistently upheld the right of every citizen to vote and its decisions have invariably struck down Southern attempts to bar black voters. Demonstrations have brought the issue before the public. The battle goes on, and further civil rights legislation has been passed to implement the Constitutional rights of Negroes.

One of the more recent amendments, the twenty-fourth, which was adopted in 1964, was created to circumvent one of the methods which had long been used to keep poor blacks from the polls. This amendment states that no citizen shall be denied his right to vote "by reason of failure to pay any poll tax or other tax."

It is a curious fact of American history that the Constitutional amendments to give black males the right to vote were passed long before any women could cast their ballots for government leaders and other officials. Not until 1920 were women granted voting rights through the nineteenth amendment. Adoption of this amendment came only after long and often bitter campaigning by militant women whose strength was greatly enhanced by the various "suffragette" organizations around the country. The most famous leader of the suffragettes was Susan B. Anthony, who began her political career by organizing the Women's Temperance Society of New York. Miss Anthony, who was born in Adams, Mass., in 1820, was editor of a publication which advocated female suffrage and other reforms of benefit to women. Unfortunately Susan Anthony died in 1906, fourteen years before the nineteenth amendment was adopted, but her work, which was widely ridiculed by both men and women of her time, did much to achieve the important rights which members of her sex now enjoy.

It is worth noting that reforms in America have generally been achieved against seemingly impossible odds. Rights for black citizens had to be voted for by white citizens who already enjoyed those rights. Suffrage for women was passed by the men who owned the exclusive voting rights at the time.

With the upheavals of the last decade, the prophetic words of Gouverneur Morris and George Mason seem to echo with hollow mockery in the roped-off gallery of Independence Hall. The reverberations of Mason's cry, particularly, remain to haunt us: *"Providence punishes national sins by national calamities."*

Yet those who argue that, because of current injustices, the Constitution has outlived its usefulness seem bent on destroying the nation's greatest repository of justice. It is always a fatal error to blame a system for the shortcomings of its human operators. The evil in people is the very reason for the existence of law, and if all men were honest, fair-minded and unprejudiced, there would be no need for a Constitution or for the legislation passed and executed within its framework.

America's great document still stands as the bulwark of freedom and justice despite the human frailties of the men who framed it and of those who have attempted to interpret it for more than 180 years. It has been the model for free governments throughout the world, for state constitutions, and for the United Nations charter. It has survived financial crisis, insurrection, a great civil war and the perpetual attacks of political extremists. If the human rights it was designed to protect are ever lost, it will not be because the Constitution has failed America but because Americans have failed the precious heritage given to them by the men who argued and sweltered and worried during the long, hot summer months of 1787.

Chapter Nine

The Immortal Document

The engrossed copy of the
Constitution is on display in
the National Archives in Washington, D.C.
The first page is reproduced here
with the remainder on subsequent pages.

The Constitution of the United States

PREAMBLE

WE THE PEOPLE of the United States, in order to form a more perfect Union, establish justice, insure domestic tranquility, provide for the common defense, promote the general welfare, and secure the blessings of liberty to ourselves and our posterity, do ordain and establish this Constitution for the United States of America.

THE CONGRESS

ARTICLE I

SECTION 1. All legislative powers herein granted shall be vested in a Congress of the United States, which shall consist of a Senate and House of Representatives.

SECTION 2. The House of Representatives shall be composed of members chosen every second year by the people of the several States, and the electors in each State shall have the qualifications requisite for electors of the most numerous branch of the State Legislature.

No person shall be a representative who shall not have attained to the age of twenty-five years, and been seven years a citizen of the United States, and who shall not, when elected, be an inhabitant of that State in which he shall be chosen.

Representatives and direct taxes shall be apportioned among the several States which may be included within this Union, according to their respective numbers, which shall be determined by adding to the whole number of free persons, including those bound to service for a term of years, and excluding Indians not taxed, three-fifths of all other persons. The actual enumeration shall be made within three years after the first meeting of the Congress of the United States, and within every subsequent term of ten years, in such manner as they shall by law direct. The number of representatives shall not exceed one for every thirty thousand, but each State shall have at least one representative; and until such enumeration shall be made, the State of New Hampshire shall be entitled to choose three, Massachusetts eight, Rhode Island and Providence Plantations one, Connecticut five, New York six, New Jersey four, Pennsylvania eight, Delaware one, Maryland six, Virginia ten, North Carolina five, South Carolina five, and Georgia three.

When vacancies happen in the representation from any State, the executive authority thereof shall issue writs of election to fill such vacancies.

The House of Representatives shall choose their Speaker and other officers; and shall have the sole power of impeachment.

SECTION 3. The Senate of the United States shall be composed of two senators from each State, chosen by the legislature thereof, for six years and each senator shall have one vote.

Immediately after they shall be assembled in consequence of the first election, they shall be divided as equally as may be into three classes. The seats of the senators of the first class shall be vacated at the expiration of the second year, of the second class at the expiration of the fourth year, and of the third class at the expiration of the sixth year, so that one-third may be chosen every second year; and if vacancies happen by resignation, or otherwise, during the recess of the legislature of any State, the executive thereof may make temporary appointments until the next meeting of the legislature, which shall then fill such vacancies.

No person shall be a senator who shall not have attained to the age of thirty years, and been nine years a citizen of the United States, and who shall not, when elected, be an inhabitant of that State for which he shall be chosen.

The Vice President of the United States shall be President of the Senate, but shall have no vote, unless they be equally divided.

The Senate shall choose their other officers, and also a President pro tempore, in the absence of the Vice President, or when he shall exercise the office of President of the United States.

The Senate shall have the sole power to try all impeachments. When sitting for that purpose, they shall be on oath or affirmation. When the President of the United States is tried, the Chief Justice shall preside: And no person shall be convicted without the concurrence of two-thirds of the members present.

Judgment in cases of impeachment shall not extend further than to removal from office, and disqualification to hold and enjoy any office of honor, trust or profit under the United States: but the party convicted shall nevertheless be liable and subject to indictment, trial, judgment and punishment, according to law.

SECTION 4. The times, places and manner of holding elections for senators and representatives, shall be prescribed in each State by the legislature thereof; but the Congress may at any time by law make or

United States; If he approve he shall sign it, but if not he shall return it, with his Objections to that House in which it shall have originated, who shall enter the Objections at large on their Journal, and proceed to reconsider it. If after such Reconsideration two thirds of that House shall agree to pass the Bill, it shall be sent, together with the Objections, to the other House, by which it shall likewise be reconsidered, and if approved by two thirds of that House, it shall become a Law. But in all such Cases the Votes of both Houses shall be determined by yeas and Nays, and the Names of the Persons voting for and against the Bill shall be entered on the Journal of each House respectively. If any Bill shall not be returned by the President within ten Days (Sundays excepted) after it shall have been presented to him, the Same shall be a Law, in like Manner as if he had signed it, unless the Congress by their Adjournment prevent its Return, in which Case it shall not be a Law.

Every Order, Resolution, or Vote to which the Concurrence of the Senate and House of Representatives may be necessary (except on a question of Adjournment) shall be presented to the President of the United States; and before the Same shall take Effect, shall be approved by him, or being disapproved by him, shall be repassed by two thirds of the Senate and House of Representatives, according to the Rules and Limitations prescribed in the Case of a Bill.

Section. 8. The Congress shall have Power To lay and collect Taxes, Duties, Imposts and Excises, to pay the Debts and provide for the common Defence and general Welfare of the United States; but all Duties, Imposts and Excises shall be uniform throughout the United States;

To borrow Money on the credit of the United States;

To regulate Commerce with foreign Nations, and among the several States, and with the Indian Tribes;

To establish an uniform Rule of Naturalization, and uniform Laws on the subject of Bankruptcies throughout the United States;

To coin Money, regulate the Value thereof, and of foreign Coin, and fix the Standard of Weights and Measures;

To provide for the Punishment of counterfeiting the Securities and current Coin of the United States;

To establish Post Offices and post Roads;

To promote the Progress of Science and useful Arts, by securing for limited Times to Authors and Inventors the exclusive Right to their respective Writings and Discoveries;

To constitute Tribunals inferior to the supreme Court;

To define and punish Piracies and Felonies committed on the high Seas, and Offences against the Law of Nations;

To declare War, grant Letters of Marque and Reprisal, and make Rules concerning Captures on Land and Water;

To raise and support Armies, but no Appropriation of Money to that Use shall be for a longer Term than two Years;

To provide and maintain a Navy;

To make Rules for the Government and Regulation of the land and naval Forces;

To provide for calling forth the Militia to execute the Laws of the Union, suppress Insurrections and repel Invasions;

To provide for organizing, arming, and disciplining, the Militia, and for governing such Part of them as may be employed in the Service of the United States, reserving to the States respectively, the Appointment of the Officers, and the Authority of training the Militia according to the discipline prescribed by Congress;

To exercise exclusive Legislation in all Cases whatsoever, over such District (not exceeding ten Miles square) as may, by Cession of particular States, and the Acceptance of Congress, become the Seat of the Government of the United States, and to exercise like Authority over all Places purchased by the Consent of the Legislature of the State in which the Same shall be, for the Erection of Forts, Magazines, Arsenals, dock-Yards, and other needful Buildings;—And

To make all Laws which shall be necessary and proper for carrying into Execution the foregoing Powers, and all other Powers vested by this Constitution in the Government of the United States, or in any Department or Officer thereof.

Section. 9. The Migration or Importation of such Persons as any of the States now existing shall think proper to admit, shall not be prohibited by the Congress prior to the Year one thousand eight hundred and eight, but a Tax or duty may be imposed on such Importation, not exceeding ten dollars for each Person.

The Privilege of the Writ of Habeas Corpus shall not be suspended, unless when in Cases of Rebellion or Invasion the public Safety may require it.

No Bill of Attainder or ex post facto Law shall be passed.

No Capitation, or other direct, Tax shall be laid, unless in Proportion to the Census or Enumeration herein before directed to be taken.

No Tax or Duty shall be laid on Articles exported from any State.

No Preference shall be given by any Regulation of Commerce or Revenue to the Ports of one State over those of another: nor shall Vessels bound to, or from, one State, be obliged to enter, clear, or pay Duties in another.

No Money shall be drawn from the Treasury, but in Consequence of Appropriations made by Law; and a regular Statement and Account of the Receipts and Expenditures of all public Money shall be published from time to time.

No Title of Nobility shall be granted by the United States: And no Person holding any Office of Profit or Trust under them, shall, without the Consent of the Congress, accept of any present, Emolument, Office, or Title, of any kind whatever, from any King, Prince, or foreign State.

Section. 10. No State shall enter into any Treaty, Alliance, or Confederation; grant Letters of Marque and Reprisal; coin Money; emit Bills of Credit; make any Thing but gold and silver Coin a Tender in Payment of Debts; pass any Bill of Attainder, ex post facto Law, or Law impairing the Obligation of Contracts, or grant any Title of Nobility.

No State shall, without the Consent of the Congress, lay any Imposts or Duties on Imports or Exports, except what may be absolutely necessary for executing its inspection Laws: and the net Produce of all Duties and Imposts, laid by any State on Imports or Exports, shall be for the Use of the Treasury of the United States; and all such Laws shall be subject to the Revision and Controul of the Congress.

No State shall, without the Consent of Congress, lay any Duty of Tonnage, keep Troops, or Ships of War in time of Peace, enter into any Agreement or Compact with another State, or with a foreign Power, or engage in War, unless actually invaded, or in such imminent Danger as will not admit of delay.

Article. II.

Section. 1. The executive Power shall be vested in a President of the United States of America. He shall hold his Office during the Term of four Years, and, together with the Vice President, chosen for the same Term, be elected, as follows:

Each State shall appoint, in such Manner as the Legislature thereof may direct, a Number of Electors, equal to the whole Number of Senators and Representatives to which the State may be entitled in the Congress: but no Senator or Representative, or Person holding an Office of Trust or Profit under the United States, shall be appointed an Elector.

The Electors shall meet in their respective States, and vote by Ballot for two Persons, of whom one at least shall not be an Inhabitant of alter such regulations, except as to the places of choosing senators.

The Congress shall assemble at least once in every year, and such meeting shall be on the first Monday in December, unless they shall by law appoint a different day.

SECTION 5. Each house shall be the judge of the elections, returns and qualifications of its own members, and a majority of each shall constitute a quorum to do business; but a smaller number may adjourn from day to day, and may be authorized to compel the attendance of absent members, in such manner, and under such penalties as each house may provide.

Each house may determine the rules of its proceedings, punish its members for disorderly behaviour, and, with the concurrence of two-thirds, expel a member.

Each house shall keep a journal of its proceedings, and from time to time publish the same, excepting such parts as may in their judgment require secrecy; and the yeas and nays of the members of either house on any question shall, at the desire of one-fifth of those present, be entered on the journal.

Neither house, during the session of Congress, shall, without the consent of the other, adjourn for more than three days, nor to any other place than that in which the two houses shall be sitting.

SECTION 6. The senators and representatives shall receive a compensation for their services, to be ascertained by law, and paid out of the Treasury of the United States. They shall in all cases, except treason, felony and breach of the peace, be privileged from arrest during their attendance at the session of their respective houses, and in going to and returning from the same; and for any speech or debate in either house, they shall not be questioned in any other place.

No senator or representative shall, during the time for which he was elected, be appointed to any civil office under the authority of the United States, which shall have been created, or the emoluments whereof shall have been increased during such time; and no person holding any office under the United States, shall be a member of either house during his continuance in office.

SECTION 7. All bills for raising revenue shall originate in the House of Representatives; but the Senate may propose or concur with amendments as on other bills.

Every bill which shall have passed the House of Representatives and the Senate, shall, before it becomes a law, be presented to the President of the United States; if he approves he shall sign it, but if not he shall return it, with his objections to that house in which it shall have originated, who shall enter the objections at large on their journal, and proceed to reconsider it. If after such reconsideration two-thirds of that House shall agree to pass the bill, it shall be sent, together with the objections, to the other House, by which it shall likewise be reconsidered, and if approved by two-thirds of that House, it shall become a law. But in all such cases the votes of both Houses shall be determined by yeas and nays, and the names of the persons voting for and against the bill shall be entered on the journal of each House respectively. If any bill shall not be returned by the President within ten days (Sundays excepted) after it shall have been presented to him, the same shall be a law, in like manner as if he had signed it, unless the Congress by their adjournment prevent its return, in which case it shall not be a law.

Every order, resolution, or vote to which the concurrence of the Senate and House of Representatives may be necessary (except on a question of adjournment) shall be presented to· the President of the United States; and before the same shall take effect shall be approved by him or being disapproved by him, shall be repassed by two-thirds of the Senate and House of Representatives, according to the rules and limitations prescribed in the case of a bill.

POWERS GRANTED

SECTION 8. The Congress shall have power to lay and collect taxes, duties, imposts and excises, to pay the debts and provide for the common defense and general welfare of the United States; but all duties, imposts and excises shall be uniform throughout the United States;

To borrow money on the credit of the United States;

To regulate commerce with foreign nations, and among the several States, and with the Indian tribes;

To establish a uniform rule of naturalization, and uniform laws on the subject of bankruptcies throughout the United States;

To coin money, regulate the value thereof, and of foreign coin, and fix the standard of weights and measures;

To provide for the punishment of counterfeiting the securities and current coin of the United States;

the same State with themselves. And they shall make a List of all the Persons voted for, and of the Number of Votes for each; which List they shall sign and certify, and transmit sealed to the Seat of the Government of the United States, directed to the President of the Senate. The President of the Senate shall, in the Presence of the Senate and House of Representatives, open all the Certificates, and the Votes shall then be counted. The Person having the greatest Number of Votes shall be the President, if such Number be a Majority of the whole Number of Electors appointed; and if there be more than one who have such Majority, and have an equal Number of Votes, then the House of Representatives shall immediately chuse by Ballot one of them for President; and if no Person have a Majority, then from the five highest on the List the said House shall in like Manner chuse the President. But in chusing the President, the Votes shall be taken by States, the Representation from each State having one Vote; A quorum for this Purpose shall consist of a Member or Members from two thirds of the States, and a Majority of all the States shall be necessary to a Choice. In every Case, after the Choice of the President, the Person having the greatest Number of Votes of the Electors shall be the Vice President. But if there should remain two or more who have equal Votes, the Senate shall chuse from them by Ballot the Vice President.

The Congress may determine the Time of chusing the Electors, and the Day on which they shall give their Votes; which Day shall be the same throughout the United States.

No Person except a natural born Citizen, or a Citizen of the United States, at the time of the Adoption of this Constitution, shall be eligible to the Office of President; neither shall any Person be eligible to that Office who shall not have attained to the Age of thirty five Years, and been fourteen Years a Resident within the United States.

In Case of the Removal of the President from Office, or of his Death, Resignation, or Inability to discharge the Powers and Duties of the said Office, the same shall devolve on the Vice President, and the Congress may by Law provide for the Case of Removal, Death, Resignation or Inability, both of the President and Vice President, declaring what Officer shall then act as President, and such Officer shall act accordingly, until the Disability be removed, or a President shall be elected.

The President shall, at stated Times, receive for his Services, a Compensation, which shall neither be increased nor diminished during the Period for which he shall have been elected, and he shall not receive within that Period any other Emolument from the United States, or any of them.

Before he enter on the Execution of his Office, he shall take the following Oath or Affirmation:—"I do solemnly swear (or affirm) that I will faithfully execute the Office of President of the United States, and will to the best of my Ability, preserve, protect and defend the Constitution of the United States."

Section 2. The President shall be Commander in Chief of the Army and Navy of the United States, and of the Militia of the several States, when called into the actual Service of the United States; he may require the Opinion, in writing, of the principal Officer in each of the executive Departments, upon any Subject relating to the Duties of their respective Offices, and he shall have Power to grant Reprieves and Pardons for Offences against the United States, except in Cases of Impeachment.

He shall have Power, by and with the Advice and Consent of the Senate, to make Treaties, provided two thirds of the Senators present concur; and he shall nominate, and by and with the Advice and Consent of the Senate, shall appoint Ambassadors, other public Ministers and Consuls, Judges of the supreme Court, and all other Officers of the United States, whose Appointments are not herein otherwise provided for, and which shall be established by Law: but the Congress may by Law vest the Appointment of such inferior Officers, as they think proper, in the President alone, in the Courts of Law, or in the Heads of Departments.

The President shall have Power to fill up all Vacancies that may happen during the Recess of the Senate, by granting Commissions which shall expire at the End of their next Session.

Section 3. He shall from time to time give to the Congress Information of the State of the Union, and recommend to their Consideration such Measures as he shall judge necessary and expedient; he may, on extraordinary Occasions, convene both Houses, or either of them, and in Case of Disagreement between them, with Respect to the Time of Adjournment, he may adjourn them to such Time as he shall think proper; he shall receive Ambassadors and other public Ministers; he shall take Care that the Laws be faithfully executed, and shall Commission all the Officers of the United States.

Section 4. The President, Vice President and all civil Officers of the United States, shall be removed from Office on Impeachment for, and Conviction of, Treason, Bribery, or other high Crimes and Misdemeanors.

Article III.

Section 1. The judicial Power of the United States, shall be vested in one supreme Court, and in such inferior Courts as the Congress may from time to time ordain and establish. The Judges, both of the supreme and inferior Courts, shall hold their Offices during good Behaviour, and shall, at stated Times, receive for their Services, a Compensation, which shall not be diminished during their Continuance in Office.

Section 2. The judicial Power shall extend to all Cases, in Law and Equity, arising under this Constitution, the Laws of the United States, and Treaties made, or which shall be made, under their Authority;—to all Cases affecting Ambassadors, other public Ministers and Consuls;—to all Cases of admiralty and maritime Jurisdiction;—to Controversies to which the United States shall be a Party;—to Controversies between two or more States;—between a State and Citizens of another State;—between Citizens of different States;—between Citizens of the same State claiming Lands under Grants of different States, and between a State, or the Citizens thereof, and foreign States, Citizens or Subjects.

In all Cases affecting Ambassadors, other public Ministers and Consuls, and those in which a State shall be Party, the supreme Court shall have original Jurisdiction. In all the other Cases before mentioned, the supreme Court shall have appellate Jurisdiction, both as to Law and Fact, with such Exceptions, and under such Regulations as the Congress shall make.

The Trial of all Crimes, except in Cases of Impeachment, shall be by Jury; and such Trial shall be held in the State where the said Crimes shall have been committed; but when not committed within any State, the Trial shall be at such Place or Places as the Congress may by Law have directed.

Section 3. Treason against the United States, shall consist only in levying War against them, or in adhering to their Enemies, giving them Aid and Comfort. No Person shall be convicted of Treason unless on the Testimony of two Witnesses to the same overt Act, or on Confession in open Court.

The Congress shall have Power to declare the Punishment of Treason, but no Attainder of Treason shall work Corruption of Blood, or Forfeiture except during the Life of the Person attainted.

Article IV.

Section 1. Full Faith and Credit shall be given in each State to the public Acts, Records, and judicial Proceedings of every other State. And the

To establish post offices and post roads;

To promote the progress of science and useful arts, by securing for limited times to authors and inventors the exclusive right to their respective writings and discoveries;

To constitute tribunals inferior to the Supreme Court;

To define and punish piracies and felonies committed on the high seas, and offenses against the law of nations;

To declare war, grant letters of marque and reprisal, and make rules concerning captures on land and water;

To raise and support armies, but no appropriation of money to that use shall be for a longer term than two years;

To provide and maintain a Navy;

To make rules for the government and regulation of the land and naval forces;

To provide for calling forth the militia to execute the laws of the Union, suppress insurrections and repel invasions;

To provide for organizing, arming, and disciplining the militia, and for governing such part of them as may be employed in the service of the United States, reserving to the States respectively the appointment of the officers, and the authority of training the militia according to the discipline prescribed by Congress;

To exercise exclusive legislation in all cases whatsoever, over such district (not exceeding ten miles square) as may, by cession of particular States, and the acceptance of Congress, become the seat of the Government of the United States, and to exercise like authority over all places purchased by the consent of the legislature of the State in which the same shall be, for the erection of forts, magazines, arsenals, dockyards, and other needful buildings;—And

To make all laws which shall be necessary and proper for carrying into execution the foregoing powers, and all other powers vested by this Constitution in the Government of the United States, or in any department or officer thereof.

POWERS DENIED

SECTION 9. The migration or importation of such persons as any of the States now existing shall think proper to admit, shall not be prohibited by the Congress prior to the year one thousand eight hundred and eight, but a tax or duty may be imposed on such importation, not exceeding ten dollars for each person.

The privilege of the writ of habeas corpus shall not be suspended, unless when in cases of rebellion or invasion the public safety may require it.

No bill of attainder or ex-post-facto law shall be passed.

No capitation, or other direct, tax shall be laid, unless in proportion to the census or enumeration herein before directed to be taken.

No tax or duty shall be laid on articles exported from any State.

No preference shall be given by any regulation of commerce or revenue to the ports of one State over those of another: nor shall vessels bound to, or from, one State, be obliged to enter, clear, or pay duties in another.

No money shall be drawn from the Treasury, but in consequence of appropriations made by law; and a regular statement and account of the receipts and expenditures of all public money shall be published from time to time.

No title of nobility shall be granted by the United States: And no person holding any office of profit or trust under them, shall, without the consent of the Congress, accept of any present, emolument, office, or title, of any kind whatever, from any King, Prince, or foreign State.

SECTION 10. No State shall enter into any treaty, alliance, or confederation; grant letters of marque and reprisal; coin money; emit bills of credit; make any thing but gold and silver coin a tender in payment of debts; pass any bill of attainder, ex-post-facto law, or law impairing the obligation of contracts, or grant any title of nobility.

No State shall, without the consent of the Congress, lay any imposts or duties on imports or exports, except what may be absolutely necessary for executing its inspection laws: and the net produce of all duties and imposts, laid by any State on imports or exports, shall be for the use of the Treasury of the United States; and all such laws shall be subject to the revision and control of the Congress.

No State shall, without the consent of Congress, lay any duty of tonnage, keep troops, or ships of war in time of peace, enter into any agreement or compact with another State, or with a foreign power, or engage in war, unless actually invaded, or in such imminent danger as will not admit of delay.

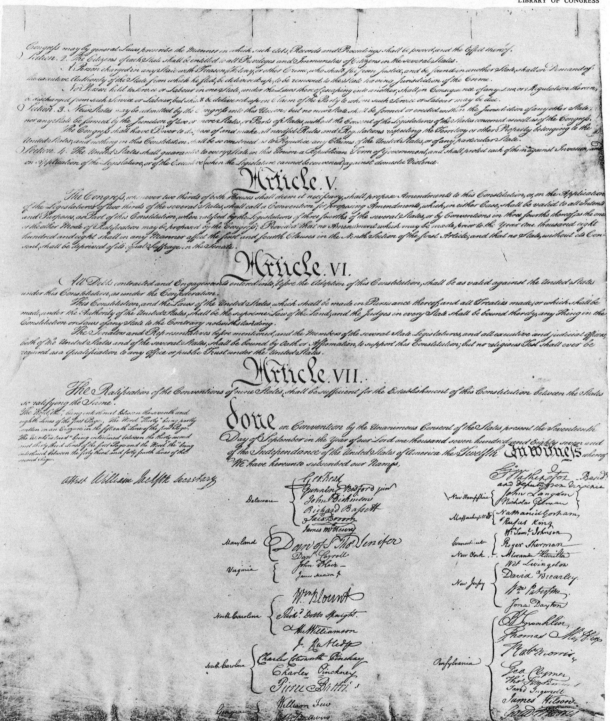

THE PRESIDENCY

ARTICLE II

SECTION 1. The executive power shall be vested in a President of the United States of America. He shall hold his office during the term of four years, and, together with the Vice President, chosen for the same term, be elected, as follows:

Each State shall appoint, in such manner as the legislature thereof may direct, a number of electors, equal to the whole number of senators and representatives to which the State may be entitled in the Congress: but no senator or representative, or person holding an office of trust or profit under the United States, shall be appointed an elector.

The electors shall meet in their respective States, and vote by ballot for two persons, of whom one at least shall not be an inhabitant of the same State with themselves. And they shall make a list of all the persons voted for, and of the number of votes for each; which list they shall sign and certify, and transmit sealed to the seat of the Government of the United States, directed to the President of the Senate. The President of the Senate shall, in the presence of the Senate and House of Representatives, open all the certificates, and the votes shall then be counted. The person having the greatest number of votes shall be the President, if such number be a majority of the whole number of electors appointed; and if there be more than one who have such majority, and have an equal number of votes, then the House of Representatives shall immediately choose by ballot one of them for President; and if no person have a majority, then from the five highest on the list the said House shall in like manner choose the President. But in choosing the President, the votes shall be taken by States, the representation from each State having one vote; a quorum for this purpose shall consist of a member or members from two-thirds of the States, and a majority of all the States shall be necessary to a choice. In every case, after the choice of the President, the person having the greatest number of votes of the electors shall be the Vice President. But if there should remain two or more who have equal votes, the Senate shall choose from them by ballot the Vice President.

The Congress may determine the time of choosing the electors, and the day on which they shall give their votes; which day shall be the same throughout the United States.

No person except a natural born citizen, or a citizen of the United States, at the time of the adoption of this Constitution, shall be eligible to the office of President; neither shall any person be eligible to that office who shall not have attained to the age of thirty-five years, and been fourteen years a resident within the United States.

In case of the removal of the President from office, or of his death, resignation, or inability to discharge the powers and duties of the said office, the same shall devolve on the Vice President, and the Congress may by law provide for the case of removal, death, resignation, or inability, both of the President and Vice President, declaring what officer shall then act as President, and such officer shall act accordingly, until the disability be removed, or a President shall be elected.

The President shall, at stated times, receive for his services, a compensation, which shall neither be increased nor diminished during the period for which he shall have been elected, and he shall not receive within that period any other emolument from the United States, or any of them.

Before he enter on the execution of his office, he shall take the following oath or affirmation:—"I do solemnly swear (or affirm) that I will faithfully execute the office of President of the United States, and will to the best of my ability, preserve, protect and defend the Constitution of the United States."

SECTION 2. The President shall be Commander in Chief of the Army and Navy of the United States, and of the militia of the several States, when called into the actual service of the United States; he may require the opinion, in writing, of the principal officer in each of the Executive Departments, upon any subject relating to the duties of their respective offices, and he shall have power to grant reprieves and pardons for offenses against the United States, except in cases of impeachment.

He shall have power, by and with the advice and consent of the Senate, to make treaties, provided two-thirds of the Senators present concur; and he shall nominate, and by and with the advice and consent of the Senate, shall appoint ambassadors, other public ministers and consuls, judges of the Supreme Court, and all other officers of the United States, whose appointments are not herein otherwise provided for, and which shall be established by law: but the Congress may by law vest the appointment of such inferior officers, as they think proper, in the President alone, in the courts of law, or in the heads of departments.

The President shall have power to fill up all vacancies that may happen during the recess of the Senate, by granting commissions which shall expire at the end of their next session.

SECTION 3. He shall from time to time give to the Congress information of the state of the Union, and recommend to their consideration such measures as he shall judge necessary and expedient; he may, on extraordinary occasions, convene both houses, or either of them, and in case of disagreement between them, with respect to the time of adjournment, he may adjourn them to such time as he shall think proper; he shall receive ambassadors and other public ministers; he shall take care that the laws be faithfully executed, and shall commission all the officers of the United States.

SECTION 4. The President, Vice President and all civil officers of the United States, shall be removed from office on impeachment for, and conviction of, treason, bribery, or other high crimes and misdemeanors.

THE JUDICIAL POWER

ARTICLE III

SECTION 1. The judicial power of the United States shall be vested in one Supreme Court, and in such inferior courts as the Congress may from time to time ordain and establish. The judges, both of the supreme and inferior courts, shall hold their offices during good behaviour, and shall, at stated times, receive for their services, a compensation, which shall not be diminished during their continuance in office.

SECTION 2. The judicial power shall extend to all cases, in law and equity, arising under this Constitution, the laws of the United States, and treaties made, or which shall be made, under their authority; to all cases affecting ambassadors, other public ministers and consuls; to all cases of admiralty and maritime jurisdiction; to controversies to which the United States shall be a party; to controversies between two or more States, between a State and citizens of another State, between citizens of different States, between citizens of the same State claiming lands under grants of different States, and between a State, or the citizens thereof, and foreign States, citizens, or subjects.

In all cases affecting ambassadors, other public ministers and consuls, and those in which a State shall be party, the Supreme Court shall have original jurisdiction. In all the other cases before mentioned, the Supreme Court shall have appellate jurisdiction, both as to law and to fact, with such exceptions, and under such regulations as the Congress shall make.

The trial of all crimes, except in cases of impeachment, shall be by jury; and such trial shall be held in the State where the said crimes shall have been committed; but when not committed within any State, the trial shall be at such place or places as the Congress may by law have directed.

SECTION 3. Treason against the United States shall consist only in levying war against them, or in adhering to their enemies, giving them aid and comfort. No person shall be convicted of treason unless on the testimony of two witnesses to the same overt act, or on confession in open court.

The Congress shall have power to declare the punishment of treason, but no attainder of treason shall work corruption of blood, or forfeiture except during the life of the person attainted.

CONCERNING THE STATES

ARTICLE IV

SECTION 1. Full faith and credit shall be given in each State to the public acts, records, and judicial proceedings of every other State. And the Congress may by general laws prescribe the manner in which such acts, records and proceedings shall be proved, and the effect thereof.

SECTION 2. The citizens of each State shall be entitled to all privileges and immunities of citizens in the several States.

A person charged in any State with treason, felony, or other crime, who shall flee from justice, and be found in another State, shall on demand of the executive authority of the State from which he fled, be delivered up, to be removed to the State having jurisdiction of the crime.

No person held to service or labour in one State, under the laws thereof, escaping into another, shall, in consequence of any law or regulation therein, be discharged from such service or labour, but shall be delivered up on claim of the party to whom such service or labour may be due.

SECTION 3. New States may be admitted by the Congress into this Union; but no new State shall be formed or erected within the jurisdiction of any other State; nor any State be formed by the junction of two or more States, or parts of States, without the consent of the legislatures of the States concerned as well as of the Congress.

The Congress shall have power to dispose of and make all needful rules and regulations respecting the Territory or other property belonging to the United States; and nothing in this Constitution shall be so construed as to prejudice any claims of the United States, or of any particular State.

SECTION 4. The United States shall guarantee to every State in this Union a republican form of Government, and shall protect each of them against invasion; and on application of the legislature, or of the executive (when the legislature cannot be convened) against domestic violence.

FINAL PROVISIONS
ARTICLE V

The Congress, whenever two-thirds of both Houses shall deem it necessary, shall propose amendments to this Constitution, or, on the application of the legislatures of two-thirds of the several States, shall call a convention for proposing amendments, which, in either case, shall be valid to all intents and purposes, as part of this Constitution, when ratified by the legislatures of three-fourths of the several States, or by conventions in three-fourths thereof, as the one or the other mode of ratification may be proposed by the Congress; provided that no amendment which may be made prior to the year one thousand eight hundred and eight shall in any manner affect the first and fourth clauses in the Ninth Section of the First Article; and that no State, without its consent, shall be deprived of its equal suffrage in the Senate.

ARTICLE VI

All debts contracted and engagements entered into, before the adoption of this Constitution, shall be as valid against the United States under this Constitution, as under the Confederation.

This Constitution, and the laws of the United States which shall be made in pursuance thereof; and all treaties made, or which shall be made, under the authority of the United States, shall be the supreme law of the land; and the judges in every State shall be bound thereby, anything in the Constitution or laws of any State to the contrary notwithstanding.

The senators and representatives before mentioned, and the members of the several State legislatures, and all executive and judicial officers, both of the United States and of the several States, shall be bound by oath or affirmation, to support this Constitution; but no religious test shall ever be required as a qualification to any office or public trust under the United States.

ARTICLE VII

The ratification of the conventions of nine States shall be sufficient for the establishment of this Constitution between the States so ratifying the same.

Done in convention, by the unanimous consent of the States present, the seventeenth day of September, in the year of our Lord one thousand seven hundred and eighty-seven, and of the independence of the United States of America the twelfth.

In witness whereof, we have hereunto subscribed our names.

GEORGE WASHINGTON
President, and Deputy from Virginia

New Hampshire
John Langdon
Nicholas Gilman

Massachusetts
Nathaniel Gorham
Rufus King

Connecticut
William Samuel Johnson
Roger Sherman

New York
Alexander Hamilton

New Jersey
William Livingston
David Brearley
William Paterson
Jonathan Dayton

Pennsylvania
Benjamin Franklin
Thomas Mifflin
Robert Morris
George Clymer
Thomas Fitzsimons
Jared Ingersoll
James Wilson
Gouverneur Morris

Delaware
George Read
Gunning Bedford, Jr.
John Dickinson
Richard Bassett
Jacob Broom

Maryland
James McHenry
Daniel of St. Thomas
   Jenifer
Daniel Carroll

Virginia
John Blair
James Madison, Jr.

North Carolina
William Blount
Richard Dobbs Spaight
Hugh Williamson

South Carolina
John Rutledge
Charles C. Pinckney
Charles Pinckney
Pierce Butler

Georgia
William Few
Abraham Baldwin

Attest: William Jackson, *Secretary*

The Bill of Rights as passed by the first Congress contained twelve amendments. The first two, concerning the number and salaries of congressmen, were never ratified. The remainder were ratified and became a part of the law of the land in 1791.

LIBRARY OF CONGRESS

Amendments to the Constitution

THE BILL OF RIGHTS

The following ten amendments were proposed at the first session of the first Congress of the United States and were ratified by December, 1791.

AMENDMENT I

Congress shall make no law respecting an establishment of religion, or prohibiting the free exercise thereof, or abridging the freedom of speech or of the press, or the right of the people peaceably to assemble, and to petition the government for a redress of grievances.

AMENDMENT II

A well regulated militia, being necessary to the security of a free State, the right of the people to keep and bear arms shall not be infringed.

AMENDMENT III

No soldier shall, in time of peace, be quartered in any house without the consent of the owner; nor in time of war but in a manner to be prescribed by law.

AMENDMENT IV

The right of the people to be secure in their persons, houses, paper and effects, against unreasonable searches and seizures shall not be violated; and no warrants shall issue but upon probable cause, supported by oath or affirmation, and particularly describing the place to be searched, and the persons or things to be seized.

AMENDMENT V

No person shall be held to answer for a capital or otherwise infamous crime, unless on a presentment or indictment of a grand jury, except in cases arising in the land or naval forces, or in the militia, when in actual service in time of war or public danger; nor shall any person be subject for the same offense to be twice put in jeopardy of life or limb; nor shall be compelled, in any criminal case, to be a witness against himself, nor be deprived of life, liberty or property, without due process of law; nor shall private property be taken for public use without just compensation.

AMENDMENT VI

In all criminal prosecutions, the accused shall enjoy the right to a speedy and public trial, by an impartial jury of the State and district wherein the crime shall have been committed, which district shall have been previously ascertained by law; and to be informed of the nature and cause of the accusation; to be confronted with the witnesses against him; to have compulsory process for obtaining witnesses in his favor, and to have the assistance of counsel for his defense.

AMENDMENT VII

In suits at common law, where the value in controversy shall exceed twenty dollars, the right of trial by jury shall be preserved; and no fact tried by a jury shall be otherwise reexamined in any court of the United States, than according to the rules of the common law.

AMENDMENT VIII

Excessive bail shall not be required, nor excessive fines imposed, nor cruel and unusual punishments inflicted.

AMENDMENT IX

The enumeration in the Constitution of certain rights shall not be construed to deny or disparage others retained by the people.

AMENDMENT X

The powers not delegated to the United States by the Constitution, nor prohibited by it to the States, are reserved to the States respectively, or to the people.

OTHER AMENDMENTS

AMENDMENT XI

Submitted by Congress to the state legislatures in March, 1794, duly ratified, and proclaimed in January, 1798.

The judicial power of the United States shall not be construed to extend to any suit in law or equity, commenced or prosecuted against one of the United States by citizens of another State, or by citizens or subjects of any foreign State.

AMENDMENT XII

Submitted by Congress to the state legislatures in December, 1803, duly ratified, and proclaimed in September, 1804.

1. The Electors shall meet in their respective States, and vote by ballot for President and Vice President, one of whom at least shall not be an inhabitant of the same State with themselves. They shall name in their ballots the person voted for as President, and in distinct ballots the person voted for as Vice President, and they shall make distinct lists of all persons voted for as President, and of all persons voted for as Vice President, and of the number of votes for each, which lists they shall sign and certify, and transmit sealed to the seat of the government of the United States, directed to the President of the Senate. The President of the Senate shall, in the presence of the Senate and

House of Representatives, open all the certificates and the votes shall then be counted. The person having the greatest number of votes for President shall be the President, if such number be a majority of the whole number of Electors appointed; and if no person have such majority, then from the persons having the highest numbers, not exceeding three, on the list of those voted for as President, the House of Representatives shall choose immediately, by ballot, the President. But in choosing the President, the votes shall be taken by States, the representation from each State having one vote; a quorum for this purpose shall consist of a member or members from two-thirds of the States, and a majority of all the States shall be necessary to a choice. And if the House of Representatives shall not choose a President, whenever the right of choice shall devolve upon them, before the fourth day of March next following, then the Vice President shall act as President as in the case of the death or other constitutional disability of the President.

2. The person having the greatest number of votes as Vice President shall be the Vice President, if such number be a majority of the whole number of Electors appointed, and if no person have a majority, then from the two highest numbers on the list the Senate shall choose the Vice President. A quorum for the purpose shall consist of two-thirds of the whole number of Senators, and a majority of the whole number shall be necessary to a choice.

3. But no person constitutionally ineligible to the office of President shall be eligible to that of Vice President of the United States.

AMENDMENT XIII

Submitted by Congress to the state legislatures in February, 1865, duly ratified and proclaimed in December, 1865.

1. Neither slavery nor involuntary servitude, except as a punishment for crime, whereof the party shall have been duly convicted, shall exist within the United States, or any place subject to their jurisdiction.

2. Congress shall have power to enforce this article by appropriate legislation.

AMENDMENT XIV

Submitted by Congress to the state legislatures in June, 1866, duly ratified, and proclaimed in July, 1868.

1. All persons born or naturalized in the United States, and subject to the jurisdiction thereof, are citizens of the United States and of the State wherein they reside. No State shall make or enforce any law which shall abridge the privileges or immunities of citizens of the United States; nor shall any State deprive any person of life, liberty or property, without due process of law, nor deny to any person within its jurisdiction the equal protection of the laws.

2. Representatives shall be apportioned among the several States according to their respective numbers, counting the whole number of persons in each State, excluding Indians not taxed. But when the right to vote at any election for the choice of Electors for President and Vice President of the United States, Representatives in Congress, the executive and judicial officers of a State, or the members of the Legislature thereof, is denied to any of the male inhabitants of such State, being twenty-one years of age, and citizens of the United States, or in any way abridged, except for participation in rebellion or other crime, the basis of representation therein shall be reduced in the proportion which the number of such male citizens shall bear to the whole number of male citizens twenty-one years of age in such State.

3. No person shall be a Senator or Representative in Congress, or Elector of President and Vice President, or hold any office, civil or military, under the United States, or under any State, who having previously taken an oath as a member of Congress, or as an officer of the United States, or as a member of any State Legislature, or as an executive or judicial officer of any State, to support the Constitution of the United States, shall have engaged in insurrection or rebellion against the same, or given aid or comfort to the enemies thereof. But Congress may, by a vote of two-thirds of each House, remove such disability.

4. The validity of the public debt of the United States authorized by law, including debts incurred for payment of pensions and bounties for services in suppressing insurrection or rebellion, shall not be questioned. But neither the United States nor any State shall assume or pay any debt or obligation incurred in aid of insurrection or rebellion against the United States, or any claim for the loss or emancipation of any slave; but all such debts, obligations, and claims shall be held illegal and void.

5. The Congress shall have the power to enforce, by appropriate legislation, the provisions of this article.

AMENDMENT XV

Submitted by Congress to the state legislatures in February, 1869, duly ratified, and proclaimed in March, 1870.

1. The rights of citizens of the United States to vote shall not be denied or abridged by the United States or by any State on account of race, color, or previous condition of servitude.

2. The Congress shall have power to enforce this article by appropriate legislation.

AMENDMENT XVI

Submitted by Congress to the state legislatures in July, 1909, duly ratified, and proclaimed in February, 1913.

The Congress shall have power to lay and collect taxes on incomes, from whatever source derived, without apportionment among the several States, and without regard to any census or enumeration.

AMENDMENT XVII

Submitted by Congress to the state legislatures in May, 1912, duly ratified, and proclaimed in May, 1913.

1. The Senate of the United States shall be composed of two Senators from each State, elected by the people thereof, for six years; and each Senator shall have one vote. The Electors in each State shall have the qualifications requisite for Electors of the most numerous branch of the State Legislatures.

2. When vacancies happen in the representation of any State in the Senate, the executive authority of such State shall issue writs of election to fill such vacancies: Provided, That the Legislature of any State may empower the executive thereof to make temporary appointment until the people fill the vacancies by election as the Legislature may direct.

3. This amendment shall not be so construed as to affect the election or term of any Senator chosen before it becomes valid as part of the Constitution.

AMENDMENT XVIII

Submitted by Congress to the state legislatures in December, 1917, duly ratified, and proclaimed in January, 1919, as going into full force and effect January 16, 1920.

1. After one year from the ratification of this article the manufacture, sale or transportation of intoxicating liquors within, the importation thereof into, or the exportation thereof from the United States and all territory subject to the jurisdiction thereof for beverage purposes is hereby prohibited.

2. The Congress and the several States shall have concurrent power to enforce this article by appropriate legislation.

3. This article shall be inoperative unless it shall have been ratified as an amendment to the Constitution by the Legislatures of the several States, as provided by the Constitution, within seven years from the date of the submission hereof to the States by the Congress.

AMENDMENT XIX

Submitted by Congress to the state legislatures in June, 1919, duly ratified, and proclaimed in August, 1920.

1. The rights of citizens of the United States to vote shall not be denied or abridged by the United States or by any State on account of sex.

2. Congress shall have the power, by appropriate legislation, to enforce the provisions of this article.

AMENDMENT XX

Submitted by Congress to the state legislatures in March, 1932, duly ratified, and proclaimed in January, 1933.

1. The terms of the President and Vice President shall end at noon on the 20th day of January, and the terms of Senators and Representatives at noon on the 3rd day of January of the years in which such terms would have ended if this article had not been ratified; and the terms of their successors shall then begin.

2. The Congress shall assemble at least once in every year, and such meeting shall begin at noon on the 3rd day of January, unless they shall by law appoint a different day.

3. If, at the time fixed for the beginning of the term of the President, the President elect shall have died, the Vice President elect shall become President. If a President shall not have been chosen before the time fixed for the beginning of his term, or if the President elect shall have failed to qualify, then the Vice President elect shall act as President until a President shall have qualified; and the Congress may by law provide for the case wherein neither a President elect nor a Vice President elect shall have qualified, declaring who shall then act as President, or the manner in which one who is to act shall be selected, and such person shall act accordingly until a President or Vice President shall have qualified.

4. The Congress may by law provide for the case of the death of any of the persons from whom the

House of Representatives may choose a President whenever the right of choice shall have devolved upon them, and for the case of the death of any of the persons from whom the Senate may choose a Vice President whenever the right of choice shall have devolved upon them.

5. Sections 1 and 2 shall take effect on the 15th day of October following the ratification of this article.

6. This article shall be inoperative unless it shall have been ratified as an amendment to the Constitution by the Legislatures of three-fourths of the several States within seven years from the date of its submission.

AMENDMENT XXI

Submitted by Congress to state conventions in February, 1933, duly ratified, and proclaimed in December, 1933.

1. The eighteenth article of amendment to the Constitution of the United States is hereby repealed.

2. The transportation or importation into any State, Territory, or Possession of the United States for delivery or use therein of intoxicating liquors, in violation of the laws thereof, is hereby prohibited.

3. This article shall be inoperative unless it shall have been ratified as an amendment to the Constitution by conventions in the several States, as provided in the Constitution, within seven years from the date of the submission hereof to the States by the Congress.

AMENDMENT XXII

Submitted by Congress to the state legislatures in March, 1947, duly ratified, and proclaimed in February, 1951.

1. No person shall be elected to the office of the President more than twice, and no person who has held the office of President, or acted as President, for more than two years of a term to which some other person was elected President shall be elected to the office of the President more than once. But this Article shall not apply to any person holding the office of President when this Article was proposed by the Congress, and shall not prevent any person who may be holding the office of President, or acting as President, during the term within which this Article becomes operative from holding the office of President or acting as President during the remainder of such term.

2. This Article shall be inoperative unless it shall have been ratified as an amendment to the Constitution by the legislatures of three-fourths of the several

states within seven years from the date of its submission to the States by the Congress.

AMENDMENT XXIII

Submitted by Congress to the state legislatures in June, 1960, duly ratified, and proclaimed in April, 1961.

1. The District constituting the seat of Government of the United States shall appoint in such manner as the Congress may direct:

A number of electors of President and Vice President equal to the whole number of Senators and Representatives in Congress to which the District would be entitled if it were a State, but in no event more than the least populous State; they shall be in addition to those appointed by the States, but they shall be considered, for the purposes of the election of President and Vice President, to be electors appointed by a State; and they shall meet in the District and perform such duties as provided by the twelfth article of amendment.

2. The Congress shall have power to enforce this article by appropriate legislation.

AMENDMENT XXIV

Submitted by Congress to the state legislatures in September, 1962, duly ratified and proclaimed in January, 1964.

1. The right of citizens of the United States to vote in any primary or other election for President or Vice President, for electors or President or Vice President, or for Senator or Representative in Congress, shall not be denied or abridged by the United States or any State by reason of failure to pay any poll tax or other tax.

2. The Congress shall have the power to enforce this article by appropriate legislation.

AMENDMENT XXV

Proposed by Congress July, 1965, ratification completed February, 1967.

1. In case of the removal of the President from office or of his death or resignation, the Vice President shall become President.

2. Whenever there is a vacancy in the office of the Vice President, the President shall nominate a Vice President who shall take office upon confirmation by a majority vote of both houses of Congress.

3. Whenever the President transmits to the President pro tempore of the Senate and the Speaker of the House of Representatives his written declaration that he is unable to discharge the powers and duties of his office, and until he transmits to them a

Old House Chamber in the U.S. Capitol where the House of Representatives met for many years prior to 1857. Painting by Samuel Morse shows a night session.

written declaration to the contrary, such powers and duties shall be discharged by the Vice President as Acting President.

4. Whenever the Vice President and a majority of either the principal officers of the executive departments or of such other body as Congress may by law provide, transmit to the President pro tempore of the Senate and the Speaker of the House of Representatives their written declaration that the President is unable to discharge the powers and duties of his office, the Vice President shall immediately assume the powers and duties of the office as Acting President.

Thereafter, when the President transmits to the President pro tempore of the Senate and the Speaker of the House of Representatives his written declaration that no inability exists, he shall resume the powers and duties of his office unless the Vice President and a majority of either the principal officers of the executive department or of such other body as Congress may by law provide, transmit within four days to the President pro tempore of the Senate and the Speaker of the House of Representa-

tives their written declaration that the President is unable to discharge the powers and duties of his office. Thereupon Congress shall decide the issue, assembling within forty-eight hours for that purpose if not in session. If the Congress, within twenty-one days after receipt of the latter written declaration, or, if Congress is not in session, within twenty-one days after Congress is required to assemble, determines by two-thirds vote of both houses that the President is unable to discharge the powers and duties of his office, the Vice President shall continue to discharge the same as Acting President; otherwise, the President shall resume the powers and duties of his office.

AMENDMENT XXVI

Proposed by Congress in March, 1971; ratification completed June 30, 1971.

1. The right of citizens of the United States, who are 18 years of age or older, to vote shall not be denied or abridged by the United States or any state on account of age.

2. The Congress shall have the power to enforce this article by appropriate legislation.

Bibliography

Augur, Helen, *The Secret War of Independence*. Duell, Sloan & Pearce, New York, 1955.

Beard, Charles A., *The Republic, Conversations on Fundamentals*. The Viking Press, New York, 1943.

Becker, Carl, *The Declaration of Independence: A Study in the History of Political Ideas*. Alfred A. Knopf, New York, 1960.

Becker, Carl, *The Declaration of Independence*. Peter Smith, New York, 1933.

Bowen, Catherine Drinker, *Miracle at Philadelphia*. Little, Brown and Company, Boston, 1966.

Boyd, Julian, *The Declaration of Independence: The Evolution of the Text*. Princeton University Press, Princeton, 1943.

Boyd, Julian P., ed., *The Papers of Thomas Jefferson*. Princeton University Press, Princeton, 1950.

Brotherhead, William, *The Book of the Signers*. W. Brotherhead, Philadelphia, 1861.

Burnett, Edmund C., ed., *Letters of Members of the Continental Congress,* 8 vols. Carnegie Institute of Washington, Washington, D.C., 1921-36.

Chidsey, Donald Barr, *The Birth of the Constitution, An Informal History*. Crown Publishers, Inc., New York, 1964.

Chidsey, Donald Barr, *The Dramatic Story of the First Four Days of July 1776*. Crown Publishers, Inc., New York, 1958.

Chinard, Gilbert, *Honest John Adams*. Little, Brown and Company, Boston, 1933.

Editors of AMERICAN HERITAGE, *The American Heritage Book of the Revolution*. American Heritage Publishing Co., Inc., New York, 1958.

Editors of AMERICAN HERITAGE, *History of the Making of the Nation*. American Heritage Publishing Co., Inc., New York, 1968.

Farrand, Max, *The Framing of the Constitution of the United States*. Yale University Press, New Haven, 1922.

Ford, Worthington Chauncey, *Journals of the Continental Congress 1774-1789*. Government Printing Office, Washington, D.C., 1904.

Goodrich, Charles, *Lives of the Signers of the Declaration of Independence*. Reed & Company, New York, 1829.

Hawke, David, *A Transaction of Free Men: The Birth and Course of the Declaration of Independence*. Charles Scribner's Sons, New York, 1964.

Hendrick, Burton J., *Bulwark of the Republic, A Biography of the Constitution*. Little, Brown and Company, Boston, 1937.

Irving, Washington, *Life of George Washington.* G. P. Putnam & Co., New York, 1857-59.

Lodge, Henry Cabot, ed., *The Federalist, A Commentary on the Constitution of the United States,* reprinted from the original text of Alexander Hamilton, John Jay, and James Madison. The Knickerbocker Press, New York and London, 1888.

Lossing, B. J., *Biographical Sketches of the Signers of the Declaration of Independence.* Davis, Porter & Co., Philadelphia, 1866.

Madison, James, *Journal of the Federal Convention.* Scott, Foresman and Co., Chicago, 1898.

Malone, Dumas, *The Story of the Declaration of Independence.* Oxford University Press, New York, 1954.

McGee, Dorothy Horton, *Famous Signers of the Declaration.* Dodd, Mead & Company, 1955.

Miller, John C., *The Federalist Era, 1789-1801.* Harper & Brothers, New York, 1960.

Mitchell, Broadus and Mitchell, Louise Pearson, *A Biography of the Constitution of the United States.* Oxford University Press, New York, 1964.

Ross, George E., *Know Your Declaration of Independence and the 56 Signers.* Rand McNally & Company, Chicago, 1963.

Rossiter, Clinton, *1787, The Grand Convention.* The Macmillan Company, New York, 1966.

Sanderson, John, and Waln, Robert, Jr., *Biography of the Signers to the Declaration of Independence,* 9 vols., R. W. Pomeroy, Philadelphia, 1820-27.

Sinclair, Merle, and McArthur, Annabel Douglas, *They Signed for Us.* Duell, Sloan and Pearce, New York, 1957.

Tansill, Charles C., ed., *Documents Illustrative of the Formation of the Union of the American States.* Prepared by Library of Congress, Government Printing Office, Washington, 1927.

Thompson, Charles O. F., *A History of the Declaration of Independence.* Published by the Author, Bristol, R.I., 1947.

Tourtellot, Arthur Brown, AMERICAN HERITAGE — *We Mutually Pledge to Each Other, Our Lives, Our Fortunes and Our Sacred Honor.* American Heritage Publishing Co., Inc., New York, December 1962, Vol. XIV, Number 1.

White, Leonard D., *The Federalists.* The Macmillan Company, New York, 1959.

Whitney, David C., *Founders of Freedom in America.* J. G. Ferguson Publishing Company, Chicago, 1964.

Index